Why the Homeless Have No Chance:

The Dismantling of Success

Our focus on employment rather than housing got everybody indoors and caused our demise.

By Jeff Grunberg

Published in eBook format by eBookIt.com
http://www.eBookIt.com

ISBN-13: 978-1-4566-3504-6 (ebook)
ISBN-13: 978-1-4566-3823-8 (Amazon Print)
ISBN-13: 978-1-4566-3575-6 (Other Print)

Dedication

What's worse than no cash-on-hand and none coming in? The landlord turns the key, but the real culprit is the disconnection, which defines insanity. As one shelter resident told me, "Man's got to have people behind him." So, while maybe it is true that no man is an island, it's relative. Some people are offshore, cut off from the main, not exactly floating. This book is dedicated to them.

Author's Note

This book is entirely based upon real events. As a participant-observer in the center of the story, ultimately a target of false narratives, when under attack I'd oftentimes be reactive, so be it, but I was there. I was there as the participant witness and most importantly, no one can tell this story better, or with more truth. A lot of people did a lot of good things. Some didn't. Most of the bad guys' names and some descriptive details have been intentionally changed, because having had their chance to talk already, they went first, they don't deserve even the negative notoriety that revealing their true identities might bring. Why give them another opportunity for subterfuge?

~ ~ ~

Dark is not just the number of homeless people and those on the brink, but also the absence of an "open wide your hand" approach to their unmet needs. Instead, they are treated more like their problems are a given, as in "the poor you will always have with you." Once in the system, what are they supposed to do? Act retired? Sit in repose, that's what, in wait for the housing to come. The housing that should by all rights come. However, the wait has proven to be indeterminate, and nobody just wants to sit around. I know that for a fact. Dark also is the shadow cast upon the homeless services industry, the gaze of those in charge, their ways of seeing from which certain expectations emerge. More proof that this social problem is socially constructed.

One

What had been taken as a given became unreliable. Turns out, you really can't know a book by its cover. For example, just because our social service programs, aimed at helping homeless people off the street and into jobs and housing, came under investigation by the Manhattan District Attorney's office, the Office of the City Comptroller, the City-Council Speaker's office, the Inspector General of the New York City Department of Homeless Services, a federal prosecutor, the Department of Housing and Urban Development known simply as "HUD," a leading homeless advocate, and a number of more private investigations, including sizeable scrutiny, New York City style, from among countless dailies and weeklies, newspapers across the color spectrum, blue, red, etc., none of them following their mandate for black and white news, was not proof that we fell short of attaining what one came to call "unparalleled success" in finding housing and employment to homeless adults. To the contrary. Only that there were some who wanted our work stopped. Immediately. Retroactively? No good deed goes unpunished, they say. More sarcasm: Guess we never should have gotten all those people indoors.

By our fifth year, right before the worst of the attacks began, with an employment focus, we helped place hundreds of people into jobs and hundreds more into affordable apartments. For those not wanting professional help, not even from our on-site professional staff, we still enrolled them as members and offered use of a self-help library. We set ourselves up, in part, to be there for people who wanted to use our facilities minimally, and/or to remain anonymous if they wished. Clearly, some were in hiding – we allowed for that. To almost everybody's liking, we had metal detectors at our front doors and cameras in the stairwells, and we intervened to break up every argument or fight, altercations you'd expect when hundreds of exhausted people mill about often at wit's end. We had great food, three squares, home-cooked on site and served in a sit-down cafeteria, small round tables, tablecloths, capacity for personal storage in the back, bathrooms, and showers too. We had so many homeless people coming to us that we soon became the largest multi-services drop-in-center in the country.

~   ~   ~

We were open 24/7, year-round. Importantly, we were co-ed. Even more so, half of our staff consisted of formerly homeless people earning living wages, not the prevailing minimum wage of $3.80-4.25 but twice that, plus paid sick days, paid vacation, and health insurance benefits too. We had a medical clinic, a mental health unit, and a sizeable social services staff. This consisted of a dozen or more social workers and case managers, plus sometimes up to fifteen part-time graduate school interns. There was plenty of support staff, and employment trainees, not to forget a couple of hundred volunteers from the corporate community each year as well. Busy place.

~   ~   ~

Throughout the building, people were experiencing homelessness, or homelessness withdrawal, there being a veritable mix of personal development levels and success, Norman Mailer's "wad" caught up in a slew of interactions, right there, in front of each other. They could self-define differently from what they might be labeled, and be defined differently by each other, their stratified peers. Spontaneous cluster sampling?

~   ~   ~

In the tall hallways winding up six flights towards the roof, above us all, were stunning murals of Roman archways and tall vines, muted colors with bright blue skies. And on the roof, adjacent to the rooftop vegetable garden, was *"The Human Being."* It was the work of New York artist, Steve Cosentino. Look at it online; it's beautiful. Majestic and poignant, 35 feet wide by 65 feet long, that big, not only that, but it was also made from discarded clothing! A portrait of a man looking upward, a shout-out to the buildings all-around us, their occupants looking down on our rooftop, on us, of course. The building below that spectacular roof, that was us, was abuzz.

~   ~   ~

Well, too bad...it shouldn't have been us. First, we had no business getting them indoors where they'd be hidden from view. That's what they said. Much worse, it wasn't what we did as it was who we were. And who was that? Some of the richest of New York's rich were our underwriters, our founders, and they made their money as landlords and property owners. Holy shit! Holy shit is right, not just a figurative enemy, but to many in the business of helping the homeless, *the* figurative enemy! In truth, in the back of mind always, explained away repeatedly but still lurking, were remnants of this same thought. I could feel its logic, an emotional position really, like holding every doctor guilty for the mal-practicing ones, these property managers represented all the wealth-building horrors ever committed by the worst of them. However, the sociologist in me wanted to focus on the relationship in this midtown instance between extreme wealth and extreme poverty. It was their concentration of midtown wealth that empowered some to try to prevent us from continuing with our outreach work. I took the decision to work for these property owners because this sentiment was unproductive in terms of helping anyone. It was somewhat hypocritical too, given that every one of our detractors sought similar financial support from many of the same people. Symbolic Interactionism. Microsociology.

Not to discount financial competition by any means, there was yet another angle to take. Their chant, "housing, housing, and housing," hadn't delivered, yet still they got their funding. To their own underwriters, indeed to the American public and much of the world, they sold the idea that they knew just how to resolve homelessness. "Housing, housing, housing" pushed all the right levers. But it has been forty years. By both policy and inclination, they are still wanting everybody to forever-wait. Not fair.

It might have hurt us that Newt Gingrich liked us. No understatement. It triggered immense antagonism. Hey, don't blame us for that. He was on his way to becoming the Republican Speaker of the House and had been on the lookout for news to fit his congressional television show, his personal vision-quest for influence, when he visited New York City for a few days. Basically, he just showed up. He had decided to visit a few programs in different parts of the city, ours included. He was very much into the business district concept, which gave us our start. Problem was, once Newt was back in Washington, although it didn't amount to more than a sentence or two, he sang our praises, in particular our approach, direct, targeted, and like I said, hands-on. He liked our program's emphasis on employment.

Another thing. It may not have helped us either that another nationally known Republican, who was not just New York's mayor, stumbled upon us too. By then already famous for his law-

and-order personality, Rudy Giuliani spied our programs more than a few times during his first mayoral campaign against David Dinkins. For example, he visited our Center to serve a meal. He walked into the former high school's gymnasium turned lounge and out of the 150 or so homeless people in the room, at least 100 started booing him. Apparently fearless among the catcalls, he stood there and took it. Political determination was what it was. His being there was not such an unusual campaign event, but if he walked out, that would have been a story to tell. Several people chose to engage him. He engaged right back. He hung in there, he said, because he liked our emphasis on employment too. Ironic, but once *that* got out, our reputation took a further hit, and that he stayed interested in getting our perspective for a little while even after taking office, lots of faxes back and forth, phone calls too, and not just one or two meetings in his city hall basement bunker. But within a year or so, not to worry, he decided we weren't worth the trouble, that we were becoming a certain kind of liability. My guess was that he discovered that things in the "homeless world" weren't going to be up to him alone, that there was a putative force greater than his, which to this day heads up the city's social services to the homeless. Unnamed. Mayor Giuliani would have to kowtow to "The Board," not a process, can we agree, that he'd likely participate in? He couldn't have known this beforehand because to know that he'd have to have been in the industry. The Board doesn't announce or introduce itself, not then, not now. You could say that except for his law-and-order approach to homelessness in public spaces, an unnecessarily authoritative approach, and his development of an NYPD Outreach Team, where authority and compassion turned the police officer into more of a stepfather offering comfort through the imposition of a strict structure, other than these efforts, which were successful in bringing people indoors, he pretty much turned away from homelessness.

~ ~ ~

Momentum against us was additionally aided and abetted by the fact that future Supreme Court Justice Judge Sonia Sotomayor ruled against our training program for which we were sued. Like other programs around the city, we were paying stipends to our trainees. Should have been paying minimum wages, our attackers said. But it was a training program. Law firms, graduate programs, and numerous social services agencies in every city were doing the same thing. They still are. They pay stipends to their trainees for showing up each day to perform meaningful "work." Resume building. The desire for upward mobility operationalized. Too bad. Serving in NY's Southern District at the time, believing the very worst about us, unexamined during a half-day hearing, amicus briefs ignored, testimony limited by structure, the judge went ahead and agreed with The Board, her hopeful summary statement aside.

~ ~ ~

None of this proves that we were coming from the political right, either. Me? Never. For more, refer to "the fifth party system" or "the New Deal." Them? You'd be surprised at how many were lifelong Democrats. No, that would be a very false assumption. What happened is that it irked a few people to discover that we were embracing equal opportunity, true marketplace choice, self-direction, and personal responsibility. Apparently, those phrases were not exclusively owned bon mots. Admittedly, they can, by some, be used as a cudgel to negate, not in our case, to the contrary, these words presented with great intimacy. In real life, people are literally moved by them. In our economic system, without the first two, equal opportunity and true marketplace choice, the others, self-direction, and personal responsibility, are more unlikely to be experienced.

~ ~ ~

Our deemphasizing the upfront use of professionals was taken as a slap in the face of the social service professional community, was never meant to be all that. It was just us being pragmatic, we thought, and fairer to the homeless person, which it was, and we were successful carrying it out. Truth is, this story, about what works to alleviate homelessness, even with all the headlines and flashy posturing, has remained largely hidden from the tax-paying public. No more.

That's right, certain advocacy groups attacked us before we even got started. They knew where we were coming from, or so they thought, our book cover, and they did not like us. Others, less focused, sharing common interests, smelling blood in the water, signed on. Still others, too busy to discern, discerned anyway. Most went with the narrative provided them, the easy way out. With the papers paving the way for the television news, as always, it was a collective project for a surprising number of people, a not-so-silent conspiracy. It got loud. There were multiple head nods, many knowing scratches of chinny chin chins, eye rolls, fingers coming together, and lots of rat-a-tat-tats. That's just how it all went down. What's the opposite of a degradation ceremony? Self-admiration.

Born to rule, referred to here as "The Board," they came together to comprise a power move. In our case, we were on their turf, and so we became their targets. Better put, they came into that part of town to target its business community. Not such a bad move; for that was where the wealth inequality would be most vivid, but come on, they could have paid a little attention to outcome, no? In fact, they were formulated for political action prior to our existence, 7-8 years earlier. Ultimately, "The Board" caused us, and ultimately, it uncaused us as well.

With their food line strategically placed in the middle of midtown, in the middle of what was to become a business improvement district, they approached one and all with the confidence of a tornado, beyond shock and awe. No conspiracy theory here. They'd become the moral arbiters of the nation's response to this emergence of so many needy people at our feet. They were in large part self-ordained. Not owners of the house so much as squatters. In the position to greatly influence, even to "control" logistics and fiscal direction. A funny play on words, they "domesticated" the homeless industry. But these were the early years, and they were only going to grow, to become the thought leaders and the power brokers too, roles emerging from the vacuum caused by a rift between the increasing number of people living in our shelters, off the grid, all but disconnected, and the mainstream which chugs along without them.

We were, to be realistically humble, no more than one of many born to help. Our problem was, however, that we were birthed in a seedling tray started by a business district not entirely from the heart; maybe for some it had more to do with the economics of revitalization.

Oversight of our work from within was shared by the Business District's leadership to include a handful of highly accomplished social service careerists forming subcommittees of their own making, along with city reps as ex officio members, etc. Outside the BID, our work was monitored by the city's Department of Business Services and funded and audited by what the city then called its "Human Resources Department." We were also subject to feedback from Community Boards #3, #4, and #5, each of whom were sufficiently concerned enough to "invite" us to nearly every one of their monthly meetings.

They put that food line there, and then they went after the property management community for its every reaction to it. Sort of a "candid camera" type of situation. They were being "punked," as they say, the homeless as fodder, The Board, as always, gaining power.

What did Dylan sing, "The executioner's face is always well-hidden?" Yes, but oddly enough, in the case of BIDs, the landlords do show their faces, so maybe they aren't the executioner? But then again, yes Bob, when it comes down to it, the processes that render a person homeless are not in each case so clear, at least not to the person. It is all so well-hidden. They do blame themselves but really, is that right? Or is that the only "right" that matters? We can't forget another of Dylan's songs, "Who Killed Davey Moore?" Obscurity.

When homeless people, their sheer numbers staggering, hundreds for sure, began to overwhelm midtown where some of the business district's most venerable and valuable buildings stood, these property owners were not happy with how many seemed to be literally living on their anything but private, privately-owned land, their building alcoves, their doorways, and their ATM vestibules. "The homeless weren't born here, they came here, and many were brought here," we explained to them. "Okay," they'd respond, "but if they're going to be here, can they at least be indoors?" Bingo. No stretch there, even the people living on the street wanted that. Everybody wanted that, right? So, I was hired to figure out how to make it happen. *That* excited me. We eventually established the idea that we would seek progress by way of each homeless person's buy-in, one by one. For so many good reasons, we settled on "employment" and its many devices. This formed our response to midtown homelessness and spelled big trouble for us.

~ ~ ~

Surely, our employment-as-a-fix bias may have differed from the approach most people in our business took, no doubt, but the hundreds of people on the food line were the ones in crisis, not any of us, those who ran the food line, or the social service power brokers who were "for" the homeless, certainly not my employers who were entirely focused on their business district. Yet that's not to say we weren't warned, we were, about the tie-in between the influence of the early advocates for the homeless and their rage, a direct relationship, which maybe we never really came to understand, certainly not to respect. Our mistake, or the central reason for our success?

~ ~ ~

An amazing discovery. The people waiting for food on that line wanted to be indoors, however, the people running the line wanted something quite different; they wanted the outdoor food line to stay put. Put. What? "In your face," they'd scream at our outreach workers. They were fighting us over what they called our "arrogance." "They have the right to be outside," they insisted. How dare we try to get them to come indoors? How dare we.

~ ~ ~

Years later now, think of it, The Board's power is still firmly intact. This, despite the rise of homelessness over these last forty years, that's right, under their vigilant watch. We ask here, hasn't their time come? Guess not, because even with all this failure, they find victory. Their persistence has become the story. Their effort is all. Funny how it works though, despite their power and their comfortable leather chairs, no pleather for them, upon reading this book, they will experience what psychologists call "negative arousal," adrenal gland be warned. They'll read it Evelyn Wood style, a quick scan, and they'll grow like the Hulk. This time, whatever dust they raise will be entirely on them, and when it begins to settle, the facts will speak even louder than the rhetoric, their harp, no matter its volume. The rooster will wake us up to their thousands of failures, not to their relative few successes. The homeless "system" must change its course.

A relatively small cadre of non-profit social service executives clutch onto the bulk of today's grant money. They literally run the industry based upon what social psychiatrist Robert Jay Lifton might call a "malignant normalcy." The belief system put forth has created a "reality" which is accepted by the public without scrutiny, the ultimate outcome being extended suffering. For it all, they obtain a position atop one of humankind's highest moral grounds, that of helping the poor and homeless. They go unquestioned and without scrutiny because their work is "good." However, a closer look shows that all along they've been dealing in fractions. Just about nobody is getting housed. Functional fixedness. Their approach is one that hasn't worked, but for the fewest people. Not fair. Where's the hope? Where's Edmund Husserl when we need him the most? What about Pragmatic Buddhism? Taking and sending.

The public handle on the massive homeless industry has become tightly chained to the wrists of The Board, an arrangement that doesn't benefit anyone else, like homeless people for example. Forty years later, there are more people in New York City homeless shelters than ever before, and it's not so much about how many people drop-in as it is how so few get out, except for those few who accept being "cornered" into unemployment, with any kind of finality. To the people named "homeless," the label makes it sound like they are going to get something like a home, which they don't. The homes haven't come. Safe to say, they won't.

~ ~ ~

Labeling this tragic social problem this way, for example, "homelessness," has immeasurably slowed everybody down, an albatross then, amounting to little more than spin. Dr. Lifton was talking specifically about current politics with an eye on World War II, okay, we can't take this that far, but it's a slice of that same pie.

~ ~ ~

BUSINESS GROUP HIRES GOON SQUADS TO BEAT THE HOMELESS. That was the headline that flogged us for years. Wow. The power of The Board is built to be felt, its imprimatur extending even after its accusations, which had fueled our downfall, were found months later by our most famous investigator to be, in his word, "fanciful." That meant what? That it was a fiction. Made up. Conjured. Problem was, we were already in the "If smoke, then fire," category. The public "lived" with the idea that we had possibly committed these crimes for so long, that even after they were shown to have been made up, barely shown actually, as the acknowledgment was hidden on page 16, lower right corner near the crease, they were still "believed." By then, we were tainted enough to cause our supporters to pull away. What did they take with them? Their funding. Even though there was no evidence to prove we did anything nefarious, they were still scared. We took great care to lay that out for them. They "got it," they said, yet, sorry, they simply had to defund us.

We had to disprove a negative, and we failed. This, even though The New York Civil Liberties Union itself said that they would have known if a roving gang was beating the homeless on midtown streets. No matter. We stood accused and, if you stood by us, you would have had to stand accused too. Better to join a conspiracy of silence instead, avoid the controversy, just turn your back and leave the room. Didn't the Seinfeld Show culminate with the four lead characters being found guilty of violating the Good Samaritan law? Our founders had had enough. Even for them, these attacks on us amounted to an unacceptable hit to their reputation. Better to cut and...well, the business improvement district spun us off. Before going, over several weeks of intense phone work and lunch meetings, in close concert with The Board itself, they sold us out to a new board of managers, and then they greatly reduced their financial support, and then they left.

Is public shaming the best way to counter public success? Seems so. They wanted to stop our work, and they did, by accusing us of heinous crimes and unethical behavior. Furthermore, maybe worse, they manipulated the media with their messaging. They dragged it out. By the time their charges had to be dropped for "lack of evidence," the public had become convinced. The trial was over. It was declared that to continue helping the homeless, we needed to be more closely watched. By whom? By them. The Board. The Board? Yes indeed, very true, they won custody of us.

Wait, couldn't we have self-adopted? Oh well, guess not, *our* success was now going to be *their* success. Sigmund Freud, 1948, "Even paranoiacs do not project arbitrarily." Joseph Heller, 1961, in his book *Catch-22*, "Just because you are paranoid, does not mean people aren't after you."

~   ~   ~

The damage had been done. But the investigation concluded that the charges were fanciful, as in "obviously intentional," right? Proven false. Wow. So, do we now get all our funding back? And the people who perpetrated this on us, will they be rebuked and exiled, or charged with a crime, same thing? No? The opposite? What do you mean our funding will go to them? Our work's to be diminished, and theirs is to be increased? But they made it up. Isn't that a crime? Too late.

~   ~   ~

What would John Dewey say? Come on, every investigation they perpetrated upon us, their way to gain free publicity for their cause, came up empty, lots of talk but empty, so they had to find another way. In fact, they would not give up until they succeeded in shutting us down, ultimately eliminating the last person standing, in this case, yours truly. That's one reason why the homeless have no chance and still don't, nothing to do with me, per se, though with my tendency to feel "put upon," I might have made it harder on myself. It's just that success outside the box gets trampled upon all the time. That's why it remains outside. And the homeless, them too? They don't have a chance because they are not given one. They must stay in the box, too. Outside. Ironic.

~   ~   ~

Unable to earn any kind of living, kept useless towards their own ends, unplugged, disconnected, in wait for "Housing First," this story began as the late CUNY sociologist Charles Winick called it: "Private property owners as grassroots organizers." Wow. Talk about hitting the nail on the head. That was the story. Help can come from unexpected sources. Embrace it? Apparently not.

Two

A focus on housing to the virtual exclusion of employment, rather than the other way around, sides with those who view homeless people as incapable of work. We didn't see it that way. Not just a play on words, we saw employment as a more workable solution. Same money, spent differently, producing a different outcome. More to the point, give homeless people a suitable income, and they'll house themselves, we said.

~ ~ ~

Uh-oh, something different. Reflecting on today's homeless crisis, as we watch out for reductionist thinking, we look back to the years 1989 to 2005 to consider why so many people who were living on the street at that time, while refusing all other rescue efforts, responded to us so positively? Perhaps to us, it was no surprise at all. For sure, they came off the streets in numbers that turned the old schoolhouse on East 44th street into the biggest drop-in center in the country, walk-in traffic, right there, dead center, midtown Manhattan, New York City, New York.

~ ~ ~

Soon, there were only a few people living outdoors in the whole neighborhood, midtown east. It went from hundreds to just several. Everybody else was inside with us. We were bursting from the seams, the stuff of opportunity. We had no beds to offer on-site, we weren't allowed to have that, that is, we were told by the city that we could only offer chairs to sit in, no beds. We were a drop-in-center; at the time, one of eight in the city, chairs only. Of course, we offered a safe place, if not to sleep, to at least doze on and off through the night, to large numbers of people, but still, not good, no beds. Nevertheless, they were our customers. Our social service efforts, like so many others relying on such traffic, the walk-in kind, went many of the same ways that retail businesses go, by the way, whose customers should be treated as if "always right." You do want the sale, don't you? It's about attitude. Yet, we also know that consumers must be educated. This all makes for good business, for on the back of our customer's choices, we believed that our success would come and, guess what, the business district got the midtown revival they wanted. For sure.

Prior to that, all kinds of outreach had been attempted in midtown but to little avail; there even was a drop-in-center established at our same location, before ours. No dice. Nothing worked. It appeared that the people approached in and around Grand Central Terminal could not be reached. For their unwillingness to go along with "the program," they gained a reputation as the "most resistant." They were referred to as the "young and restless." It was said that many had been expelled from their shelters for rule breaking. These were the ones nobody wanted, drawn from the ranks of the ones nobody wants, so it was ironic to think of them as resistant too; weren't they the ones who had been thrown out? Not wanted, why *would* they want back in?

They were "too difficult" to work with, so it was said, and to the dismay of the local retail shop owners trying to make a lot of bucks, frightfully, quite suddenly, as their numbers doubled, pedestrian traffic went way down. There was The Board's massive food line, proudly tagged as "the biggest" by the people who ran it next to the terminal, on Vanderbilt Avenue, set up to clash with the community it was placed into. Timed to coincide with the 5pm rush hour, arguably always just around the bend, right there next to the huge transportation terminal. "Excuse me, Ma'am, could you help me with some carfare to get home?" Double meaning.

The Vanderbilt food line was set up so that the poor people on it could "join forces" with Grand Central Terminal's poor; now indeed the numbers were bigger than anywhere else. The media was on it. As they watched the line grow, they watched the community sag too, and they shared what they saw. Local businesses complained to the city, which opened a part-time overnight drop-in-center in the nearby St. Agnes Church schoolhouse, but most of the people stayed on the street anyway. A small number of reporters began to follow the failed outreach efforts, the police crackdowns, and the political declarations more closely. Piece by piece, they "tracked" this growing social problem without much insight – their focus was on the visage. Did we say nothing was working? Well, everybody got fed, which was good, and a few people picked up a few dollars in handouts, and for sure, some did go indoors, but even then, they seemed to come right back, certainly to be "replaced." If the sound on the television set were off, it would look like ecstatic joy, but sorry, the sound was perpetually turned on, and it indicated great sorrow at the spectacle of so many in need. The people handing out the bags of food were on center stage, telling the story, educating everybody, their importance growing like the problem itself. They had the run of the territory, literally owning midtown "homelessness" – owning everything but the blame. They were in every camera shot, thriving on "the set," in vitro. Did I say the media was on it? The newspapers had little else to draw on, their reporters like sponges soaking up the "knowledge" of these young volunteers or their intrepid leaders; plenty of sincerity to go around, a sad picture. Prior to this food line, the focus was mostly on the plight of the homeless during the Thanksgiving to Christmas season. Great idea then to establish a massive food line even if at the expense of these real people who, manipulated by their relentless hunger, with little else to think about, would be more than happy to upturn their lives to make the trek. Anything for that sandwich. In the abandonment of what was their previous comfort zone, they'll walk that extra mile or two if they had to, their feet throbbing, their food source apparently on the move. The Great Reroute.

~ ~ ~

About six years or so later, at the peak of this food line's spectacle and glory, so cynical, in we came. We were a brand-new kind of social service agency, a public/private, not-for-profit agency established to benefit our founding profit-makers, very wealthy and prestigious were they, talk about prime location, no doubt some of the richest people in the country, and in this prominent world-city, they were some of the most prominent. They seemed to own all the buildings everywhere, The Empire State Building, The Chrysler Building, The Graybar Building, The Waldorf-Astoria Hotel, The Citi-Corp Center, The Lincoln Building, The Ford Foundation Building, and what was then the Pan AM building, now MetLife, almost every building adjacent to the blocks surrounding the great Grand Central Terminal, up and down the east side of Fifth Avenue all the way over to Second Avenue, in total, about two tenths of a square mile. These were the founders of the Grand Central Partnership Business Improvement District. And they formed a spin-off non-profit social services corporation to help the area's homeless.

~ ~ ~

Our agency's success could only mean one thing to the business improvement district (BID): Those hundreds of people living on midtown's streets would no longer be there. Where then? On their own, the BID might never have thought past this, their central problem, who knows, but they did know enough to engage social services experts who saw success as going well beyond just getting everybody off the street, while knowing it had to start with that. Happy to see the BID stepping up? No, there were several people who were not in the least bit happy.

~   ~   ~

What is a BID? A business improvement district whose boundaries are drawn by the owners of the properties to be included within it. Its purpose is to beautify its area. In the case of Grand Central BID, roughly from 35th to 48th street, from 2nd avenue to 5th, its boundaries had some very wiggly lines, common to a process where not every owner is willing to commit. In the end, for the BID to become a reality, more than half of the owners would have to vote to pay a self-imposed, brand-new tax, enforceable by law. In Grand Central's case, about 11 cents per its 70 million square feet, or about $7.6 million annually. Overseen by the city's Department of Small Business Services, the BID must follow a pre-approved plan for improvements to their area. On their behalf, then as now, relevant NYC commissioners crow: "BIDs are invested in their communities and their local leadership helps small business corridors grow and succeed." Collectively then, BIDs are in perpetual trouble-shoot mode, precisely the reason for their existence, to upkeep, maintain and repair, upgrading always, no graffiti, pick up the litter right away, repaint the "street furniture" constantly, the mailboxes, benches, and news boxes too. All of it, the great effort, is aimed at drawing in tourists and retail shoppers, improving what they call "the footprint" of small businesses, expanding their capacity to earn, etc., and lastly, not the least, lowering vacancy rates. In this midtown "space," they also set out to double the street-lighting, hang building-corner planters flowering in their display, and install into every sidewalk corner about 25 square feet of polished stone, wheelchair accessible ramps with granite inlays. Beautiful.

Oh, and that food line. Herein, you could credibly argue, is the start to our story. In the case of this BID, there was written into their contract a requirement that they address the homelessness that lay within its confines. And so, it came to pass that in their politically approved, often publicly negotiated budget, they were going to invest $250,000 annually to their homeless effort, about 3% of their largess. It was a huge start, about $250,000 more at the time than any BID was doing anywhere else. Can't we say that Mayor David Dinkins knew exactly what he was doing when he insisted on it? It's just that the food line had become very noisy, as in "media noisy," a national embarrassment, to the city too. Not surprisingly, a man whose counsel just about every mayor sought, he was close to Mayor Dinkins, an historical figure in city social services history, was next on the scene.

To pull their homelessness plan together, the BID tapped one of New York's most revered social services giants, the then 80-year-old Dr. James Dumpson, a former New York City Welfare commissioner, the first African American person to ever hold that position, at different times the head of nearly everything important to the field, still very active. He was a Visiting Professor at Fordham, a Senior Consultant at New York Community Trust, and about a year after I began working with him, he was named Chairman of the Board of Health and Hospitals Corporation. Most notably, most brilliantly, he had always been able to avoid membership on The Board. Somehow, he remained his own, a rare and special thing for a person to achieve, given the heights to which he'd risen. As for me, I was hired by Dr. Dumpson first as a consultant for about six months to the business district starting in August 1988, then for about six months as a part-time program director, and then full-time by

August 1989. It worked out perfectly this way, because I was not so ready to make the move initially, to leave my hospital job, and to work for people in that stratosphere. It took me a year to decide. But I relented and was named the BID's Vice President for Social Services, and soon, once we established ourselves as a stand-alone non-profit agency, I was named the Executive Director of its newly born social service agency. Exciting times: excitement to come. In an office adjacent to the former city chief of street cleaning, Tom Gallagher, the BID's vice president for sanitation, and down the hall, the retired director of Washington D.C.'s Holocaust Museum, Arthur Rosenblatt, the BID's vice president for art and design, in a tall building on east 43rd street, I sat with a great view, big picture windows. Manhattan at large. I sat between the two corner offices of the two people who made our success possible. In one, sat a former two-star chief of police, who before his retirement had served as Manhattan Chief of Detectives and Queens borough commander, Richard Dillon, the business district's vice president for security, and in the other, the former head of Community Board #5, Dan Biederman, the president, and co-founder of the Grand Central BID.

Dr. Dumpson remained my go-to for twenty years on all matters "midtown homelessness," almost right up until what we can still say was his untimely passing at 103 years old. Amazing.

We would try to get to know every single person who appeared to be living on midtown's streets, or waiting on that big food line, or anyone of the several additional food lines that sprung up from time to time. They'd be clear as to who we were, our motives as well; couldn't fool anyone anyway. What are their perspectives? The pace would be conversational. We'd get what we could get, all the perspectives adding up to a whole story, ongoing. The questions would come organically. We would also speak to all the storekeepers and whichever property managers we could catch up with, along with many of the residents, passersby, and commuters, same methods, a persistent opportunistic presence, our strategy. Would old premises hold up? Later for that. Did we even have to say that, as it turned out, that the extremely poor people who came to midtown on their own, as well as those that were literally placed there by their advocates, did not want to live outside, that they did so because they saw no satisfactory alternative? They came from all over the city, many of them new to midtown.

Off to the side, Dr. Dumpson confided he was not sure how the BID might take to the longer-term aspects of our job. If we succeeded in bringing people indoors, what then? They'd be indoors and we'd want to help them. That takes time. Another thing, besides all that, our success, so brash, was going to be seen as very threatening. Some very powerful people, he said, were going to be very upset. "Forge on."

Still helping the BID only ten hours per week, I was not at the time willing to leave where I was then working fulltime, Columbia-Presbyterian Hospital, so the consultant position was just right. I was enjoying what I was doing too much; we had established a psychiatric program inside the dreaded Fort Washington Armory, which had 1000 homeless men living there, a mental health effort that has since tripled in size even as the shelter's overall population has been reduced, still there, now run by another agency. I really did enjoy the people I reported to, the whole setting, working a couple of layers under Dr. Herb Pardes, former head of the NIMH, and other famed writers and researchers. I was not eager to leave for the unknowns of this large business district. Leaning forward nonetheless, energized, and focused, on the other side, I was highly motivated by Dr. Dumpson as well as other of the BID's heavy hitters, many of whom normally would not be involved in the "homeless" picture. This was some kind of great opportunity – an adventure in every sense of the word. Personalizing it further, I figured I had yet another chance to rescue people from street life. Hands on. A professional challenge. Could I do it? Hey, instead of here, can we continue this conversation inside, perhaps at our Center?

There was a quantitative side to our work too; we ran surveys, did counts, and looked-for evidence everywhere as to what was working or not from an outreach perspective. Was anyone being especially successful in getting people indoors and off the streets? There were several different social service agencies out there trying. Often, they were simply waiting for individual "break-through moments" when a person finally would agree to come indoors for help. And again, occasionally, they'd succeed, but we wanted to do better than that. So, by necessity as well as professional inclination, we took the time to sit down for prolonged conversations with these agencies. And with the homeless too, needing their buy-in, of course we sought their take on things. Surprise: they said nobody had even done that! Their take? People talked to them, but it was always more perfunctory than real. Nobody looked to them, they said, as if they were not worthy enough to speak on their own behalf. There was always the "right" answer, and if you didn't give it, well, they'd keep asking until you did, a series of interactional power plays with them on the outs. We sensed their despair. We knew that for outreach to work they'd have to want to come inside; we saw no other way. It was totally up to them. Now, what did they want? Good news, their appreciation for what one person called our "ground-up approach" was palpable, that we talked "regular" to them, straight at them. Hovering low to the ground in the negative zones, disconnected, there was still a heartbeat. It was not too late?

Not doing well on the Adlerian continuum of social interest, disconnected from the very world we took for granted, it was obvious they needed help plugging into and eradicating all six degrees of separation rather than just the one they were dealing with, locked away with downwardly mobile others. They had been lured there, as we said, by food line advocates who chose, without asking, on the behalf of all homeless, to fight an apparently unwinnable fight, affordable housing for everybody. Was it an abundance of compassion that brought the line to midtown? No, they were dropped off," as it were, in midtown, true, and worse, there was no home they could return to. There weren't going to be any homes for them in the foreseeable future either. Empty promises were adding up. Bad math.

If you ask them, weird that nobody did, the homeless blamed themselves for their situations. They knew it was going to be up to them to fix it. Who else? Yet, they were in no position to achieve much of anything, 80% were men, 20 to 50 years old, in midtown without any money, without connections, nobody to phone, no phone, searching for a lucky break. Facts are facts. They were there on the streets of midtown seemingly impervious to outreach efforts. We were going to figure out what it was going to take for them, on their terms, to come indoors with us. Maybe it has as much to do with what they wanted from providers as it does what they didn't want to give up. For sure, indoors they've got to live under the rules of others. But how could it be, in this country especially, that we do not see them for what they most basically are? "Consumers."

Consumer rights include the "right to be informed: availability of information required for weighing alternatives, and protection from false and misleading claims in advertising and labeling practices," and the "right to choose availability of competing goods and services that offer alternatives in terms of price, quality, service." Businessdictionary.com

Seen by passersby as illegitimate, what if we turned that around and established legitimate reasons for them to be in midtown? We could change people's negative perceptions, that's what. With services in our Center offered to all comers, we grouped them in "types" of membership - we asked that each choose a type of membership that would spell out the degree of involvement they anticipated needing. To some degree then, like everyone else in midtown, they'd be there because they belonged, our place being their reliable destination end point. Normalization. They would blend into the fabric instead of standing out, literally. The massive Grand Central Terminal, being smack center midtown, was always where people mingled on their way to somewhere else. Well now, they too were in midtown for proprietary reasons. They were members of our Center. They were engaged in a business-for-self endeavor and would be respected for that. On the way somewhere, tending to their business of survival, were they not then as legitimate as anyone else? Just asking.

When we interviewed the late novelist in our book *Beyond Homelesness*, Jerzy Kosinski did not disappoint. He said, "Why not regard them as we might any failed businessman?"

We opened a Multi-Services Drop-In Center two blocks away and offered free memberships to all comers, allowing them to choose whichever scope of services, from all to none, that they wished to receive. Their pace. We were intent on hiring as many people as we could, drawn from the pool of our visitors. It had to be that way.

Three hots and a cot? Is that all? How about something beneficial to the long term as well? Okay, a thought in the form of a question: If an industry of services worth billions of dollars, 2 billion in New York alone, has been formed around their plight, shouldn't the homeless themselves get most of the jobs generated?

We had detractors. That's right. It's too tame to call them that, more like conquistadors. From the first meet, instead of turning towards us, leaning forward, "Thanks, we can use the help," they were up against us, leaning backward, "Leave the homeless alone." We threatened their food line – we did, but we thought in a good way, trying to help everyone indoors, just two blocks away. Maybe they'll stay indoors and get whatever help they want, we said. Our willingness to help homeless people directly, somehow fueled the notion that we were up to no good; that we were acting "against type?" Oh yeah, we were their enemies, they figured, and they treated us that way from Day One. It was a set up and I walked right into it. Class warfare. We made the calls, it's just that they wouldn't take them.

The most civil thing we could do is restore their consumer rights. It'd be as if they had insurance that every program accepted, and for which they'd not need a referral. That way, they'd have complete access to the industry's array of services. Liberation. Choice. Treatment decisions. The right to pick their service providers or to change course at any time? Civil rights.

Wouldn't you know it, our biggest detractors, the most avowed, started things off for themselves in 1981, following a court victory that named them the walk-in auditors of a brand-new city policy. Three meals, and a homeless shelter bed at night, "three hots and a cot," was now every person's right, a right that the city was required now to fulfill, upon demand. That could be a very good thing, but why appoint anyone permanently as watchdog? Permanently. Where's the quality control on them? Was this an animal that gave birth to itself? The Board. Its members were consistently chosen as the talking heads in nearly every newspaper article about homelessness from then on. The briefcases of these self-made superheroes bulged with potential lawsuits, their thing, some yielding important results, others just plain harassment, Saul Alinski style. Saul would not have appreciated how disingenuous they were to the whole of the facts I would hope. Often, their moves were merely public relation moves, the threat being their legal bite, notoriety for "the cause," the prize. The start-up social advocacy agency that The Board founded to carry out their court-appointed oversight, invented the scandals at the heart of this story, inventions which spurred our slow demise.

Reframing was their modus operandi. What we called outreach, they said was really an effort to "hide the problem indoors." That our homeless and formerly homeless outreach workers were really "goons," who we organized into "goon squads." Their goal was not to bring people indoors for help as we claimed, but "in an effort to sanitize midtown, to harass and beat other homeless people up, to chase them away from our district." When we paid homeless attendees five dollars for spending time at a monthly outreach breakfast fair, which we held to showcase service programs, they said it was a case of our "bribing them to get out of town." They referred to our program as being something akin to a "back to Africa" approach. Why would a newspaper print that observation without visiting or at least calling us? Why not start off neutral, even skeptical, and take time to investigate the matter? Were they beholden to The Board for its soundbites? Guess so. The Board didn't stop there. There's more.

At our Multi-Services Drop-In-Center, we had security guards at the front door, just there, and a walk-through metal detector as well. If they were needed for some reason, we'd know where to find them. We'd call and they'd come running. But they stayed there so that the rest of the building could be kept relatively mellow, quiet please, somebody might be trying to catch up on sleep. Climbing to the higher floors. A former high school, there was an internal winding staircase, very wide, airy, tall ceilings, six floors high. You could climb up the dozen or so staircases, two of them between each of the floors, straight up to the roof, which itself was looked down upon by some of the city's highest structures. A thousand windows seemed to be looking on. A sea of concrete and steel surrounding our "little" 30,000 square foot building. Inside, each floor had two or three big classroom-sized rooms. As I said, no security except at the front door. No problem. People were nice. We knew that if women felt safe there, we were probably doing something right for everybody.

Is the system rigged? You decide. They labeled the problem, shaped the argument, and "taught" certain reporters what to see upon close inspection, one side of one angle. Okay, perhaps they were not exactly terror-cells, but they wielded a moral compass like emboldened warriors. Not to fall in line, which is where we came in, was risky.

We weren't supposed to succeed; better to think we didn't.

Meanwhile, then as now, resulting from various and combined efforts, most homeless people are indoors. Yet, then as now, there are thousands of people living outside, literally under our noses, their status degraded, curbside. Elusive to the public, their impoverished appearance is all. To the contrary, about 90% of New York's homeless were usually indoors. Like their outdoor counterparts, not doing well, still they may have been saved from the worst, street life, equally for its degree of disconnectedness to the economic mainstream as well as for its intrinsic dangers. Sometimes though, indoors means no more than a bed in a large shelter, which present great difficulties to their residents as well. Degenerative experiences, en masse.

Shelters help us see two distinct groups of homeless single adults. There is one group usually indoors, and another group usually outdoors. The official NYC mayoral counts of homeless people on the streets from February 2003 all the way to February 2016 have indicated two to four thousand people, mostly single adults, some couples, living on New York City streets, subways, and parks. So, there are as many as ten times the numbers of disconnected single adults living in shelters than outside where people tend to be even more disconnected than them.

While it is not so simple as saying that they are homeless because no one will have them, almost by definition that is true. As sociologist Peter Rossi wrote, it is "apparent that the network of kith and kin is the last line of defense against homelessness." He went on to recommend "aid to families with dependent adults."

When single homeless men and women do make the choice to enter the public shelter system, they must tolerate its rules and accept the interventions of its social services staff. For those hundreds who, perhaps by disposition alone, are simply not willing to succumb, the only time they might come indoors for the night is when they must, if hospitalized, arrested, or when the temperature drops below freezing, their hands forced by the police. Interestingly, when they come into a few dollars, they will take a room or a bed somewhere, a most important point, because that's what money in-the-pocket does. This fact speaks to another, that they wish to be indoors. Yet, they are saying "no" to outreach workers. Good reasons for a bad decision? Or are they good decisions? In any case however, because they are living outdoors, they can be thought of as comprising what Peter Rossi called the "literal" homeless; what we're referring to in more relative terms as "usually-outdoors."

How you define homelessness affects the count, which affects the funding. The broader the definition, the higher the numbers. Enough passion and soon you'll find yourself counting the "invisible" homeless. For sure, the higher your numbers, the greater the demands you can make politically. The greater the demands, even greater grows your dissatisfaction, all of it a powerful impetus to forge ahead. Despite the ineffectiveness of the approach. Not to worry, there's always going to be a call for a humanitarian "re-doubling" of the effort. "We just can't give up." Typically, the funding flows because the funders don't want to give up either. Sadly, the process speaks to expectations too. They get dumbed down – people do not expect different outcomes. Is there no alternative? Ironic how things work out; "alternative approaches," ours and others, find their life in this ineffectiveness.

We turn to what sociologist Joseph Blau referred to in 1992 as the best estimate available. Completed by The National Alliance to End Homelessness, its findings fell somewhat in the middle of The Board's political speculations and the city's undercounts. They concluded that 2.1 million people experience homelessness for at least part of the year, while 735,000 are homeless on any given day. In 1999, the National Law Center found a similar relationship between the numbers homeless yearly, 2 million, to daily, 700,000. And in April 2016, the National Alliance once again found similar numbers, with just under 600,000 people homeless at any given time. However, in every year in the past 20 years, the number of people living doubled-up is increasing. We could speculate the latter resulted, in part, from the bad name shelters have earned, that it does not necessarily point to an actual reduction in homelessness. Speculation. But instead, suppose we just accept these last numbers without that caveat, meaning that 25 years after the 1992 first count, there were 135,000 less homeless people. The questions of experimental validity and/or of the research tool's margins of error aside, of the 735,000 considered to be homeless at any given time in 1992, in each of the years that followed, 5400 people on average found a place to live? That's either 1 in 374, based on the 2 million per year, or 1 in 136, based on the 735,000. But maybe the better point is the turnover, about two out of three homeless people cycle out of homelessness each year. At any given time, most people who have been, or will be, homeless are housed, as in "found a roof over their heads for the night." At least that. Three times as many as not. There are then, as we've said, two categories of homeless single adults, which are based on a gross understanding of where they spend their time:

Group One - The Indoor Homeless

Homeless at various times during the year, most of their time even when homeless is spent indoors.

Group Two - The Outdoor Homeless

While they might obtain housing at various times, Joseph Blau found that these people live outdoors 80% of the time.

One major difference between living outdoors and living indoors is that mortality rates are four times higher on the streets. Perhaps we are speaking more of a continuum, a narrowing field from the start, those who escape the streets at one end, and those who die on the streets at the other.

Peter Marcuse wrote how today's homelessness differs from that of all earlier periods: "Today's homelessness is a long-term, not a temporary or transitional, phenomenon." For one fifth of the nation's single homeless population, with men outnumbering women 4:1, that is evidently true. Historically, people who are displaced settle where they will be most tolerated, even if only for a little while, and often only until the community rises to expel them.

For the outdoor homeless person, the more reliable locations are in or near transportation facilities. Fast-paced activities, around-the-clock access, and transient populations offer minimal social resistance. For those who wanted to set up a table to sell books or even to panhandle, there's abundant opportunity. A homeless person new to New York, there being no more Bowery, often just stays where the buses or trains drops him off. In fact, that's where this story's sharpest focus is on, midtown Manhattan, a trapezoidal mile of midtown stretched between two large transportation facilities, Penn Station and Grand Central Terminal.

Three

Twelve years before these midtown adventures, I had visited an island within an island, set apart, called "The Bowery." About one square mile in size with New York's oldest street, Bowery Avenue, running through it, an area that Teddy Roosevelt compared to hell about a hundred years ago. In the late 1970s, when researching down there one evening, besides dozens of restaurant-fixture wholesale shops, I counted nine taverns within just a few short blocks of each other. Keeping with our John Donne theme, among these nightspots, scattered about, were lodging houses with beds enough for hundreds of local castaways. Brownstones everywhere, grouped together and stand-alone, a sprawling human warehouse, always a "room" available. The Bowery, then, as a whole institution. Living made more manageable, self-contained, that is, a man had options, crummy options, but he did not have to sleep on the street. He could rent out, one night at a time, a super-cheap, chicken-coop-wired, and windowless cubicle just that much bigger than the tiny, single, very possibly lice-infected bed within it. All this, yet the landlords deigned to pass themselves off as risk-takers. "We're in a dirty business," they'd say. For sure, they charged very little for what little they offered, yet their profit margin went a long way in paying down their mortgages and growing their equity. Their "hotels" were booked to near-capacity year-round, and beyond that on bad weather nights. To the men, the small rectangles were seen as at least two or three dollars better than the streets, overnight accommodations scaled to affordability. Affordable housing? That's dark. That was also how broke they were. Yet, from wherever you stood late at night or early morning, you could also see people who looked like they couldn't afford even that. Maybe they simply did not want to ask the city for a free ticket into one of those coops, the "buy-in" too big of a price to pay, even if not exactly coming from their empty pockets. For more, see Lionel Rogosin's 1956 docufiction film, *On the Bowery,* or for a washed down version, any one of the 48 Bowery

Boys films put out around the same time. The area was what investigative journalist Diane Jeantot once referred to as where the "socially quarantined" stayed. The Bowery.

Written in 1933, *Down and Out in Paris and London,* by George Orwell, was the first book that stopped us in our tracks. We read and reread it for his own participant observation perspective, the first book that confirmed our work so thoroughly. We felt a little lighter in our step. Orwell described the two faces of receiving, that "we love the giver for giving to us in an hour of need but simultaneously, we hate the giver for seeing us in this state." He demonstrated the structural arrogance of doing "for" someone as opposed to the more practical and humanistic approach of doing something alongside someone, in other words, "with them." In its negation of the opportunity to establish a relationship, a connection born from reciprocity, doing "for" someone without wanting anything but compliance in return, provides the "groundwork" for what ethno-methodologist Harold Garfinkle called a "status degradation ceremony." It partially fulfills the social formula necessary for shame. If you were in the business of helping someone through their recovery, for example, it makes the task much more difficult for the person if they are expected to jump through the hoop of this often-demeaning structure. Nobody willingly hands you the reins to their life, not usually. Next, we looked at the book that inspired Orwell to write his, that is, Jack London's *People of the Abyss,* written in 1902. In disguise, London set out to do exactly what Giamo and I did, only about 75 years earlier. Looking further back into the past, London's book too had an inspiration of its own. Jacob Riis' mostly photographic study *How the Other Half Lives.* It came out 10+ years before London's book, around 1890, which was roughly when, yet another great book came out, to wit, *The Open Boat and Other Stories* by Stephen Crane's. Especially two of its stories, *Men in the Storm,* and *Experiment in Misery.*

Within the first year of spending that kind of time down there, meeting with many different people, hundreds of hours in conversation, an idea took hold. That each of the men knew it was up to them to escape their place on skid row. Nobody was going to rescue them. Their perspective. The world as they saw it. Yet, they were immobile. Unemployed. Let go.

Most alcoholics in New York were not in the Bowery. Why them? Boom, another floodgate of questions. And through it all, we were quickly accepted by our subjects. What did a gathering in a Bowery tavern have in common with any other all-night cocktail party in any other part of town? People looking past each other, looking inward, blankly, maybe nowhere? Were they friendly teammates engaged in locker room banter? Hardly, for the ultimate showstopper was "Yeah, well you can't spell bum without 'u' in it." Another one: "Don't mind me, I have optical mitosis. My ass is connected to my eyes, and it gives me a shitty outlook on life." All of it, adding up to a perpetual circle in a downward vacuum, life with a slow flush, life on the edge, Sisyphus no longer a myth.

Once, after attending a seminar on fieldwork at the 116th street campus of Columbia University, I approached the speaker, the famed anthropologist Margaret Mead, for an up close and personal question. She was surprisingly short, sitting there behind a low desk at the front of the converted classroom, so even though I was only 5'9" myself, I had to bend way down. Virtually in a squat then, after telling her about our study, I asked her if she thought Ben and I should spend an overnight in a Bowery hotel to see what it was like. I will never forget her answer: "How else are you going to know what the cockroaches do?" Classic anthropology, which she helped invent. As if in a Donald Goines novel, experiencing the inner city within the inner city, a parallel universe, everything being the same except different, here we were with people who were literally part of a hidden tribe stuck in an inverse relationship with "uptown." It seemed to be defined by how literally cut off from "society proper" they were. But for our fieldwork approach, subtle but sure, we'd know very little about them.

By 1981, that same area, four city blocks by ten, an expanse of streets at the southernmost end of Third Avenue, the Bowery, had been discovered by the real estate community. Like skid-rows everywhere, New York's own was now in the process of being reclaimed by mainstream prospectors who viewed it merely as a series of building plots, as under-utilized real estate, and taking it a step further, New York City style, towards the reality of gentrification and under-capitalized air-rights.

Everyone else is protected by sheet rock, brick, window shade and curtains. They've got vices too, vices they feed; hidden from view, even from each other. Audience segregation.

Why the Bowery? The Bowery was somewhere to be somebody. A lesson learned. For these men, where else?

In the Fall of 1977, a Bowery resident said to me "I'm not here because of problems. I got no mother and no father. Listen here, could ya? I was born an orphan; got no relatives and I was never married. Man, I don't got no problems." No problems to speak of. W.E.B. Du Bois. Double Consciousness.

~ ~ ~

Margaret Mead, Jack London, Stephen Crane, George Orwell, Jacob Riis, Sutherland and Locke, Harper Lee, Donald Goines, David Shapiro, Alfred Adler, Virginia Satir, Carl Rogers, Leon Festinger, Harold Garfinkle, Herbert Gans, Anderson, Peter Rossi, Knut Hanson, James Baldwin, Lionel Rogosin, Jerzy Kosinski, SE Hinton, Richard Wright, Henry Miller, Maya Angelou, Harriet Beecher Stowe, Bob Dylan, George Seligman, Carl Whitaker, Lionel Rogisin. Street corner society.

Four

Most homeless people have decided that New York's one-billion-dollar public and private shelter system offers accommodations that are preferable to the streets. The verdict is in. If it's a choice between shelters and street life, for single adults throughout the country, shelters win out 5:1. Do shelter residents know something about street life? Firsthand knowledge. Sometimes the roof *is* all, which is not to say that people in the shelters are happy with the accommodations. They're not. See Peter Rossi's *Without Shelter*. Obviously though, to some, street life has its advantages. In the minority to be sure though, there are those who choose to remain on the streets, a cruel play on the whole concept of choice, but their choice, nonetheless. When doing outreach, it's important to revisit that decision with them. Does it still have validity in the time and place of the moment at hand?

~ ~ ~

Homelessness is happening to them. At the center of their stories, they are the primary protagonist. Whether cast in that role by a sudden fire, or from being slammed by a what became a growing snowball too big to be contained, they will feel as if they have been "in charge" all along, as in, "It happened under my watch." Managing their survival, their personal stories always from a listener's point of view, fascinating, we'd inquire, by what psychological means have they been surviving? Apparently rare, our approach, with attitude as described, we noticed, was much appreciated. In a whisper, "Psst! I want to work. I want a job. You got one?" You bet we will work on that.

~ ~ ~

Most importantly, our outreach workers were peers of the very people they approached. They were once homeless too, on the street, or in a homeless shelter, or in a drop-in center. They knew a lot about what each person might need to hear, often actually knowing the person they were speaking with, or they knew someone who knew someone who knew them. Six degrees of disconnection. We'd insist that the sort of knowledge they had, once trained to best use it, is what has helped them become some of the more perfect salespeople out there, if getting someone inside is the top priority, that is. In fact, they want to succeed more than most, their ego-drives in gear, their empathy ramped up. No surprise, drawn from their personal experiences, they are positioned to say the kinds of things successful salespeople everywhere say.

~　　~　　~

When teaching their sales brokers how to close a deal during a cold call, brokerage firms encourage them to convey three things: "I know how you feel. I used to feel that way too. Here's what I did about it." In essence, it was "I know, I felt, I did." A most compelling sales approach. And, in context, just as compelling, more at stake here, was our peer-to-peer outreach strategy, undertaken for some of the same reasons drug programs widely use former addicts as peer counselors. Again, we can turn to *The Souls of Black Folks*, think Du Bois' "Double Consciousness" and "The Veil." The outreach worker cares deeply how he is seen, especially by the person he is helping, his peer on the street, one down. With much of the groundwork having been done before their first meet, the two of them will very likely make a "connection." Perhaps by way of personal fragmentation, with each of the participants needing to profit from the experience, the encounter is "meant" to count, and it does. Experiential transformation. It was happening where everybody involved becomes one step more whole. A case of crosswinds, shared identification aside, apparently embodied in the outreach worker is a sort of next-level success, and when he or she speaks to the person on the ground, a certain kind of hope is conveyed. Hopefully, from down below comes that spark, an inner dialogue: *If he can, maybe I can.* Personal reconciliation can be revisited, fragmentation breaking down that much. Divided selves merging? Finally, there can be a sense of continuity, maybe even purpose. This is not a treatment program, but we want to help in every way we can. This is more like a healthy sales approach if you will. It touches on vital issues without condescending to the person who is one-down, the parental voice, "You need treatment. Come on." No, it starts from the ground and goes up, because that's where the person is and needs to go. And the outreach worker? He is furthering his own progress that much more, with a peer and in front of a peer, his body of work on display. This is huge for him. As for us, why can't we create a programming approach that includes paying attention to the progress of our outreach workers too? Outreach done this way can be intrinsically healing, and both the worker and the person he's helping do need to heal some. Both are in great positions to help the other. A dialectical approach. Positive reciprocity.

Who are these people who are homeless who will not come indoors, unlike their usually housed peers? Even if disconnected and living in a shelter, the "usually-housed" have chosen to be that rather than to be on the streets. In the case of the sheltered homeless, perhaps given absurd options, they've nevertheless chosen to be in an institution of some sort. If not a hospital or a program, a shelter then, an assigned bed, part of a congregate, surrounded by peers, on a caseworker's caseload. For this, they are less socially isolated than their usually unhoused peers who made a different decision, that is, to avoid the institutional settings offered, instead, to stay outside, to be literally homeless.

$\sim$ $\sim$ $\sim$

Cohen and Sokolovsky, two researchers who wrote *Old Men of The Bowery*, noted that those homeless who live on the streets had only two-thirds of the social connectedness of their community-housed peers. One-third less connected than a sheltered person. One Bowery resident who lived outdoors told them, "People are more trouble than they're worth. Ya think they're your friends then next thing ya know your shoes are gone. Living on the street is easier because you can stay away from everyone if ya want to." So, there's that. But to survive on the streets does requires a certain sort of intense dependency even if on a smaller and smaller circle of people. As that happens, social distance from everybody else increases. As this occurs, it's only natural they'd be less responsive to professional outreach efforts. Eviction psychology.

Generally referred to as street people, they will sometimes spend the overnight in a homeless shelter, but typically sleep in boxes, tunnels, doorways, park benches, even behind bushes or in trees, very often just riding the trains and snoozing, trying to find that fine line between feeling safe and being out of view, being alert to trouble, but catching some much-needed z's too. Sadly, as they continue to live outdoors, accomplishing survival, "mastering" their environment, they grow even less amenable to standard outreach efforts. Their physical safety, self-esteem, and social status too are at the lowest levels imaginable. A somewhat rigid adherence to their routines helps keep them alive. They "know" how to survive. Public judgment based on such constructs as "deserving" or "undeserving" becomes muddled, just as cause and effect does. Paradoxically, the visibility of street people is reflective of their social isolation. See Stephen Crane's *Experiment in Misery* to understand the process, often repeated daily:

> "The youth was trudging slowly, without enthusiasm...was clothed in an aged and tattered suit...By the time he had reached City Hall Park he was so completely plastered with

yells of 'bum' and 'hobo' that he was in a state of the most profound dejection."

Descent meets dissent, or is it the other way around? Howard Griffin, in *Black Like Me,* wrote about walking through familiar areas with purposely darkened skin, passing as a black man. He strolled past a social club whose solicitors worked the sidewalk calling out to all those who passed by except to him. "Tonight, they looked at me but did not see me." Invisibility results from a social process, which perpetuates exclusion. Both actors participate, but it is the person living on the street whose life is, relative to the other, on the skids, irrelevant. Always, in instances such as these, the status of the invisible person is lower than the one who does not see him.

As the late ethno-methodologist Harold Garfinkel stated: "Any communicative work between persons, whereby the public identity of an actor is transformed into something looked on as lower in the local scheme of social types, will be called a "status degradation ceremony." Such social communication, these micro-sociological processes, are what Stephen Crane's character was experiencing as he walked downtown. The process whereby one person is "degraded" at the expense or for the benefit of the other. No surprise, according to Garfinkel, this degrading process is "in accordance with socially valid and institutionally recommended standards of preference." It is the preferred way we work as a society to keep each other in place, to keep our place, often to displace. In fact, as Garfinkel pointed out, "There is no society that does not provide in the very features of its organization the conditions sufficient for inducing shame." In short, where there is status, there are battles adjusting it and, the point here, to it. Experiences are not events tied end to end, even if experiential segues provide a seamless sense. People's lives do not occur in vacuums. There is the snowball effect, the "post" in post-trauma, or perhaps it's more of a liquid quality, like the current of a stream. Proteanism embodies the flow of this liquidity. To psychiatrist and author Robert Jay Lifton, it is proteanism which allows us "the ability to stay constant in metamorphosis." It helps us feel whole. Unfortunately, he says, when combined with extreme poverty, proteanism might render the person more fragmented than whole.

Despite decades of newspaper articles, television specials, and advocacy, insiders congregate towards one end of a continuum, and outsiders to the other, remaining, to each other, unknown, both groups being worlds apart. Besides not standing alongside each other in the workplace, they are not sharing movie theater seats nor bumping into each other at social gatherings. They do not go to the same hairdressers, eat in the same places, or get examined by the same doctors. All in all, it's a situation rife for typecasting, as opinions get based solely on second or third hand information.

If an outreach worker is trying to help someone who despite laying on the ground, apparently in need, is rejecting the effort, then the situation calls for the outreach worker to step back. If this is happening often, the program that hires the outreach worker itself may need to step back. Then should come the pivot. The program needs to recognize the primary social patterns at play. As we have seen, a person experiences their exclusion from the mainstream not just from the stares, hidden or obvious, or by way of their apparent invisibility, both measures of their social distance, but by the weight of the personal shame they feel, out on display as they are, the societal degradation, ongoing. Talk about being superfluous – Hey, where is the housing? Don't I matter? Recognizing that these sociological and psychological themes can act as barriers to personal action, enabling the outreach program to prioritize its approach.

If a person spends all day in the business of survival, just like in any other business, to be successful, he must put in the time, and in time, if successful, it's probably because he has become somewhat consumed with his work. He survives because he is good at it. And, if he does it for very long, it becomes his norm, day after day. His way of life becomes his lifestyle. He lives it. He breathes it. His lifestyle? Alfred Adler wrote about the coherence of the personality, of the unity of the individual in all their expressions, "The style of life commands all forms of expressions; the whole commands the parts." He considered the differences between two pine trees, one growing in a valley and one on a mountainside; in the case of the latter, seemingly in defiance of gravity, there is a certain amount of molding to the environment, a bending toward the sun. Despite that, both remain pine trees with all but a few qualities in common; they are of different sizes, both shaped (one straight, one bent) by "society's pliers," a Dylan phrase, the sun, and the slope of the mountain, just two of many influences interacting with the tree's life forces, what Adler would call their "expressions." They are both standing tall, pointing to what will sustain them, the same, but different.

Warren Cummings was 21 years old and no stranger to New York when he entered its shelter system early in the summer of 1982. Born to working-class, black, common-law parents, he was born in the Dade County, Florida projects. His father, whose name he never learned, dropped out of sight when Warren turned three. At four, then, he and his mother moved to Brooklyn into a building where one of her sisters already lived. His mother found a job in a local Laundromat and left her son to be raised by his aunt. Two years later, she met a man who soon thereafter moved in to help raise the family, which grew by three more children over the years.

In fifth grade, around 1971, Warren was ten years old. Due to classroom behavior such as "shooting paper clips, putting tacks in the teacher's chairs, and hanging out with a crowd that did whatever we wanted to do," he was thrown out of public school and forced to attend a special school, what they called a "900" school. Faced as they saw it with innumerable disciplinary problems, according to Warren, the teachers "were allowed to hit you if you didn't do what they said you should do. They'd take their belts off and make you lean with your hands against the blackboard. If they didn't have a belt, they would use a bamboo pole."

He stayed there for three years and was allowed after graduating to re-enter the public-school system, where he finished the ninth grade.

During these public-school years, he and his school friends took part in a scam to avoid attending classes. With store bought program cards, they forged the appropriate signatures to convince their parents of their perfect school attendance records. School days were spent sneaking on the subways, for which he was ticketed on four different occasions, drinking beer, smoking marijuana, and hanging out. Finally, they would be careful to be home by 3:30 as if they went to school, with nobody the wiser.

Time for tenth grade. Now 15 years old, Warren went to that first day of school, sized up each teacher's method of signing off on the cards, and proceeded to stay absent for three consecutive months. At the beginning of the fourth month, he was caught by his mother and stepfather, who beat him. They monitored him very closely for several weeks to get him back on track.

While in high school, he found a part-time job in a supermarket, where he earned upwards of 80 dollars per week.

"On our breaks from work, on the weekends, we would throw stones at passing buses and then run away. I might have hurt people, but I really don't remember."

During his off-school hours, he hung out with Ted, an eighteen-year-old twelfth-grader who said he was a hit man for the Mafia.

"The thing was, he always had two or three thousand dollars in his pocket from hurting or killing someone for his bosses. He wanted me to join him, but I knew that if I joined, I might never get out."

His friend Ted introduced him to a different kind of fun, holding orgies in his Harlem apartment, often inviting three or four girls and several male friends to join in, one of them being Warren. Rum, beer, and reefer would be all over the place. If the girls didn't want to go along, Ted would slip some Spanish fly in their drink, and then everybody's clothes would come off. "There would be ten or more of us naked at a time," Warren said, "it was all about the party,"

When he was 17 years old, Warren's family moved south, but he refused to go with them, choosing to remain in New York. He was having too much fun as he couch-surfed, spent some nights on the street, and generally partied the days away.

When he was in twelfth grade, he was fired from his job, "for coming to work late." He quit school, and immediately landed a job in a factory where during the first week, he came to work late only once, but during his second week, he came to work late again, this time getting himself fired.

After this experience, he went south to join his family. He remembered feeling somewhat demoralized and did not feel like working right away. He needed some time off, he said.

"I was having too much fun. In Georgia, if you are from New York, you are like a celebrity. I had a radio, and women just came to me to get into the music. I wanted all of them. I just couldn't up make my mind. I didn't live with my parents then. I had taken my own room for about $20 per week."

He grew bored, eventually taking a job working "off the books," just long enough to earn carfare back to New York. There he got a job and moved into his own apartment. After four months, a girl moved in with him. Her welfare payments now had an address to come to, which proved fortunate because, three months later, he had an argument with his boss and lost his job. He returned to work at the same supermarket he had worked in as a child in school. Again, he was fired for tardiness and attitude. "He would always be picking on me. His wife didn't want kids, and he did, so he'd always be in a bad mood. Sometimes, he'd be angry at me for no reason at all."

Warren left his girlfriend and moved back down to Georgia. He landed a job upstate with his stepfather as a laborer installing windows into makeshift tin houses. He tired of that job within one month and quit. Soon, he found a position loading watermelon onto trucks, which paid him sometimes well over $100 a day, seven days a week. It lasted only two weeks due to its seasonal nature, but he amassed, he remembered, close to $1000. After this job ended, he obtained a similar job as an apple picker. But after three days, discovering that after room and board, he had only several dollars left, he quit.

"I just left one day. I turned from the foot of the ladder I had been working on, and just walked down the highway. I had no suitcase and by then, no money left."

He hit the road, hitched a ride to a local town, and applied for welfare. He was able to receive, through Traveler's Aid, a bus ticket to New York City. In New York, he soon found a factory job. He took a one-room apartment, met a woman, and invited her to move in with him.

"She was 33 years old but said she didn't want to have sex. After two weeks, I told her to get me a bottle of vodka from the bootlegger on the corner. When she came back, she found her suitcase on the sidewalk. I snatched the vodka out of her hand and slammed the door in her face."

Though he stayed at the factory job for nearly one year, he was eventually fired for continued lateness and for arguing with the boss's son. He received unemployment benefits and instead of paying rent, spent it on movies, food, and clothing. "I could have paid rent, but I didn't put my mind to it."

After being evicted from his apartment, he lived for three months on the F train, a Manhattan--Brooklyn subway line.

"I would hang out until 11:30 or 12:00 getting high with different people I'd meet. Then I would board the train like I was going home. I would ride from one end of the line to the other, from 179th street to Coney Island, and back. Sometimes, at 179th Street, the police would take me off the train and put me on the third street bus, a special bus the city operates to take homeless people to their main center. I would go down to the Bowery and stay around there for the night in some hotel. Occasionally, I would get a summons for jumping turnstiles. As soon as the cop would turn away, I would rip it up and throw it away. How was I going to pay for it? Other times, mostly during rush hour, I would get a summons for "attempting to jostle others." I would just be standing there, minding my own business, with a can of beer or rum in my pocket, and they would give me a ticket. A lot of times there would be warrants too."

Once he was arrested for sneaking on a train. The arresting officer checked the computer and made note of outstanding warrants. Warren was sent to Rikers Island for six months for, like he said, "jostling others." "It was okay there because I saw hundreds of different people I knew from where I grew up. Some were there for murder; others were going upstate for something. Some of them said that they would rather be in Rikers than at a shelter because they got bigger portions of food there."

When he was released, during this period between the summers of 1983 and 1984, Warren had four jobs, each lasting less than a week. The first two involved picking potatoes in North Carolina. He went in a van with 15 others to work on whichever farm was hiring. In both cases he did not like the conditions and quit after several days. "I left because the outdoor bathrooms were cold and there was no toilet paper or soap." The other two jobs were in factories and lasted only three days each.

"I quit the first factory job because they had rules like you couldn't go to the bathroom between breaks. And if you were late even a few minutes, they would send you home."

The second job lasted for such a short time because he and the boss fought over his being late his first two days there. On the third, "I realized I would be late, but when I got there, I started defending myself and arguing with him. He fired me for being too aggressive."

Warren's welfare case had been suspended, and he was

looking for work. He described an incident, which reflected his attitude about living amongst other homeless people: "I was hanging out in the park with some girls I had seen around. We were drinking some rum and having a good time. This guy who knows me from the shelter approached and said to me, "Hey, don't you have to get back to the shelter and sign in for your bed?" I turned to him and told him to cool it, but the time I got back to this one girl, she was walking away. You can't let the women know where you are staying. You have to let them know you are working and living on your own."

At 21 years old, Warren Cummings was living in the shelter when we met him. Like many of his sheltered peers, it was difficult to figure out how to help him. The professional who has trouble housing him doesn't want to be discouraging but doesn't want to "pile on" the bad news either. What to do? No answer. Everyone's on their own. The Board won't tell us, but there's no housing.

Given that they cannot conceive of Warren being able to hold a job that would enable him to afford rent, not believing he would pay the rent anyway, to get there, the staff works to label him "disabled," which will render him eligible for the type of housing for which he will not have to pay. Because he has no income, he would then "qualify" for housing support through the local welfare office, which would cover his 30% share of the housing, with his newly acquired federal disability benefits paying for the rest of the rent. To achieve this, the homeless person is told not to do the one thing he yearns to do. He is told, "just for now, do not work or to even look for work unless you want to lose," now get this, "your housing eligibility." This is an odd way to put it, given that everybody is supposed to be getting "housing-first." That's right though, top-priority housing goes to the disabled, and who are they, besides the obvious, it turned out that shelters are so toxic to proper functioning, that if you have lived in one for an extended length of time, even if you are able-bodied, you may be considered "functionally disabled," or shelterized, thereby qualifying you for top-priority housing. It's a rule change made to benefit the sheltered, and it has. However, it's a rule change in the face of no housing, which still means you are homeless sitting in a shelter. "You are disabled, now act like it, or else." That's not a threat. It's just the system talking. Too bad, but at least his caseworker is a nice person.

Imagine if Warren worked at a place where initially, they'd let him take all the bathroom breaks that he wanted? If he worked where coming in late was initially a teaching moment, not a reason to fire? Imagine if every "excuse" Warren found to fulfill his detachment, not just psychobabble, was nullified by the benevolence of an incentivized employer? If the bathrooms did have toilet paper and soap? Couldn't that be called "bringing John Lennon down to earth?" Could it be called, "doing the possible." Which is better? What if, given his changeability, he was offered a series of temporary positions or day jobs, where his inability to focus was much less of a problem? Did he suffer from long-term ADHD? Maybe. Instead, worried about his vulnerability, they say to him something like, "Remember what we said to you from the beginning, Warren, 'If you get a job, you will not be considered 'disabled' and you will lose your benefits, which includes this housing too.' Now, now. Deep breaths. That's better. Be still."

Five

In the 1960s, the Kerner Report reflected on the problem of civil disorder with a wisdom that today can be applied to homelessness. "To pursue our present course will involve the continuing polarization of the American community. The alternative will require new attitudes, new understanding, and above all, new will." Polarization? Insiders and Outsiders.

~   ~   ~

Able to transplant previously hidden poor people into plain sight, homelessness is as powerful a social force as any. For example, causing poverty as much as being caused by it, this is not about who lives indoors and who lives outdoors, which is each person's physical reality, it is also about a social condition. Before they came to be called "homeless," they were "Outsiders" or on their way to such a fate, a downward drift, increasingly detached, their social ties diminishing with their every step. This is best understood only in contrast to those people we can consider "Insiders," people who, even if in an economic struggle, have a complex web of people and places they can rely on. Of course, both categories are formed by the arbitrary collapsing of several other categories, which serves to prove the power of incrementalism, but for purposes of understanding this, we collapse. The point is, then, that to the degree people are in either group, Outsiders, or Insiders, they define each other. It's not just economic theory, the tale of the perennially employed versus the chronically unemployed, it's the social drift that occurs when social inclusion becomes but a dream from which homelessness emerges. While arguments abound as to who is to blame for homelessness, or who among us is the victim, it is the will of each of the members of these categories, which we should be most concerned about. Symbolic Interactionism is real. But will is something that is aroused from personal conviction, which itself is educated by social process. This is most ironic, for a person's most significant social processes come in the workplace. Yet, most able-bodied homeless people are unemployed and often kept that way or, if working, kept apart by wage and status. Once in a homeless program as a recipient of services, they are arguably kept unemployed by way of program design. That means that they are deprived of what can be considered an almost naturally occurring social force, an active verb to be sure. Inside such programs, where policy discourages work, social networking is undermined, its corrective processes thwarted. There's the deprived and the trapped, and then there's everybody else. Herbert Gans.

Homelessness is a textbook example of how extreme poverty operates as a segregating force. Social interactions occur but within a vacuum, they're insular, and they're going to stay that way mainly because of distrust and transiency, two of the most important elements of a person's survival strategy on the streets. This circularly caused conundrum is not uncommon among homeless people. In his 1989 paper, *Without Shelter*, Peter Rossi describes an early, bitterly cold, February morning scene witnessed by his research team. It was of a group of homeless people sitting inside a Chicago bus station. Staring straight ahead, no conversation at all, everybody sat still. Yet, these few moments taking shelter from the storm were in contrast, he wrote, to "...days spent alone, always on the move, walking from food kitchens to those places where one could stand or sit without being hassled - a library, a train station, a park bench." They sat with others, but it was more of the same, they sat as if alone. Around the same time, wouldn't you know it, a New York City mayoral commission found a substantive number of homeless people "have grown up isolated from mainstream social and economic life." Despite their new-found visibility, they had become literally detached from the life-sustaining social networks of mainstream society, online or off. Until this detachment is resolved, much of today's social work and public dollars spent will continue to be in vain.

Social Standing. Despite over four decades of newspaper articles, news bulletins and television specials, and advocacy, Insiders and Outsiders remain unknown to each other. The results?
They are worlds apart. Besides not standing alongside each other in the workplace, they are also not sharing movie theater seats nor meeting each other at social gatherings. They do not go to the same hairdressers, eat in the same places, or get examined by the same doctors. All in all, it is a situation ripe for typecasting where opinions based solely on second and third-hand information, or by what is seen briefly, are formed by each every day.

Inside. For most people on the Inside, from the time of birth onward, the basic issues of survival do not scratch through to the surface of everyday life. Decisions as to where to sleep are rarely crucial, and when made, involve equally comfortable and safe alternatives. Being "broke" rarely impacts upon the availability of food and can be remedied without the slightest consideration of an anti-social action. While there are many on the Inside who live below their potential and truly suffer from that, if you are an Insider, living "on the edge" is more a conceptual choice than an economic reality.

Being freed-up from survival worries does not guarantee that Insider life will come easy. Often, there will be much stress and of course there are no guarantees, that is, one does not always obtain the pleasures one seeks. The benefits that come with the business of comfort can be plenty, but they do not necessarily protect against suffering and can cause intense pre-occupation. Still, for an Insider, social isolation derives from a state of mind rather than from a structural reality. The socially connected Insiders are unlikely to ever be homeless, to even come that close to "dropping onto the streets." They may be poor, they may "supply" the shelter system with enough overnight stays to sustain the industry and then some, but most are somehow "covered" by their resources, by others and the quality of their connections to them, hard to set a number, but put it this way, 99.5% of American citizens are not homeless. While we don't know it for a fact, because the statistics have been steady within a range, we can say that they are not likely to become homeless either.

Within each category, Insiders and Outsiders, as Henry David Thoreau wrote, "the mass of men leads lives of quiet desperation." This is not to be minimized, as half of America may live near or below the poverty line, but for the sake of this discussion, we say that most people are perhaps barely able to afford their unaffordable housing, no doubt the reliability of roof over head is always "iffy," but okay, they are inside. Once on the Inside, steadily working or not, even relatively passive people can stay relatively comfortable. People with serious drinking problems, with psychiatric problems, even those who get hospitalized, will not become homeless. People can come out of prison with their comfort only marginally interrupted, can commit otherwise serious blunders, experience tragedy, get fired or get divorced, and still, even while their blood pressure climbs, or their health fails, their basic comforts will remain intact. How can this be so? How can life on the Inside literally promise relative stability for so many, even during troubled times? There can be those tougher economic times during which their numbers may greatly shrink, still, what is responsible for such relative comfort? The simple answer lies in complicated social processes. On the Inside, peer group members engage quite naturally in the perpetuation of their comfort and in their constant hustle for more. Opportunities, resources, and choices are there for the taking. See Elijah Anderson's "cosmopolitan canopies." Not just public parks, or coffee shops, but also The Facebook Marketplace, Nextdoor.com, Swap Meets, Barn Sales, Flea Markets, Uncle Johnnie, and his contacts, even your friend's cousin's cousin. The accountant where Auntie Mary used to work knows someone who knows someone, not to worry, you're a shoo-in. Dad's former assistant is looking for people; you're on the inside track for one of the positions. Go to Bob's Haircut Salon and mention me, tell him I'm the one that used to work with his son, you'll get a discount. Hey, relax, I know the best doctor – he will make time to see you, let him know I recommended you. And so forth. Paraphrasing the famous phrase, "When you ain't got nothing, you got nothing to exchange...."

This Insider trading of ideas, of job, housing, medical information, and all sorts of referrals, even tidbits of self-improvement gossip along the sharing of contacts is invaluable and life-sustaining. Not only do people on the Inside live longer, but their stability and opportunities for upward mobility is almost ensured by both the frequency and variety of social interactions. And while it can be argued that these processes may result in an obsession with comfort that may work to the detriment of others less fortunate, it will not be very productive to try and stop them. They serve as irreducible facts of life. That is, at every social, developmental, and economic point along the circumference of their compass, people perpetuate themselves, keeping their self-definitions alive and their perspectives confirmed as the years go by, their community standing intact, all of it, the results of some very personal and socially based processes.

Outside. When we conducted our survey of people standing on the Vanderbilt Avenue food line, close to 60% reported less than $100 income in the previous month. Recent studies have shown that while in this country about fifty million people live below the poverty line, there are one and a half million people who live on less than $2 per day. Clearly, they are not gainfully employed.

Peter Rossi, in *Down and Out in America*, pointed out that "The income of the homeless is not a steady stream; it is intermittent and unpredictable, meaning for many days in the week, weeks in the month, months in the year, many homeless people have no income at all. It is no mystery why the homeless are without shelter; their incomes simply do not allow them to enter effectively into the housing market." Not even the job market.

Usually born into it or along its borders, fewer than ever of today's homeless have dropped from significantly higher economic and social ranks. The themes of outsider status and interpersonal transiency are subsumed by "the hustle" to survive in ways that magnify everyday problems associated with poverty. Their social-worked lives, the redundancies of their daily imperatives at such a primitive level, the repetitive solutions have rendered their sense-of-selves as possible agents of change to a descending minimum. Add to this a housing market which does not have room enough, an employment market which prioritizes from the Inside out and what results is equivalent to being socially and economically ostracized from Insider culture, the media often being the only link. It is not long before their personal sense of "ownership" of their lifestyle becomes distorted. Either they blame themselves for everything, or they blame everybody else. Feelings of helplessness, powerlessness, and uselessness.

As social gravity will have it, their peer support systems contain others in their same unstable situation.

Life on the Outside means few opportunities to get Inside. Only through acts of war, small-time lottery winnings, and other isolated instance of happenstance do opportunities for short visits to the Inside appear. Long stays are rare. Nevertheless, even while some Outsiders are sometimes heard to espouse negative attitudes toward life on the Inside, especially the pressure to compete with one's own accomplishments as well with those of others, by and large, most feel they deserve at least the option of life Inside, and if truly given a choice... It's called "purposeful work" for a reason.

Mythology. There are at least three significant myths which guides the way Insiders "see" homeless people. One. Homeless people do not want to work. In his essay, *No Man Can Live with The Terrible Knowledge That He Is Not Needed*, Elliot Liebow wrote that unemployment does not "like air pollution or God's gentle rain, fall uniformly upon everyone, nor does it strike randomly at our labor force. Unemployment is directional and selective; it strikes particularly at those at the bottom of our society." As he points out, in Marxist theory, work is a fundamental condition. From a Freudian perspective, it is man's strongest tie to reality. In a capitalist system, as Liebow writes, "It is also through work that the individual carries out those social roles that define him as a full and valued member of his society." Read that quote again. Close to 75% of whites believe that blacks prefer to be on welfare than to work. They're wrong. Several welfare programs require people to be working to be eligible and that hasn't stopped too many people from applying, just the opposite. People may hate being told what to do, but they would rather work than not. Despite this, many continue to believe that people receiving governmental assistance are more likely to be lazy than hard-working. Cognitive dissonance. The truth is, this myth that homeless people don't want to work defies the facts, as we found out when we conducted our food line survey. 75% of the people interviewed were African American. In that survey, we discovered that nearly 70% reported having worked steadily within the past two years, and 40% in the last month. How much did they want to work? When asked what help they needed the most, there was a virtual tie between employment, 89.5%, and housing, 90%. A virtual tie. Yet something on which we can hardly make an impact, the housing situation, is "worked" on to the exclusion of employment, the thing we can immediately make an impact on. Nothing must be built. No land or air rights in the way. The jobs are there. Inside.

Another myth. Homeless people all have drinking problems. Yet, 225 billion retail dollars were spent in 2016 on alcohol alone. It is unlikely that this came out of the pockets of the homeless. Here's a sampling of to what degree alcohol is in the lives of others: the Centers for Disease Control reports that 58% of men report drinking alcohol in the last 30 days, with 23% of adult men reporting binge-drinking 5 times a month, averaging 8 drinks per binge. In fact, close to 80% of college students report drinking regularly, with a fourth of them regular binge-drinkers. White to black, America's population ratio is about 5 to 1, yet whites outnumber blacks 7 to 1 in liquor law arrests and nearly 9 to 1 in arrests for driving under the influence. That's a lot of people drinking and making very bad decisions while under the influence. While a higher percentage of homeless people report drinking problems, about 30%, compared to the general population, around 10% - debatable, since 27% report recent binge-drinking, but still...nevertheless most homeless people do not have this as their defining problem. No doubt, it is not to be minimized, that excessive or addictive drinking or drugging negates meaningful activity and undermines good health. It increases the likelihood of downward mobility for Insiders and Outsiders alike. Not to be overlooked either is the fact that in all walks of life, alcohol use is often related to the availability of otherwise productive social activities and opportunities. That is, recreational alcohol might serve to mediate friendships and opportunity as well as to treat their absence.

Another myth. Homeless people are short-sighted. Probably so, but not, as this myth would have it, to a fault. That is, long-term planning is an incremental luxury relative to the size and stability of one's economic and social network. Being able to handle day-to-day exigencies increase capacity for long-term planning, often leading to it. If a person wishes to extend himself into the future, practically speaking, lamentations and other acts of the imagination aside, he will only succeed at this to the extent that his present situation "permits" it. To the contrary, we can think of homeless people as somewhat preoccupied against this end. As they are busy timing their travels to fit the requisite number of soup kitchen schedules to fill out the week, on-demand social worker meetings, clothing giveaways, all the while keeping their search for the instant labor opportunity on track, thinking in the long-term can be counterproductive. Irregular sleep patterns, sometimes virtually none, their surroundings that unreliable, also will detract from productivity. And, they are extremely poor, no cash or credit to draw on. From the outside looking in, it does not appear that Insiders care much about what homeless people are going through. What, they have too much on their plate, pun intended? While there is increased anger towards aggressive panhandlers, and sporadic violent acts carried out against some homeless individuals, these are exceptions to the rule. Most Insiders are not comfortable with the spectacle of homelessness, but panhandlers would not be out there if people did not give. Bus and train terminals would not be so jammed with homeless people if vendors of all sorts and other retailers did not handout free coffee, or a dollar or two for the completion of minor chores, or if publicly funded social service agencies didn't send outreach teams out there to proliferate goods and services. Newspapers would not run stories on homelessness if there was nobody out there paying attention. The stuff of humanity. The stuff of hope?

Social networking. Speaking of the facts, the social distance between those who live on the one side and those who live on the other permits for mystification of the other. Problem is, it is not likely that organic social processes will ever bring the Outside in. And in this land of Insiders, unless there is an intervention, there comes the inevitable passing of time and the further hardening of perspectives. What to do? Unravel the ways that homelessness is socially constructed.

The differences between the homeless and the almost-homeless and the never-to-be homeless is more than an issue of economics. How well are they socially networked and with whom? That's the concern here. Inevitably, social lines get drawn and barriers constructed. For too many, homelessness is abstract.

The disconnection is real. If Outsiders came to know and be known by a wider variety of people at various socio-economic levels, and in this context even each other, the economic and political reality of "homelessness" would change. It would probably be renamed too.

Perhaps networking between Insiders and Outsiders must be compelled? In return for tax breaks equivalent to 20 hours of the person's salary, in effect paying for their time, can we ask people to volunteer, and therefore for their employers to release them 20 hours annually at a qualifying social service agency? At tax time, proof of such efforts can be submitted. Or maybe it can be a year of community service when you turn 21? Should we not require candidates for political office to prove they've done that? Connectivity works for Insiders. It will work for Outsiders as well. Enough? No. The best solution is employment. The social engine.

There are voices which call for the "lift yourself up by your bootstrap" approach. They are from those for whom the concept of an "insurmountable problem" is too metaphysical. Maybe they speak less in sympathetic tones and more in challenging ones meant to uplift, in that case a potential lifesaver. In fact, it is the person with the bootstrap approach who is likely to seize upon opportunity when it does finally present itself, who is likely to best avoid negatively slanted self-fulfilling prophecies, whose vigilance against destructive environmental influences promotes perseverance. If these voices speak during times of meager opportunity however, they will have a vacuous unrealistic quality, and will heighten despair. For those who feel that to challenge the individual is to put the cart before the horse, and instead choose to challenge the government, or attack Insiders for their status, the wait will be long and the pickings few.

To say that housing will solve the problems that homeless people have is to mystify, to ignore the essence of social process, the dynamic, evolving circularity of relationships which comprise each micro-social moment. It is to introduce a new myth that states that failure is just the flip side of the overnight success.

Six

At times, I want to appear therapeutically non-congruent. You've come to me uninterested in receiving treatment, you say, yet here I am, running an outpatient psychiatry program for a hospital and here you are, sitting across from me exhibiting symptoms. You have intentionally walked into our suite of offices, clearly marked as such, and you have willing come to sit there. Or you enter a shelter where I am running the social services program. You say that you do not want or need help, yet you walk into the waiting room, sit down, and wait to be called. You ask to speak to the director. You walk in, sit down, and tell me that you don't think you need any help. You want to be in our program, you say, just no treatment or help, please, you say. Yet, right in front of me, I see that you are talking to yourself, and you are pacing back and forth in front of my office in apparent stress. You are not hiding that. What do I do? First, I assume a double-message and then, to begin the process of overriding your ambivalence, I begin to cobble together a relationship between the two of us. If you can be successful with me, that will be transferable to others of my staff. Success with us all will reinvent or grow your sense of yourself as a protagonist, in charge, socially confident among those of your peers with whom you have the most in common. Perhaps your ambivalence towards treatment will be the common denominator. Why shouldn't you be skeptical? Hopefully though, when you walk away from our meeting you will have had a positive experience without necessarily feeling you've been treated for anything at all, this even as I was trying to affect your social life. At the end of the day, or the session, I want you to leave my program with things on your mind, certainly not empty-handed, so maybe there'll be a new motto to live by, a new way to look at some aspect of your life or perhaps an awareness made more intense by our having met for those few moments. At the least, a memory of shared laughs, perhaps some meaningful exchange we can look back on, one that made future ones just that much more inevitable. I do not want you to forget me easily, and when we next meet, we will continue weaving our relationship peppered by reminders of previous encounters. I suspect that as time passes, you will grow with confidence in your social abilities...you've handled "us" well. You handled me effectively, and I am the director, in one sense no small accomplishment, a strategic victory. Your general goals having been achieved, your "social interest" ramped up, your input having been substantial, you've got something going now. As he strives to belong, and to feel significant, this is truly an Adlerian moment. He has done. He can do. Maybe beginning to see things a certain way differently, you bring your experiences from within our program, those successes, out into the world. Our relationship needs to stand out. I must genuinely like you, and you need to like how I like you.

Post-graduate, at The Institute for Mental Health Education, while earning a certification in family therapy, we came to understand the idea of circular causality. Up until then, everything was seen in terms of linear causality and there was always a need to find *the* cause, as if there were only one culprit.

Paul Casserino, a brilliant psychologist who had been trained at Smithers Alcohol and Rehabilitation Center at Roosevelt Hospital and who was running a sprawling social services department in one of the city largest shelters, an 816-bed facility on Ward's Island, where we met, showed me how effective spontaneous humor could be. He used humor to relax people, never at their expense, instead to uplift them, to disarm them, to jumpstart insight-oriented conversation...fantastic to watch him in action. Surprising how humor could underscore sincerity. Seemed that the person felt good about the fact that someone was trying to "make" him laugh. He experienced personal significance. At that moment, he was the center and the target of attention. His response mattered, his laugh. It worked in the way alcohol worked to lubricate interactions at a dinner gathering. Humor facilitated conversation. In the Bowery, alcohol mediated relationships. Humor could do that too.

There must be something right away that can be found about him that reflects positively, something he can take personally. It must be real, based on what is occurring right there and then – his seriousness, his steadfastness, his survival abilities, perhaps how he explains his situation, or something he has said that was particularly practical, for example. We can both do something different now, something better.

You are now here, actively participating. Less isolated than before we met, you are alive, a survivor no doubt, your skill-set and personal strengths are obvious in your participation with me, my staff, and some select subgroup of your peers. You've made many decisions, many, and most do not need any sort of revisiting. You may have made some bad ones, or others may have made them for you, no choice there, but mathematically, realistically, given the cards in your hand, there was no other way you could have ended up anywhere but right here, right now, in a homeless shelter, talking to me, involved with us. This conversation is proof that this is a new start and that it will be successful because of your social abilities. You "brought" yourself here, to my desk. It is happening because of your personal qualities. You are a particularly interesting person to us. Nothing grandiose here, no blame for the past, no past as prologue, just an up-close look at "what is real," right now, right here. You are experienced. You are here at my desk, right? This is a new moment, our moment. If I am being dramatic, well, it is not me that is dramatic, it is your life we're talking about here. That is dramatic. You can't write yourself off. Okay, maybe right now it seems that your past can be prologue, can be, but it's not the whole story. Even your diagnosis is but a snapshot of a moving picture.

You are in a homeless shelter, true, however you could be sitting in some dark corner somewhere like a lot of other people here might do, but you're not doing that. You are here, something that you made happen. Negative self-backtalk can't be trusted; it's too simplistic. Inside even what you may label as your larger "failure," your "homelessness," were multiple smart micro-decisions that may have literally kept you alive, for instance, that did bring you here to sit at my desk. Let's treat it that way – you're a complicated person who deserves more than you've gotten...nobody's fault, we're not going to go there. Now, let's get the ball rolling...

I don't want to be lumped with the others who have tried to help him. He could be stuck. Just in case he is, I want my work to unstick him. I am intrigued by the workings of his mind, I am. I want to notice in what ways he is different than others that I have met. Running a program of so many others similarly positioned, when I am drawn into a conversation with him, and I am drawn, what I see in him, indeed what I like about him must be specific to him. I position myself to like. I want to like each person and if I can't, it's on me...he may or may not respond, but I will do the work no matter the obstacles we face, whether it's the space or time frame in which we meet, the circumstances, my position, his position, whatever. Everybody has qualities worth noting, strengths that are obvious in him. I must be on my toes, on the lookout for pivotal moments and this is one of them, our first couple of meetings. I want to look for and reflect that perception he has of himself as being in crisis, not just in a bad spot, but let's be real, in crisis. Let's take it to be as dramatic as it is. We're going to be that serious. I want to bring that reality out, no denial here, but to help him realize that his situation is more an active verb than a period at the end of some sort of sentence he is serving. I do that, and he will, from those moments on, take back the lead. I want him to reflect onto himself. I don't want to minimize. Here, I refer to all of Carl Rogers, not the part that has been transmuted into "motivational counseling," but the part that intervenes, that prompts a person to take the lead. If I can't capitalize on them, "our" moments, then it makes our next affiliative moment less likely. In that sense, it really is on me. It is my profession, what I do, and what I am supposed to do. The segues must be relatable to the conversation at hand. It's called making something happen out of the something that is happening. Push, pull, draw out, prompt, maybe even confront. Managing the reflexes. Reflective conversations are only part of that. The more effectively I can use our relationship as a treatment tool, the better. Sigmund Freud. Negative experiences cannot always be avoided, but where possible they too will be capitalized on. No choice. The negative can be redefined, let's say, to create a positive experience, perhaps a positive experience of apology or regret, part of the foundry from which self-awareness can be mined. Learning from experience, pedestrian knowledge being the most accessible, our ups and downs as we work together become a focus, his personal philosophy always at the core of our discussions. References to it helps it grow. His capacity for personal oversight increases, his executive function becoming all that more efficient. Ultimately, I want to help codify his experience into a wisdom. Henry Stack Sullivan. Carl Whitaker. "Yes, okay, in some ways you are trapped in this place. That happens to a lot of people. But look around. Most people are not as aware as you seem to be. You're walking back and forth in front of our program with your eyes halfway open. The cup is half full? You are not disinterested, but you are not nosey either, the perfect blend of the two, yet you see most everything. Back and forth. Back and forth. Nothing escapes your notice. A lot of people may be losing time, but your awareness, which is Step One, puts you in an advantageous position from the start. Why don't we sit down and discuss strategy?"

A great start when first meeting someone is an open-ended, cut to-the-chase question. "So how did you end up here?" Or another: "So, just how have you been able to survive all this?" Both seek the perspective of the person at the center of the storm, acknowledging the seriousness of the moment, feeling his pain, and what the person already suspects about himself, that he is indeed the star of his story, his role, the protagonist. He matters. If he is suffering from low self-esteem, these questions can help throw a cognitive wedge between his self-definition and the situation he's in and can serve to reduce some of the "noise" of self-blame. They move him toward the next open-ended, cut-to-the-chase question. "What are you going to do about it?" William Glasser and Reality Therapy. These questions are linked with each other and make up the length of our approach, social-networking therapy. He is not going to do this alone. We will connect him with like-minded peers. He will see the connections for himself. He will gravitate towards them; his self-imposed isolation having met its endpoint. His sense of personal agency will be socially reinforced by the peers among whom he stands. It'll happen. He will capitalize on these moments, it's only natural, and off we go…

Considering someone disconnected is not as ambiguous as it seems. You're on the phone talking but there's no one on the other end. Just the echo of your own voice. Homelessness is like that, a process of disconnections adding up. In some ways, more visible than anyone else on the street, in the open, or perhaps in a congregate shelter, either way, on your own, here because of whatever it is you've done, or so you think, you feel to be part of an unknown crowd of people and not part of another. You have no privacy. There's no exit. No one you can call. You feel like an extension cord with no outlet to plug yourself into. I see you in the hallway. I approach. "Hey, good to see you. I was wondering if you would stop by. Come on in…you know, I was thinking about something you said the other day…" Oh my god, he noticed me, maybe I'm not invisible. He's been thinking about me. Maybe I do count for something. It's not that easy, but it's a start.

"It is the client who knows what hurts, what problems are crucial, what experiences have been deeply buried. It began to occur to me that short of my inappropriate need to demonstrate my own cleverness and learning, I would do better to rely upon the client for the direction of movement in the process." Carl Rogers. The person comes for help wanting to improve his trajectory – he wants not just movement but upward movement, a new momentum, wind in his sails. The client will dictate priorities and draw up the action plan. If given a chance, as professionals, we will be there to make sure he has clear eyes on himself, and we trust that in his strong hands his future has its best chance. His self - his future - his hands.

In a shelter, running a program, what with the turnover and the many pressures, we've got only a little time to work with a disconnected person – what to do? Certainly, the idea that he should be given one assigned case manager to interact with, picked not by him but by someone else, an arranged marriage, who "determines" his or her readiness to work, who then acts as his sole conduit to the mainstream, is antithetical to what he needs to overcome. Yet, this arrangement is literally insisted upon. It is an industry practice. The assigned case manager works on only what is "brought" to him or her. It's called "motivational counseling." But our work is crisis work, not long-term, far-reaching therapy. Is that even needed, we ask? If we do not treat what they are experiencing as a crisis, then we are taking that from them. Disconnection from self? While their own tendency might be to downplay their situation, rendering it as their new normal, we should avoid feeding into that mentality. Here, we are not going to downplay anything. Their situation is complicated, too important to put it or them all into a one-solution fits all category. We're going to confront their situation from their perspective. Not housing-first so much as them-first. Imagine that, case managers with no housing to offer nonetheless sit down at their desks with their homeless clients selling it. Both are thinking that there is nothing to do but wait. This is a profound waste of time. Profound.

Social networking therapy attempts something different. It asks the person-in-need to develop a working relationship, not with one case manager but with everybody on the team, the professionals, and the paraprofessionals as well. It asks that every staff person, whether it be the nurse, the dayroom assistant, the recreation therapist, the case manager, the psychiatrist, or the director, to work out a productive relationship with each "client" in the program. This simple change of relating to many instead of just to one, by multiplying his social network sevenfold allowing him to "pick" his springboard relationship, an evolving choice that may very well come to include the entire staff, our goal, speeds up his bounce back. It increases the likelihood that he will feel "liked" enough to return to the program the next day, which he will not do if he doesn't. That happens a lot and almost always, when it does, the blame is placed on the client for his "resistance." To the contrary, we give him these many relationships and we don't think of him as difficult if he does not want to talk to this or that one of us; of course, he can pick and choose, and turn towards or away from this or that staff person at any time. His call. But we tell him or her that we believe that to the degree he can figure out how to get the most out of each one of us, each with our specialties, he "becomes" more self-made, more "ready," for what the world might have to offer him. We are not going to "match" him with just one person for all these reasons. Another thing. We will observe who among their peers she or he tends to spend time with. As part of our effort to help her then, we might try to "add" them to our "team." We say "add" even though these people were already on his or her team. For example, treatment for her disconnection consists of her figuring out a workable relationship with all seven of the staff and all her peers with whom she chooses to associate. This is her current social network and though we expect it to grow exponentially, this is what we've got to work with, and so we do. The focus is less on her personal psychological makeup and more on its sociological context, to include all the players within it. Here, Kurt Lewin meets Leon Festinger.

He can take on all the blame he wishes to, but the "solution" to any dilemma he will experience is going to lie within his hopefully ever-expanding social circle. Surprising then, isn't it, that it is tradition within psychiatric treatment circles to try to keep an outpatient apart from his "negative" influences, usually achieved by asking him not to hang with his friends, certainly not with other patients. However, to even try to keep patients apart from their very own social circles renders you less credible and makes treatment less likely to take hold. Keeping them away from their so-called negative influences is, by and large, a psychiatrist's pipe dream, but as our friend Bob Dylan sings, "In order to dream, you've got to be asleep." It just will not happen. Given access, he or she will hang with their peers, their friends, real reference points in flesh and blood. Better that we "encourage" him stand up to negative influences among his friends, more effective to bolster the positives. Hey, perhaps you can let us meet them too? Maybe we can influence the way everybody in your social circles interact. We should try. It's called, "social networking therapy" for a reason.

We can accept the decision to stay on the street as being made in a world of descending choice even if we strongly believe it is the wrong one. Because we accept it, it does not necessarily reduce our efforts to convince them otherwise, the primary reason we perform outreach. But what would make the job easier? What if what awaited them indoors would resolve their sense of being "out of it?" Disconnected. Degraded. Floating over concrete. What if what awaited them indoors was a real pathway to employment, which by the way contained numerous social-networking pivot points? Would they come in then?

Seven

In April 1989, just before we started, former NYC Human Resources Administration Commissioner William J. Grinker said that despite a variety of outreach efforts the city had made little progress in getting people off the streets in the previous year. "We know at this point that many of the techniques that we have tried have not been all that successful." "We know," he said.

This was the commissioner talking common industry knowledge. "We know..." he said. Yet, he was ignored by just about everyone in the outreach business, they, who just keep on keeping on. Why is that? Why didn't the commissioner make more of his findings? Why keep the funding in place, and why support what he knew to be ineffective? Afraid of a little upheaval? Afraid of "The Board?" Did he find some measure of professional satisfaction in sitting back and waiting to be proven right, again and again? But what about us? We were taking it all to heart. Maybe he didn't know what else to do, but we were going to try a few things.

~ ~ ~

What were the current unworkable methods at the time? Typically, workers in an outreach program, defined as an organized attempt to bring homeless street people indoors, will spend months and sometimes years working to gain the trust of one individual. The program staff might go so far as to lay blankets at the person's feet or place food or other products against a nearby lamppost or gutter, an effort they hope will warm-up the person to the idea of accepting first them, then hopefully, a referral to their social services agency. Condition them to stay there and what, utilize something like a trail of food leading them to their program?

Kind of a reverse Hansel and Gretel? It is so difficult to simply walk away from someone in need, and if you want to see the person again, a little food does go a long way, they say. "See you again tomorrow? Same time, same place?"

In 1982, one program's Executive Director described its technique in providing outreach this way: "Two of us approach an individual and after greeting him we attempt to explain the nature of our work. The technique is to give him a paper bag containing a sandwich, fruit, two cigarettes, and a flyer identifying our program's services. Coffee, additional food, hygiene kits and clothing are also available at our Winnebago parked within sight. Clients are encouraged to come to the Winnebago or to our office at designated hours to visit us." That's it. Not bad at all; not intrusive; not demanding; meets them where they are, respectfully distant – just doesn't work as an outreach tool. Can we say that too much of that can border on the neglectful? After all, apart from the demeaning cruelty, subtle, that comes with using their hunger against them to ultimately squash their own view of themselves in favor of yours, food does provide sustenance. The people lying in the grass, the wounded. The professional workers in an outreach program, the hunters? No mistake, the hunters have the credibility to act as they do. They get publicly funded, don't they? Again, we ask, why is that? Are commissioners indeed too hands off? Too much respectful distance? Dr. Dumpson, the Welfare Commissioner under Abe Beame, explained to us in our book *Beyond Homelessness* that it is the role of the commissioner to educate the mayor, not to simply follow the bouncing, political, red rubber ball. Guess that just does not happen enough.

It's odd that "small returns" has become policy as if it is the best anyone can do. Oh, the poor homeless person, they say, so weak and vulnerable, so in-denial, so very incapable really, much too disabled to work, for now a blanket and a cup of soup is enough. What's to come? Housing, housing, and housing, that's what. Seven years later, some of the results of this same program's efforts were reported in Cohen and Sokolovsky's book, *Old Men on The Bowery*. They found that after many visits to their many outreach locations, "about 25% of the street clients finally accepted an invitation to come to the project office where they received anything from a cup of coffee to a room, financial aid, or psychiatric care." Over many months. Many visits. 25% success. As one agency recently stated in a six-month summary of its outreach efforts in a city park, "All of the homeless need clothing, toilet articles, food, hygiene items, which all the outreach workers seek to provide as a first step in their contact." Later in that same report, the agency indicated that it would continue to "stress long periods of outreach to build trust between client and worker." The 1994 year-end report of this same outreach program presented somewhat discouraging results. With an annual budget of $125,000, the agency was charged with trying to bring in, during the spring and summer, up to 200 homeless people, and in winter, up to 50 men and woman, living in Riverside Park, on New York's Upper West-Side. In its first eighteen months however it succeeded in bringing indoors just 35 people, or 14%, only half of whom accepted their referrals to treatment, about 7% of their target population. This was considered a good enough start. The state-of-the-art program was subsequently refunded, their work not yet done. Their lack of success met expectations. They needed to keep trying. More funding for that.

In other nearby action, five outreach programs, each separately funded and, due to privacy concerns, purposely not in coordination with each other, had been serving Madison Square Park, a small park on Manhattan's lower eastside about ten blocks south of where we were operating. "We must assure client privacy," they said. So, everybody knows this or that person. All five programs are "working with him." However, they just can't talk about it with each other. Privacy at five times the expense. The expense of failure times five. Wait. What would they be saying to each other anyway? A diverse sampling of five identical points of view? They're operating on the same premise. Everybody is in denial, the root cause of resistance to treatment, which they were offering. A six-month review revealed that collectively, they made 306 visits to the park. This resulted in 272 different people being contacted. Building trust. And for that, a 15% success rate. They described the population as follows: "Very service resistant. Interested only in sleeping and being left alone at night. Many of the homeless population use alcohol and drugs."

This was like the report of the NYC Human Resources Administration commissioner five years earlier. Five years earlier yet still being "discovered" today. Perpetual eternity. The commissioner spoke up:

> Unfortunately, life on the streets tends to complicate an individual's ability to accept services. Programs need to develop additional approaches to engage this resistant population.

In most of these programs, the outreach worker or the program director decides what kind of help the person in distress needs. Once they are assigned a case manager, that person serves as the homeless individual's sole conduit to mainstream society. In the case of the newly defined "intensive case manager," the ICM, they are given around-the-clock responsibility, "for the sake of continuity of services." If the case manager and their client avoid any rifts, in the best of situations, they will work together in relative isolation from others. The case manager is fearful of "negative influences" and often will implore their "client" to minimize contact with his or her peers. For privacy's sake, they will consider any information that is gathered from the client, in the form of case notes or treatment plans, to be confidential and privileged. In the "solutions" section of his report, the New York City Commissioner had called for more case management. In his statement of program goals: "Staff must be trained and should be provided with a job description that expects substantive case management." Yet the doctor-patient, role-based relationship that outreach service professionals often mimic, no matter how enlightened, is not dissimilar to the stereotypical parent-child relationship. There is one in authority and another who is expected to acquiesce to it. But wait, don't most adults resist being told what to do? The theories that follow from all that will often, according to family therapist Carl Whitaker, create false feelings of power in the social worker. Straw men.

In an interview, sociologist Peter Rossi had this to say about such traditional social service approaches to homelessness: "Case management is a real scam, a marvelous way to keep social workers from dealing with clients. All they do is deal with the 'case' and talk to each other as to how to manage it." Somali Canadian poet/rapper K'naan:

> She got on welfare and hated it
> case work a power trippin'
> and generally being degraded if
> nothing else she was treated sick
> and ineffective which is the worst thing
> that she'd been left with

So, whatever it is that our sociologists and poets know, others don't? Or they do? Is it about interpersonal power, or does it come down to social order and role differentiation? Are they that hard to side-step? Hmm...

~   ~   ~

During outreach, insistence that the client go along with the outreach professional's goals often results in a standoff. When extended over time, it is seen as proof of the client's self-destructiveness, the inherent difficulty of outreach, the fragile nature of homelessness, all of which is transmuted into a need to gain the client's trust. They know that to the client; they are seen as untrustworthy, and they construct their outreach around that. The person who is not trusted blames the person who doesn't trust them. In time, maybe this will change. Let's wait on that.

~   ~   ~

Built-in contradictions. From the outset, the outreach worker appears to be making efforts to increase the client's comfort and survivability on the street with food and blankets etc. Once establishing that, then they try to get the person to come off the street. Which is it? Maybe it's both. Maybe it's neither. To gain trust, something they feel is missing, they provide incentives for the person to stay on the streets, sacrificing the person's own safety in the end. Whether from distrust or earned caution, an ongoing refusal to come indoors is seen as part of the "denial" process. These analyses, defensible as they may be, may serve to prolong the person's street life. For as the outreach worker "waits" for the homeless person to become more trusting, time passes, and the person's street ties strengthen. Street ties? This is something Snow and Anderson described in *Down on Their Luck* as one of "the factors that influence the careers of the homeless." Outsiders who frequently lack the ability to establish social ties have by and large resolved this conflict in favor of street life. They have become habituated to their daily routines and relationships and seldom engage in serious endeavors to extricate themselves. They don't just have each other's backs, they have each other. It is what it is.

The efforts of the social services professional, who may be an expert in the trait areas most applicable, are frustrated even as their theories are "proven" accurate. As trait-centered outreach workers, their jobs are not easy. As Snow and Anderson found, the target population often has other concerns than escaping street life. While they may still have a strong desire to get off the streets, their day-to-day behavior revolves more around the activities they share with their homeless associates. However, paying attention to the homeless person's status within his peer group, and to his social standing within the larger society, informs the outreach worker to operationally understand the needs of the homeless person.

Refer here to Alfred Adler. Please. He's revered for a reason. His essays on how "social interest" interacts with "style of life" show us what our day-to-day driving forces are. As regards inclination or capacity, just because they are rejecting what you are offering them, a different life, why treat people as if they are so different? So different from you? Understanding all this helped us fashion a way to extricate and rescue them, those ones who were choosing to remain on the streets long after their trait-centered outreach workers went away. Usually homeless, they don't really want to be.

In *The People of The Abyss*, the 1903 autobiographical account of his own homelessness, Jack London commented on the social distance from the mainstream that people who live on the street experience. "There is no place for them in the social fabric, while all the forces of society drive them downward till they perish. At the bottom of the abyss, they are feeble, besotted, and imbecile. The work of the world goes on above them, and they do not care to take part in it, nor are they able. Moreover, the work of the world does not need them."

In the mid 1990's, one study interviewed close to one thousand men and women whose average age was in the mid-thirty range. 25% had been robbed while on the streets, having been threatened with a gun, knife, or other weapon, and 18% reported having been beaten. It had already been established that problems associated with street life included vascular and skin disorders of the legs and feet, coming from weather-related issues, or from not being able to properly lie or sit down when needed, all of this, besides the trauma and post-trauma coming from being mugged or raped on the streets. For a cultural reference, see Jack Nicholson and Meryl Streep in the screen adaptation of William Kennedy's novel, *Ironweed*. See what horrors Meryl's character goes through getting by during a winter storm. One prominent research group concluded that mortality rates on the streets is nearly four times that of the general population. For another cultural reference from way back, comes George Orwell's *Down and Out in Paris and London*. In one of its later chapters, he listed and discussed what he called "three especial evils" associated with street life. The first was hunger, the second, perpetual celibacy, and the third, enforced idleness. He said, "a man who has gone even a week on bread and margarine is not a man any longer, only a belly with a few accessory organs." In fact, in our survey we found that 26.2% of the area's street population reported they had recently gone hungry for two days or more. His second evil, perpetual celibacy, he said was due as much to their "besotted" condition as to the nearly 6 to 1 ratio of single homeless men to homeless women. Orwell described it this way:

For of course it goes without saying that if a tramp finds no women at his own level, those above--even a very little above--are as far out of his reach as the moon...He is absolutely without hope of getting a wife, a mistress, or any kind of woman except--very rarely, when he can raise a few shillings--a prostitute.

And while it is difficult to determine which of these conditions is worse, none could be more so than that of Orwell's third evil, enforced idleness. This likely results from the fact of unemployment. As Elliot Liebow stated:

In industrial societies, unemployment strikes deep at the heart of man. It can put a man 'out of it,' and can turn him into a caricature of himself, giving him the appearance of being stupid and lazy with no concern for the future. Faced with nothing to do, he has no place to go. He hangs around. He is superfluous, and he knows it.

Superfluous, yet in a fishbowl, no privacy. Even indoors, in the shelter system, they are on public display, within view? A breakdown of self. With the many reams of paperwork they have generated comes an unexpected source of meaning; at least it "proves" they exist as an individual. The many social service-oriented people who have interviewed, investigated, and treated them over the years speaks "inside their head" with a collective influence too. What would they tell him to do now? Their bed among so many other beds, the shared mailing address, limited belongings, little clothing, these "little" things, taken together, offer a stripped-down mentality. It speaks: "You need to be told what to do, how then, to think." They wait on lines for food, clothing, bed assignment, carfare, entrance, and exit. Lines publicize their condition and their needs making them more a part of a large, needy crowd, than an individual recognized by anyone other than that institution You must adapt and so you do. For now, this is it.

Embittered social distance from the mainstream concretizes it. Makes street life more dangerous, and that much harder to escape. Regarding the individual as inextricably socially embedded, Alfred Adler referred to the "iron logic of communal life." He said, "We refuse to recognize and examine the isolated human being." As for his perspective on his relationship to society, Adler called this, the person's "social interest." If we are to focus on the person's "habitus of life," he said, then we must turn to the person's relationship with his or her reference group. Multi-layered interactions notwithstanding, positive peer relations are essential to success.

Adlerian in nature, we developed a program approach that proved very effective inside a homeless shelter. "Social Networking Therapy." A social status-centered, team-oriented, peer-networked employment approach, which focuses on individually designed strategic plans. The trust is put in each person's naturally occurring social interest, and that the social engine of "the workplace" would keep things going in the right direction, helping to wrestle the person's life away from crisis. Personal satisfaction to come. Homelessness begone.

Eight

TOP TEN REASONS GIVEN BY HOMELESS PEOPLE FOR LIVING OUTDOORS

1. We want to remain anonymous for legal reasons.
2. We have mental health or severe substance abuse problems. We fear discovery and institutionalization.
3. We are loners, proud of our independence. We draw satisfaction from street life.
4. We are waiting out a short-term problem, or for a check that's on its way, and see no need to be further processed by "the system."
5. We choose to remain on the street with a close friend, or a pet, rather than risk losing contact.
6. We have had some negative experiences with a social worker or case manager and wish to avoid further contact with them all.
7. We are offered limited to no choice and are unaware of the variety of services available.
8. We blame ourselves for the mess we are in. We are on the street to think things out.
9. We have been thrown out of one or more places and think we're on a banned list.
10. We want jobs, but are only being offered treatment

~   ~   ~

Social Networking Therapy along with status-centered outreach can greatly impact people who give reasons 6-10. Consumer education and choice. Inclusion. On-the-job training. Employment. Employee assistance programming. Self-help.

It seems to be a common-sense proposition that one would want to escape street life. Attitude versus behavior. Cognitive dissonance. Leon Festinger. An examination of the distrust which homeless street people have for outreach efforts should produce skepticism of the labels "resistant" or "in denial." Referring to those who "refuse" services affixes blame on the homeless person for what might be a practical or rational outlook on life. He's refusing a pitch, not necessarily treatment itself. That could mean that it is the outreach worker's "resistance" that prevents successful outreach. Are they "in denial?" For all anyone knows, it happens a lot, the outreach worker operating from a commonly perceived social-standing distinction, perhaps from a position of superiority, perhaps not, maybe just a youthful idealism that has transmuted to adult righteousness, or is it never too late? Then, there's the parent-child dynamic, not a very intuitive way to work with adults. Regardless of the counseling techniques employed, it underwrites an approach that is wrong-headed, not simply faint-hearted. No. In fact, if this is even a little true, then we declare that the outreach worker's "love for our fellow man" is a pseudo condition, a posture, little more than insecurity from the inside out. Maybe that's what compassion is partially made up of, but it is belied by their own disbelief. Stop, switch it around. Micro-sociology. Ethnomethodology. Meta-communication. Harold Garfinkle. What's really being said?

Why not speak to the person's desire for social inclusion through work, to their need to craft their own accomplishments? In so far as they are unlikely to rise under such circumstances as dictated to them anyway, it becomes an approach that limits them because of how it sees them, through the prism of a disorder. The identified patient. "In the wrong," and in need of change. This approach literally holds them down. There are over 4000-5000 people right now on New York City streets that regularly say "no" to their outreach workers. Ironically aligned with people who point fingers at them, a result of the collective mire of self-blame, the person living on the street does not often have any kind of master plan beyond nitty gritty survival, a big enough task in and of itself. He is, for the moment, experiencing the dark side of his sense of personal responsibility. Yet, very often, by not accepting the help being offered, he or she is being responsible to himself. He's staying out of what he perceives as "harm's way." He'll get a job eventually, he figures. Things will work out. They always do. I think this is called, "Catch 22."

He has his own thinking. The only way is to listen to him. No choice. You don't have that kind of power. He does. Don't fight it. Don't think of yourself as an outreach worker, maybe more a job recruiter. Listen hard. 90% will say they want a job. Again, think of that same quote already applied, of the late, great novelist Jerzy Kosinski who said in our interview with him in *Beyond Homelessness*, "They failed as any businessman might. We can accept failure in that case, we make provisions for that, why not for this too?"

Nine

From the start, the homeless have not received the help they most needed, no surprise, because everyone's been pointed in a most unworkable direction. Fact-check. Given all the landlords, employers, families, and other institutions that would not have them, The Board's "folks" have lived sheltered and apart, disconnected from the main. Mind-boggling. By working against one of the most telling and primary truths the homeless must live with, one of chicken and egg caliber, their inadequate incomes, and their difficulty in getting and keeping good-paying jobs, they've been wrongfully labeled and badly treated.

~ ~ ~

They do not have homes, an essential quality of life, which obviously is true. Without a reliable income, the things they do not have are aplenty, none of which, we argue, ought to bring them a label. For one thing, that it might mobilize an ineffective response. Metaphorically, though they do not have wings, we refrain from calling them "the flightless." That could apply, but certainly, we are not going to promise that we will work on fixing their flightlessness, though we have tried that, a few people even jumping off cliffs with strap-on wings. However, if landing on our heads, squash, had any meaning, only then did we invent the airplane. What about our getting them homes? Squash. It's not possible? Well, it is possible, it's just not happening. Unfixable? It might as well be considered that. Certainly, for the homeless it seems that it is not going to happen. Perhaps because the competition is too fierce. The sheer numbers of people scrambling to find affordable housing grow every day, literally overwhelming a marketplace apparently designed to only make small supply and demand adjustments as our lives chug along. Functionalism. There'll be no gross level changes even during times of crisis. How sad. But true. And, even as we continue to try, and we should, it is time to acknowledge that given the results of our efforts, this angle needs to be scaled back more in favor of a different approach. We owe to the very people we are trying to help, those who cannot afford even the most minimal of rents.

The money needed to switch over to an income-oriented approach, hiring people, supporting them, working with employers who would need support too, etc., is now being spent on food stamps, rental assistance, emergency assistance, and emergency shelter. It's largely there. And as for employment and the generation of legitimate, hands-on income, through attrition alone, we could fill up to half of all the positions now held by workers in our nationwide shelter system and homeless social service programs from the ranks of todays' homeless. Again, the homeless should be given half of all the jobs being performed on their behalf. The remaining half of the staff, those who had been professionally trained, could offer supportive employment assistance. Planting a thought-seed. More later. We need to think "Employment."

The ratio of the number of homeless shelter residents needing housing and those finding it, depending on how terms are defined, could be anywhere from between 50:1 to 100:1. Translating that into an action plan, maybe only 1 in 50 program staff in all homeless programs should be working with homeless people to find them housing. Any more effort than that would be resources misspent, right? We do have a forty-year track record in these matters. Even if from a position of hope, we doubled the staff-side of our ratio to 2 of 50, we could still free up 48 program staffers to fight on different terms, their respective nonprofits switching-up their efforts in favor of the other end of the spectrum, that of income. What we want is for each homeless person to be able to obtain enough of it to enter the current housing market, high rents, and all, through the work they do just as they most wish. Synchronicity.

We see them as people who need a living wage job, which we can give them upon demand.   We drop the undoable, never done, in favor of what is doable, more easily done. Instead of having them wait on housing to be renovated, or for the discovery of land to build it on, or the outcome of zoning-wars, or of lobbying efforts, all of which can and should continue but on a smaller scale, why not change our approach? We can use the same money already in our hands differently. No handouts here - people would work for every penny they get. That will give everybody the wings they need. No longer flightless, they'll fly all the way to an unaffordable home, their next step. Capitalism: A Love Story, the sequel. Michael Moore.

The fact that people cannot with full-time minimum wage jobs find housing that they can afford is an indictment on skyrocketing housing costs. It's also an indictment of the minimum wage,
for the lack of access to living-wage employment, right? It's a virtual lockout, isn't it? Government entitlements, monthly payouts, emergency funds, food, legal advice, all of it helping to stabilize but effectively lacking inspiration. People are propped up but without the use of their legs. It collectively solves a primary emergency, life and death, no joke, however a lot of this could be handled by the people themselves if they had as income just a little bit of the money being currently spent "helping" them.

Community-induced self-hypnosis, arms out, zombie like, the entire industry all too willing to follow the path that The Board, their designated thought-leader, has laid out for them. It's more than just a little suspicious. Forty years now, so few housed. The good news is this: As living wages are adopted as the minimum, the working but homeless or sheltered person would get them too. Do we have to say it? It is not a living wage if you cannot live on it.

From the start, it sounded a bit too much like the absurd ideology of trickle-down economics. Just wait on the housing, their unpaid fulltime "job" apparently being to sit tight, their position to worsen, their dreams to fade. Indeed, beyond there being no housing that they can afford, that is, they have no income, there are several other very serious dimensions of their personal rubric cubes, to their peril, that are regularly ignored. For one, self-agency, which is central to people's innate need for self-determination. Innate needs. Self-determination theory. Edward L. Deci and Richard M. Ryan write about the requirement for a person's buy-in, for their perpetual right to renegotiate. Why does The Board insist on treating them so one-dimensionally? Why do we let them?

The amount of underachievement needing to be overturned is a problem we share with the homeless, we who are first responders, outreach workers, social workers, and executive directors too.

It would be a great thing if the housing came one day, yes it would, but after lo these many years, for the sake of helping these particular people right now, can we say that it will not be here soon enough, merely on the way? Rarely ordered, rarely shipped, there's no tracking number. The "housing movement" is working very hard to satisfy this need for everyone, great, but for "the homeless" it succeeds only 2% of the time, not so great. Quick math: That's 98% who don't get housing first or even last, not at all. That's just how many people show up homeless versus how many leave with a home.

The homeless have been, by dint of the politicization of their need for respite, held apart. Disconnected from the start, they are now "the sheltered." Now, they are vulnerable for real.

Prevention? Besides all of those who have don't have any kind of reliable home of their own, two million or so people experiencing homelessness," there are upwards of fifteen million others across the country living in what we can call "extremely unaffordable homes," where it costs more than half of their monthly income. But wait, there's more, many, many more people who inhabit the next category, living in plain old "unaffordable homes." Referred to in sociology as cost-burdened, it's been reported to be as much as one-third of the country, these are homes which costs 30% to 49% of person's income. If we are keeping count, we're way over one hundred million people who need affordable housing. In a tweet, "that's bad."

Setting aside the power of positive thinking just for a moment, can't one conclude the obvious? We must do something completely different – an entirely different approach. One that defines the problem differently; from one that asks them to wait to one from which they could benefit immediately. Immediate employment and related, self-directed action. Consumer empowerment. Choice. From this and these, their disconnection can end, many of the disconnects resolved.

The only ones truly in-the-know, given a voice, that's 25,000 able-bodied adults in the New York City shelter system alone, speaking the same language, across our country, overseas too, – Cape Town, Rome, Munich, Graz, Amsterdam, Guttenberg, Glasgow, London, Paris, Tallinn. "It's not fair if you don't let us work our way out of this mess." Forty years and counting.

If instead, we hired them and paid them a living wage, or worked with employers to do just that, they would have the funding to house themselves, which they would do. We'd support them, as in "supportive employment" or, while holding their jobs open for them upon their return, refer them for treatment if necessary. The forever wait would be over. And it wouldn't cost more. Has anyone ever said, "Less is more?"

Why can't homeless people benefit from the industry which has grown around them? They should get its jobs.

Has the Board's approach out forced the market force? Is housing, housing, housing the right fight, right here, right now? It's been raging for almost forty years now, the fight that will last a century. There are challenges from all sides in the courts, on regulation, de-regulation, rent control, with trade-offs on renovations and new construction, transcendent processes to the people it helps, again, a small part of the whole. It bears some fruit but, how to say it best, think of the thousands who rush the Walmart doors for Black Friday's "affordable" Xbox, only a few dozen in stock; what about everybody else? "It's backordered. Any day now." Who cares? We're talking Xboxes. Okay, what about inside the shelters? To the tens of thousands of people that knock on those doors. "We are going to try to get you housing. Sit over there. Lie down if you want, it's your right. It might make the wait easier." "Actually, it makes it really harder. Shelterization is real." "Relax; it's temporary." "No, it isn't. Sartre. No Exit." "Don't worry, we'll get you something better." "Political drivel. No, you won't." That's just how many homeless people there are how little affordable housing there is, and what little room for hope that remains for this approach, which competes with one third of all of America for whatever new housing is "created." The "homeless system" really offers shelter only, a few get lucky, and everybody else waits. Hint: Through its ownership of the "homeless problem" and its authoritarian oversight of industry practices for its correctness, The Board flourishes. Homeless people do not.

~ ~ ~

Some research. Very telling.

1. The authors of *Madness on the Streets* found that in the mental health field, the establishment bureaucracy considers work exploitative and forbids it. For example, mentally ill people who are patients in long-term hospital stays, are kept in total idleness. The authors wrote that

"patients and staff alike had been written off by an ideological movement which preferred to ignore their existence." Wow. Written off by a movement that purports to be "for" them. <u>Preferred to ignore.</u>

2. In 1993, in a book called *Down on Their Luck: A Study of Homeless People*, the authors wrote that "...the bureaucratic principle of standardization often leads to pernicious rigidity with respect to individual client needs." The truth emerges; it was always there. <u>Pernicious rigidity to client needs.</u>

3. In a book called *The Visible Poor*, a study of how homeless people were portrayed in the media in 1989, the year we started our programming, the authors concluded that pathology was minimized to showcase housing needs. <u>Pathology minimized.</u> Hmm, now why would The Board do that?

When approached for treatment, it was said that the homeless in and near the Grand Central Terminal resisted. The prevailing belief among social services professionals was that they were in denial regarding what kind of help they most needed. The idea that they needed treatment first, then housing, produced poor outreach results. It was then changed into them needing housing first, then treatment. "Housing First," is the new clarion call. Again, looking at the growing gap between those in need of housing and those getting it, we see poor results.

Maybe there's some logic to their resistance. Maybe it's time we stop fighting their resistance. Makes us ask – Who is resistant? But no, you see, the bottom line is that the professional staff has expectations, which they are required to express in their client's charts every six-months in terms of a restatement of their goals, a new set of signatures, a commitment to rehab and to good behavior. No mention of employment. It's not realistic. Not to worry...the housing will come.

If a person is living at a shelter and working somewhere for a minimum wage, increasing that to a living-wage level would cost about $15k annually. If the person is not working, and you hired them for a living wage, that would cost about $35K. The job or the increase may be a "gift," but the money would have to be gathered through work. It's a lot less than the $50k or so that it costs to "upkeep" someone who is homeless.

Their hands, their destiny. The way it is now, against the whole, there are so few housed. Yet, through the power of a living wage, the potential to house themselves is ever-present.

Replacing one never-going-to-happen solution with another, this time, employment? Wait a minute, it is already funded. We'd just have to move the money around. No land to buy. No buildings to build. Will take a change in thinking, that's all. That's all? No, it is a big deal. The real deal. They feel personally responsible for their homelessness, and they want to work their way out of it.

In the world of homeless service provision, personal problems are seen as barriers to employment. The social worker feels unable to defend that person's "job readiness." Efforts are focused instead on redirecting the homeless person to defer certain of their dreams such as employment, and to accept it as impractical. Don't resist. Don't move from that chair and you'll be okay. Let us attempt to rehabilitate you until such time that you have been fixed. Then we'll talk employment. Here we have a practical reason, based on what sounds like a solid principle, that health enables work. So, let's fix 'em first, but it is a belief that keeps disconnected people disconnected. Applied to the broad community of homeless people, it works to maintain the shelter system.

Back up. How exactly is pathology treated in the real world, in the non-homeless community? For starters, during a job interview people are not expected to show that they are problem-free. In fact, during the interview process, unless confronted by them, employers are careful not to even ask about an interviewee's personal issues. Too personal. Point is, whatever an applicant's pathology might be, unless it presents itself during the interview or comes out during the background check process, they do not become part of the discussion. People outside the homeless community are not asked to get fixed before they get hired. However, once they get the job, if problems appear to negatively impact performance in the workplace, that's a different story; then they are expected to be addressed. After being hired, however, if required by their employer to get help for a problem that is interfering with the work they are to perform, they can be referred to their employee assistance program, a benefit available in most every large company. If the social stigma is too much to overcome for them to take that route, to keep their job, to maintain the social and family status that their employment brings, they'd likely experience strong enough motivation to complete treatment somewhere, in most cases, by way of their medical insurance benefits. Here, in our reworking of the homeless service delivery system, service providers are "in the ready." Staff is already in place. Get it? For practical reasons, work has a particular power that it exercises all the time. It enables healthy decisions like taking and completing a course of treatment. Makes self-sufficiency possible.

This wrongfully labeled person doesn't need long to figure out that if he wants to work, the treatment plans constructed for him aren't going to be worth his time or effort. It does nothing to bring in an income. It doesn't even let him try to get to that next level, to at least become one the many overburdened "working poor," without work, even poorer. Instead, it's a "job later" approach, the flip side of the "housing first" doctrine. It's all about waiting on someone else's dime. Go ahead, have a seat; you can even lie down if you'd like. We will shelter and protect you, and keep you in that place over there, not to worry. In the waiting room, sitting there, next to each other, a picture emerges. Unproductivity. Demoralization. Obstruction too.

"Housing First," the new way, instead of "Treatment First," the old way, is effective when the housing is there, but ineffective when it is not. Why tout housing first if there's virtually no housing? Why treatment first if there's no housing to come?

It is the working-life that many have been turned away from while still reporting that it's what they want the most. Now their personal doubts reflect a dimmed momentum, and their self-esteem is shattered, the couch-potato effect; a couch they're literally made to sit and stay on. In many cases, won't they need physical therapy to regain use of their legs? That's right.

Sheltered in this manner, they've become even more vulnerable. The cobra-effect.

~ ~ ~

The argument for housing as a panacea suffers from its nobility.

~ ~ ~

At Fountain House, which is a New York City based, membership-driven clubhouse for mentally ill people that emphasizes work, as recounted in *Madness on The Streets*,

> One staffer told us that when a Fountain House member stopped vacuuming to listen to his voices, she said something to the effect, "I don't care if you are hallucinating, go on vacuuming." The member did just that, he vacuumed, hallucinations in tow. As the authors explained, "The emphasis is on what the client can do best, not what he does worst, or can't do at all."

Imagine that we say sarcastically, helping a disabled person become productive. Could it work for the able-bodied?

~ ~ ~

They did not have homes of their own and so they were labeled homeless, understandable but arbitrary. Not insignificant, the label has shaped the discussion, the most ardent advocates sidestepping its main shortcoming. Unrealized success. Whatever happened to pragmatic thinking? Just to mirror reality is not enough, Alice in Wonderland had it right, you've got to go beyond looking at the mirror, you must go inside it. We want to solve homelessness now, not Judy Garland's way, "one day, over the rainbow." No. Instead, think: George Herbert Meade. See: The person experiencing homelessness. Listen: To that person. Consider: The Looking Glass Self. There's me, myself, and I. Three as one. But then again, there's you and there's the other. Alfred Adler. Social Interest. And of course, there's Elliot Liebow. Let's hear it for inclusion. Employment.

The problem is that homes are not all they do not have, and we do understand that until they can get back on their feet, they will need a place to crash. Okay, so in New York, though four or five thousand are on the street, more than sixty thousand sheltered people aren't. They've got that place to crash, now what? No wings. Flightless. Isolation. Disconnection.

Ten

Having gone undetected, the initial misdirection went forward, repeatedly rethought. In just one time-loop, markers for cognitive impairment were formed. Now became later. Things were getting written in stone on a one-way track. Noam Chomsky and the cognitive revolution? False understanding was upon us, and there it has stayed for forty years. This is the story of how public perception of homeless people has been crafted. First came concern. That was supplanted very quickly by opportunistic advocacy and media underachievement. It could have become a cautionary tale to tell but didn't. Of course, the fact that our work took place in the heart of the world-famous city of New York of all places, and the fact that it involved the extremely wealthy, rather, the top tenth of the top tenth, as well as the extremely poor, the bottom tenth of the bottom tenth, is the stuff of social services charisma. It really was historical.

We don't have to imagine the landscape, the entire Lewinian field in a dust storm. Homeless people are "stuck" inside homeless shelters. Was it like being stuck inside a heavily polluted northern Chinese city, no way out? Put another way, why does this homeless problem persist? Why, they asked Ghandi, after all his adulation and fame, did he continue, still in rags, to sit at his spinning wheel? "I don't want to disappoint all the people that worked so hard to put me here."

The twenty or so industry managers who perpetrated the demise of Grand Central business district's homeless outreach effort were some of the leaders of New York's homeless service provider's ruling class. Here, we're calling them "The Board." In fact, along with its founder, still today a final moral arbiter of sorts, forever on call, they come together on an as-necessary basis. PRN. Well, okay then, *their* system is impaired. Their system, which has snubbed alternate approaches among which ours was most prominent at the time, and most hurtful to their specific cause, that of causing chaos in midtown, and their less specific one, that of solving homelessness. Homelessness is with us much in the same way as it was so many years ago when they first began their "reign." The shelters are packed. The streets are a sad home for so many still. Can't we ask why there has been such minimal success? The Board blames society, or society's richest, and we cannot say that they are completely wrong. But as the Somali rapper K'naan raps, "You can point your finger, but there's three pointing back." No more blaming. Oh, and no more waiting on the housing.

There is one thing we must do for this mindset to be properly repealed, for the thinking on this problem to go from linear to circular, for a different point of view to at least be considered, the entrepreneur's credo, so that we can begin to imagine a better outcome even in the case of long-term homelessness. We must admit that The Board has defined and framed the entire problem ineffectively. Indicted here for their arrogance, they must take their leave. More than that, they should be exiled. Usurping Anne Sexton's *All My Pretty Ones*, to them we say, "You overslept."

Standing the problem of homelessness on its head so that it can be seen differently, we could create real change. Perhaps we should start by naming the problem something that points to a solution that can be realized right away. Most poor people are not homeless, however, those that are can be considered among the most disconnected. No people behind them. No contacts that can jumpstart their reemergence. No connections of value. That's right – homelessness doesn't just worsen poverty, it causes it. Exceptions exist, and we can think of disconnection in relative terms, but compared to people who do not live in the proximity of homelessness, we can think of those who are as being "The Disconnected," and they suffer from it. Simple. If you're disconnected, and unplugged, we all know what you need. An extension-cord? More outlets?

This situation seems to require a strategic intervention aggressively aimed at reeducation, but not of the homeless person, instead, of the "other", that'd be all of us, the likely never-to-be-homeless others. How else to cut through the mindset of this complacency in caregiving, which is tied to "doing for" rather than "doing with?" Who is it then who is suffering from disordered thinking? That'd be us, not them, and apparently it is a chronic condition. Looking at it from this point of view, we can see that all along the homeless themselves have been the most grounded, no simple double-meaning here, but in the conceptualization of their situation, they've been, as the British say, spot on. They want to work. Of course, they want housing as well, who wouldn't? Really, they'll take it if it's free, or if it comes subsidized, sure, but the pathway to housing can work against that other dream of theirs, financial self-sufficiency. Because so much of today's housing typically comes with strings, such as "we consider you disabled, so we see you as unable to work, i.e., you're literally not allowed to work." So, for the person who gets this housing, this one-in-a-hundred person, out of a fear of losing their benefits, i.e., their housing, they will often be reticent to discuss their employment dreams. What?

What they want, here and now, is a job, for they understand the formula as we all do, to wit, that jobs can "pay" for the housing. That's how it gets done throughout our one-in-a-hundred economy, where dreams of being the exception often make the rule. Think "lotto." No, what they want is that job, the here-and-now being better than the over-the-rainbow. Just ask them.

If one abides by the now infamous "six degrees of connection," can't we then say that everybody is to blame for any one person's disconnectedness? Extrapolation.

The problems that seriously disconnected people have need to be resolved the same way that ours are. They will be mainstreamed not through their connections per se, but from what results from those connections once they add up. The grand sum. Life as an action verb. Not a deep stagnant pool, but a body of moving water. Supportive employment at a living wage. It is called "inclusion."

Thinking of people who languish in our shelters or on nearby street corners as primarily suffering from "disconnectedness" blames us all, as it should. It speaks to a corrective action, and just as it does for the rest of us, the 99% of us not housed in institutions or living in our cars, and more assuredly will lead to housing than today's housing-first approach, which makes everybody wait. Much of the nation's housing is unaffordable, by the 30% standard – and that's a major problem. Why isn't everybody living in unaffordable housing driven into homeless? In a phrase, "sizeable income." The size of their income, for which they likely work/hustle hours on end, grows to manage their housing costs, otherwise their housing must shrink. How low can it go? Down to zero? Income is the answer.

All too often, programs are stand-alone. They duplicate services without duplicate gain, their sensitivity to the actual problems at hand limited by a certain kind of righteous rigidity. But that can change too. Based on services offered, programs could be linked. The formerly disconnected person, instead of being stuck in the one program not of his choice, would be handed access to the entire system, his mainchance. Now, he'd have an "in" to every relevant program in the city, each of which would be offering jobs to help transform. Programs, then, can grow or shrink based on consumer choice. Beehives within beehives of activity. Employers of every strain would be encouraged, by way of a salary-sharing public/private partnership, to hire people coming from our retooled "employment" shelters or, since once hired they'd be paying rent to the system for putting them up, it might be better to call them "employment hostels." From every direction comes motivation. A true consumer-driven job market. Economy of effort. Who is disconnected now?

Re-tooled around employment and its many devices, in deference to Adler's concept of "social interest" and Liebow's plea that we lift the "terrible burden," the new system would create a brain-centered buzz, a productive breeze. A multitude of current service providers would experience more than a little anxiety, sorry for that, but what of the need for deconstruction and the subsequent rebuild? It's all necessary, and once the paychecks start rolling in, the governmental handout being replaced by the personal workout, a lot of people, half of the staff of all these programs, would start becoming "formerly homeless," their unaffordable rents now "covered." Change all around this social problem is essential if we really want to eliminate the suffering that can feed a homeless lifestyle, that is, a life that points a person towards adult homelessness instead of a life of gainful employment. Talk about disconnectedness. Please, talk about disconnectedness.

Social disconnectedness is the machinery of stigma.

Intimidated by the lack of outrage among my peers towards "the system," the delays in bringing this story forth are on me. Back then, we were led to think there'd be more to gain by not confronting others on their practices so much as by growing ours. Our good work will win the day, we figured. Well, we figured wrong.

It was clear what they needed. They said so themselves. They were realists. As the years went by, we grew increasingly determined to get money into their hands in the form of stipends, salaries, loans, newspaper sales, whatever. Always looking around for ideas, we'd adapt here and there, copying, inventing, the thing is, especially in the case of ongoing, activated stigma, silent conspiracies happen. How else could so many people who want to work be "kept" unemployed? A question based on fact. In those days, though, if we blew any kind of whistle, it would only be the ones that dogs could hear. See "cold fusion" below. So, you could say, we dogged it. My fault. We could have camouflaged our efforts better. At some level, we knew that so much as just announcing our successes would appear to some as defiance. Of course, we knew that we could have conformed to a much less successful and controversial approach, but that was not going to happen. How could we have looked in the eyes of the people who came to us for help if we did that? But we could have, I could have, steered our programs off our very local path and towards the highway. "This section of the highway is maintained by The Board." Head down. Respectable. Ineffective.

Anyway, almost from the start, the concept of "Housing First" became just one more stanza to John Lennon's masterpiece, *Imagine*. Housing should and housing could. If this and if that. Who was it who said, "It so ain't going to happen?" We said, let's prove our point. Vote "now."

Current efforts to house people are considered state-of-the-art. The term that is currently being used to defend the approach as an intelligent one is "evidence-based." This way, the people at the forefront have everyone else thinking that they know what they are doing. They say: "Would you just look at how well this person is doing now that they are housed. Look at how well that person is doing. You see. It works." Our response? "Turn around and look the other way." Look at how slow the hour-glass drips for so many. Are you looking in their eyes or right through them? Guess there can be no quarantine against this principle maladjustment, another three-lettered disease, RDD, meaning "Research Deficit Disorder." The facts are out there. Easily obtainable, just "not seen." For how long can we consider The Board's intentions honorable, or their missteps unwitting?

We can only hope that the lights will slowly turn on, that soon, whole cities will emerge from its darkness. There has been a blackout – we are waiting for power to be restored. Adapting the words of Bernie Sanders, we can see this is a rigged social services system whose thought leadership has not led us beyond the idea that we should base our work with homeless people around their need for affordable housing. In fact, this kind of thinking pulls in the reins throughout the homeless services industry. Continuing in our Bernie Sanders-like tone of voice, we say that the social services elite has benefited for too long. Not only do they have millions of dollars in contracts, extraordinary salaries and extraordinary influence and status, but often their programs are where people who are homeless are not being given the rights they deserve. Consumer rights. The question is not necessarily why do so few of them succeed, but instead, how do so many of our successful agencies get away with such little success? By showing what they've done, their *Annual Statements* hide what little they've done, the evidence. Instead, they're crafted. A public relation coup. The grant maker's dream. Meanwhile, consumer rights, supposed to be a given in a capitalist democracy, are allowed to diminish because of what? Because of their initial diagnose and the resultant label? So, the homeless are put in their place, told, not asked. They get the shelter only to remain down and out.

Calling them homeless is the result of a descriptive analysis, no insight. Why this person and not that? Why these people and not those? Among the very poor, most of whom are not homeless, there are plenty of people in no position to accumulate materialistic wealth of any shape or form, or who may have had some but ran out. We know that income is a major factor. We can also ask, what is it that has helped their never-been-homeless but equally poor peers to avoid the worst? We've said it in other ways…most alcoholics, substance abusers, mentally ill people, or even criminally involved people are not homeless. Why not? While some of these problems might be over-represented among the homeless, a lot of this bad stuff happens after a person becomes homeless. So then, what? Most of us assume that true luck is there for all of us to grab one way or the other. While a person might need to resort to shelter life amid a perfect storm of personally experienced problems, and it always involves some choice, but mostly it will be the result of actual circumstances caused by very little choice, personal responsibility notwithstanding. Don't make them wait too long for an income to generate. Things will only get worse.

Thirty-Forty years ago. The birth of The Board. The most newsworthy among them were always the most ego driven. Their heads bent from the weight of their beards and weighty thought, so thoughtful, sincere as hell, brilliant at describing things with a syrupy compassion drawn from their singular perspective. At the conceptual center of this growing intellectually incestuous crowd, always building on their own bad ideas, more self-contrived than we'd ever want to believe, exalted, they preside over a failing industry with the unwitting help of the not-so-neutral media - too bad, for this is/was/always has been a situation where success, or its lack, deserves and requires exposure.

Today, still, The Board cannot seem to get a handle on the problem of homelessness. Granted, there are echoes of Gunga Din bouncing off the city's "canyons of steel," but that's just Frank Sinatra singing Vernon Duke's *Autumn in New York* in the background. They chant three times for something people ought to have a right to but as it has turned out are only going to get in drips and drabs, "housing, housing, housing," and they know it.

They scream their words in an over-produced campaign, which in the vacuum of the black hole that it creates can be little more than evidence of The Board's effort to stay in charge. What else could it be?

We need to think of Plato's pedagogy of wisdom, Socrates' research, which is more accessible than one might think. We need to separate authority from expertise. They're distinctive.

True stories based on a fiction eventually will compound. Foundations get laid, and soon a real-life city is built. This book then is not an unscientific look at a midtown slice of turn-of-the-century homeless social service delivery so much as one beyond social science. If you step into its mirror like we did when we began to try and help homeless people in midtown, you'll think Alice left Wonderland and got a little meaner. Instantly, we became an obstacle to a plan-in-the-making that we unwittingly walked in on, a meta-communication of sorts. Guess we weren't invited to those meetings. Whenever a certain one of The Board's television-ready underlings noticed me, perhaps I walked into a meeting she was a part of, she would point her longest finger at me and scream "What do you know? You wear a suit and tie. You're just a mucky-muck businessman." Then she'd run out of the room, slamming the door behind her. In her world, by wearing the clothes of the enemy we embodied them, a primitive understanding conjured up by the way her syntaxes fired. Her syntaxes and those of her fellow Board members. Yet, the people we worked with seemed to greatly appreciate our approach and our attire. We dressed up in shirt and tie to help them, rather than doing what was more common, which was dressing down to "relate" better. The homeless people we met with saw us differently than The Board – did that matter? I suppose I was dressing like the people they felt most removed from, so the fact that we were relating was huge. Hey, he's in a sport jacket, shirt, and tie, but look, he's carrying a backpack. He's relatable! No joke. Seriously, my belief that many homeless people, especially because of the specific qualities of their demise, could work, in fact, that they needed to work to truly end their homelessness, was bad enough. But to The Board, my formal attire, typically by midday a rolled-up shirt and a loosened tie, apparently was enough to vanquish my life's work. In the snap of a cliché, I was unqualified. And by defending myself, I suppose I fell for it. They won.

We learned how status-centered outreach, based on what the homeless person wants, rather than trait-centered outreach, based on what the professional wants for them, is the most successful approach and has the best outcomes.

Close to 90% of the people we surveyed wanted a job as much as a place to live. Amazing that nobody has connected the two. We found that whether they were disabled or not, a desire to work was present. If <u>all</u> services were offered as part of a credible pathway to employment, outreach success would improve eightfold.

What about the imposition of the doctor-patient mentality, the parental demands, and the condescension? If you're on the ground looking up, that's enough evidence to indicate negative intent. If you are going to say a person has a condition called "homelessness," a snapshot of what is really a moving picture, then by the rudiments of etymology, sociologically, "home" is the solution. Yet, given their disconnections and the problems they cause, given the extent of their unemployment, their basic unemployability, sheltering them then becomes a case of prescribing the ailment. If this were purely a psychological problem, that could work out therapeutically, whereby the ailment provokes certain antibodies. However, a badly run shelter does this so poorly as to deepen the hurt. Think iatrogenic problem-solving. Sometimes it does come down to the roof and the quality of its insulating properties but calling their problem one of homelessness for the little it brings to the table other than to qualify someone for their shelter bed and a bout of institutionalized hopelessness, helps those "in-charge" more than it helps the people they so name. This points to another problem, one that precedes it. When putting forth too narrow an outreach effort, such as a trait-centered approach, the person finds themselves stuck inside an all too idiosyncratic situation. "Hey, he's been drinking," says the outreach team, "we better find a substance abuse expert." First day on the job, the expert begins with a greeting. "Hello there." Following that, the trouble begins. "We want you to go to a clinic where you can be referred to a detoxification program for a week or so, and then we'll send you to a 28-day-stay treatment program. Okay?"

"What do you mean, 'No'?"

Uh, oh, slippery slope time. If a homeless customer says "no" to the product offered, what trait will he be treated for then? His resistance. The outreach team will then meet to formalize a goal of "getting" that person to those places *they* "know" he needs but doesn't want. To the trait-centered outreach team, his not wanting the "right" thing is what keeps him on the streets. But do we really need to denigrate someone for turning down a specific offer of services? Why can't they choose their provider from a city-wide swath of providers? Consider this: Funding should only go to the programs that the homeless choose. If one consistently gets chosen over another, that former needs to grow, the latter to shrink. Consumer power.

It's in the little things. When you have consumer rights, sitting at a restaurant table for example, you are handed a menu. Many places even have a children's menu. The restaurant stocks items that the customers have shown they like, not necessarily what the owner believes they should eat. No holds barred, in most places the customer can order whatever they want, whenever they want, as much as they want. They can send things back, or ask for more, or take some to go and so forth. Done. You get what you can pay for. Well okay. But don't the problems that people on the street have fund an industry? Their problems are their currency. They have little else. Do we need to take their problems away from them too? Is that really even possible? If they are encouraged to "own" their problems, today's therapy-speak, then they have the collateral necessary on which to base their purchase. Their purchasing decisions should not be derided any more than a successful waiter mocks their customer's decisions. "You want ketchup with that? Hah. No way. Get out of here. No, really. Get out."

Eleven

Our midtown work for Dan and his district started with a study of homelessness in New York City's east side. As we saw it, our task was to solve east-side homelessness, not the cities or the nation's problem, even if we would hope to demonstrate programming that could prove meaningful elsewhere. We'd attend to micro-sociological aspects, the specific ecology of midtown's homeless situation, each person's "why," would not get as much scrutiny as their "what, where, when." That's who we wanted to speak with. Each person.

~ ~ ~

I timed my first visit midway through their food service when I expected the area would be teeming with enough activity to mask my presence. That way, I could watch from various locations within the entire scene. I could even stand on the line itself, which I did several times right up until it was my turn. Once I went all the way through, so I could taste the food; several other times, I just turned my bag over to the last person on the line. There was a wad of merging masses, dozens upon dozens of extremely poor people, who else would have traveled so long for their daily bread? Some were placid and calm, and some were highly agitated, but most seemed to be there in good spirits, on their own, not exactly interacting with those around them. The men outnumbered the women about four to one. I counted everyone I could that first night and found 211 people on one line and 53 people on another, the lines perpendicular to each other, the smaller one exclusively comprised of elderly people, the other of all ages on up to elderly. Most of the attendees were people of color, though I did count about 40 white people. There were seven servers, all white, five women, two men, all of them appeared to be of college age. There were two vans. As it turned out, one was sent by the line's very founders, early members of The Board, and the other from the

Salvation Army. Good old former Garment Center worker Gabby Cashman, advocate extraordinaire, by all appearances clearly ambivalent about her obvious drinking problem, was there too, typically joining the dinner-line events a bit after they started each evening. Gabby would have her own box of food and would walk around with it, barking at people who she felt was misbehaving, such as calling out or, Heaven forbids, reaching for the food before she handed it to them. The other thing that really sent her over the top was if a person made disparaging of sarcastic comments to her like: "This is one sorry-ass sandwich" or, "Do you have any warm soup," or worse, "Hey Gabby, got anything to drink?" Years later, in a whisper, the back of his hand shielding his mouth, one of The Board's leaders revealed to me that Gabby would at times get so unruly as to throw whole boxes of sandwiches at whoever made her angry. Why did he feel a need to whisper behind his hand? I think it's called an "abundance of caution." At one point, I visited a woman who worked in a local lunchtime pub. She had called to ask what could be done to stop the homeless people from using their doorway overnight as a toilet. I explained that I had been hired to try to figure out some solutions. Hurry please, she said, as she poured bleach into her restaurant's doorway hoping that its pungent odor would serve as a deterrent. At least it would cut down on the cleanup job the next day.

Twelve

It seemed that a thousand homeless people were living outdoors in midtown Manhattan. They were being offered help but were refusing it. Why? What was wrong? Why had outreach efforts not been more effective? Exactly how should money be spent on this social problem?

~ ~ ~

Hired to get up-close to the city's largest, dinnertime, outdoor food line, which was at the center of both a social crisis and a public relations storm, we saw about three hundred homeless people assembling each evening for a bag of food.

~ ~ ~

To the advocates who specifically chose the location of the feeding program to maximize political impact, the cause of homelessness was clear. We asked them about it. They said people were homeless because of the "system." For example, allowing greedy landlords to prevail. Better legislation was needed so that society could be restructured for better balance between the haves and the have nots. All good points. They ran the food line as a demonstration, large scale, of this victimization to the rush hour crowds. Social Problems. The Conflict Approach.

~ ~ ~

The social service agencies responded more to the personal suffering. They saw the depression, drug and alcohol issues, health, and mental health issues for what they were. The suffering and the fog of suffering. They wanted to help yet, when offering help to the homeless people who were standing on the food line, they were met with resistance if not denial, they said. To overcome this behavior, they needed specialists. Naturally, they stressed under-funding as the cause of homelessness. Good points. Symbolic Interactionism.

To the local property managers who had hired us to run our study, the advocates were politically driven, prone to exaggerate and simplistic about cause. The social workers and government agencies had big hearts but were managing things poorly. From their point of view then, the true cause of homelessness was bad management. They pointed to the number of food lines operating within blocks of each other, not just the huge one we were focused on, and their lack of coordination. As evidence, they explained how homeless people raced between them carrying armloads of food some of which they'd later sell to their very own less fortunate peers. Each food program reported their counts, no names taken; the overlapping numbers were simply added up and turned in. Funding sources looked at the reports and declared that the problem was bigger than it was, much bigger than expected. Hyperbole underwrote the lobbying efforts launched from each of these angles, which began in fever pitch from New York to Albany to Washington D.C. Meanwhile, the retailers saw homeless men and women sleeping at the foot of their storefront windows and doorways. Property values falling. Vacancy rates rising. Good points. Functionalism at work.

In sum, the food line advocates, the social workers, and the property managers all had one big thing in common; they wanted this problem fixed. Politicians too? Or were they just brokers, each out for their specific constituency? Wait a minute.

What about the homeless themselves? What about their perspective?

We formed a gathering of 50 local volunteers and trained them to run an unduplicated count and to conduct a survey. We counted 640 seemingly disconnected people on the streets, each of them alone, by themselves on that rainy March night, between 8pm and midnight. There may have been more. We interviewed, 200 of them. We paid them with $5 store coupons from a local deli, enough for a couple of sandwiches and a drink. We asked them what they wanted to get out of homelessness? 90% said they wanted housing. The same percentage, 90%, said they wanted employment. 90%. Seventy percent blamed themselves for the situation they were in. 70%. Only two percent blamed their last landlord or employer for their homelessness. 2%.

Remember how the advocates for the homeless blamed the property owners for homelessness? Well, the homeless disagreed. They disagreed with their own advocates in a very important way that can point us to a more effective approach. More on that later. But, for now, what does that say about The Board?

What else did they say they wanted? Despite eighty percent admitting to having significant problems such as mental health issues or substance abuse, only fifteen percent requested treatment. 80% to 15%. They did not see their homelessness as being caused by denial. They disagreed with their social workers too. Maybe this should be settled indoors instead of on the streets?

To review, most admitted to serious problems and blamed themselves for it, yet very few wanted treatment. That is a good case for the idea that resistance is at play. 80% to 15% indeed. However, treatment typically will not be effective if the person is relatively disinterested. They acknowledged their problems but wanted something else more than they wanted treatment for them. Two things most said say they wanted was housing and employment. Housing does make it easier to get the job and to keep it. You need an address. Besides the many personal gains, to the prospective landlord as well as the employer, it rightly boasts of stability. As well, employment can be life changing. For example, the steady paycheck makes the unaffordable apartment less so. In fact, once working, they would be much more likely to accept and complete treatment, especially if their jobs (and social status) depended on it. That is not very different from any of us. We're social animals and want to avoid shame. Oh, and most importantly, the housing hasn't come for them.

Early on, we became determined to fill half of all the jobs at our Drop-In Center from the very people coming to us for help. That would be our gold standard, something we can proudly say we accomplished. Working alongside each other like that over the years brought us unparalleled outreach success.

~   ~   ~

Because I believed homeless people can work, one of New York Magazine's investigative reporters described me as sounding like a holdout for cold fusion. He said he couldn't find anyone who agreed with my premise.

We put the need to "show up" for work as first and foremost. Ours would be an attendance-based process, something about irrefutable evidence being the most convincing. Once a person showed up repeatedly, which told us what we needed to know, we were going to find a way to work with them. Out in the open, no other way, they're in the workplace after all, "performing" in front of their peers you could say, they'd be succeeding, or at least visibly trying to. Here we ask, what besides the pocketbook did that effect? Social status.

Circumstantial peers. From the bottom they all began. And now, these homeless people were legitimate mid-towners now. Disconnections were breaking down. They were in midtown because they had to "go to work" like all the other commuters. That would give them among other things, besides an address and a place to get their mail, somewhere, you could say, to hang their hat. They came indoors and the line went away.

Conclusion: Sometimes warning signs need to be taken at face value. How the problem was seen caused everyone to overlook the obvious. For example, resistance was seen as an indication of a personal problem. Okay, but it was also a valid form of social communication. What did Freud famously say? Yes, but it is also a cigar, and we want to call our own shots, to unravel whatever it was we had been raveling. What causes a problem? What causes purple? Is it red or blue?

Thirteen

S tuck in a co-dependent relationship with their advocate-captors, it took a long while, from 1981 until 1989, before the people standing on midtown's big outdoor food line on Vanderbilt Avenue just outside Grand Central Terminal took matters into their own hands. As advocates, they wanted to raise public awareness, but of course, the people being fed didn't appreciate being drafted on stage, into a media showcase, cameras, and all. Publicized at their worst. Feeling like they're looking their worst, and they are. Of course, they stood on that line willingly. They were hungry.

~   ~   ~

Sometimes, members of The Board would stand outside our building to "try to get the homeless back," one of them said to me, "They're our homeless." "Hey, come back to our food line. This place doesn't care about you. Come on." Or they'd just stand in front of our building howling and chanting accusatory questions, no question marks, which we knew better than to answer: "HOW DARE YOU? HOW DARE YOU? HOW DARE YOU?" How dare we do what? Their front door rants against our operation occurred "spontaneously" only and always at the height of rush hour. Each day, thousands of people commuting to and from work passed by unaware that they were receiving continuing-education as to how to see us.

~   ~   ~

Everybody should have affordable housing but forty million people in this country do not. None need it more desperately than the two million or so people who can't afford not to have it. Disconnected and unlucky. Extremely poor. Lacking consumer rights, and simplistically represented by their own advocates, a top-down tyranny, which uses their plight of homelessness as political fodder. They point to the distress of shelter-life and street-life as an example of what's wrong with the system; amazing, since *they* are the system.

Fourteen

Why such an uncritical media? In a word, lunch. Again, food as the great motivator. But these were always very special, work-related lunches, Fridays were best, one reporter at a time; what we can call a relatively small food line. Who played host? The Board; always The Board. We were not there, yet did we have to be there to know that they did not dine on bologna white-bread sandwiches with a side of cold pea soup?

~ ~ ~

The Board speaks. "I call them homeless folks," they'd say, "to show that they are just like you and me." Later, in the most famous of blue papers, The Board's founder was quoted as saying much more. "If people knew the extent of their disabilities there'd be much less sympathy, but if you see them as your own uncle Harry or aunty Mae, as homeless victims of a greedy landlord, you'll likely feel more supportive." That's referred to as, "strategic planning."

~ ~ ~

About 50 million people in the USA live in housing that is not affordable to them. Half of them live in poverty. The other half don't, even if they are unable to afford their residence. Four out of five newly built apartment houses are built for luxury. In fact, excruciatingly high numbers of relatively affordable apartments are lost each year. Blame the market? But the market goes by way of demand, and the money rises and falls accordingly. Think of the "upgraded rebuild." Are we going to keep asking hundreds of thousands of people in our shelters across the country each night to wait for these trends to reverse, for their personal number to come up?

As later explained, these many lunches were necessary because of the high turnover of reporters assigned to these kinds of topic-driven stories. This way, from diligence, even sometimes if not from knowledge, they'd position themselves as the go-to person on all stories "homeless." No secret conspiracy here. It's widely known by now, to get the whole story, that readers who turn to just one source, angle, or perspective, do so at their own risk. Caveat Emptor. Wow. Is that where we are? All the news that fits.

On the rare occasion that a homeless person is "housed" by their social worker or case manager, the housing that is found for them often requires they move into communities they don't want to be in, now geographically estranged from what little social supports they did have, complete with an unaffordable commute back. They're in a community that they lack experience in, typically with housemates they may not exactly have chosen to be around, having to register with the government as a disabled person when they might not be very disabled at all, very common, and thereby, they lose time measured in years from achieving their employment goals, which is usually what they wanted in the first place. Apparently, it was not for them to decide.

Another wrinkle. Often, they do not get the treatment they need if they want it differently than it is offered, instead their "resistance" is tolerated by "compassionate professionals" who wait for them to agree with what's been prescribed. The formerly homeless tenant too is in wait, that is, for the professional to "come around" to their point of view. They want to work but can't now at the risk of losing their housing. Earn too much and you're out. True life, in most cases when living in supportive housing, once you earn a living wage, about $15-17 per hour, you are out. Why? Because that is the level of pay seen as evidence that the person can live independently. Imagine the time and money saved if that wage was offered from the start, let's say, upon entering the shelter?

Back in the day, there emerged an independent operator who we've fake-named "Gabriella Cashman." Seen in her ear-to-ear grin, pushed to its limits, Gabby was always a sneeringly angry, ear-to-ear angry, nostril flaring angry, garment-center sales executive turned failed politician. Finally measured by the weight of her silk, I suppose, she transformed herself into a successful homeless advocate. Very visibly working through an array of weighty personal issues, she was called the "sandwich woman" by some, her approach a bit primal. Back in the day, late 80's, she'd scream at people who tried to "skip" to the front of that food line, a bottle of wine possibly having drowned her own sorrows some hours earlier, its effects wearing off just as she came out to poorly feed everyone. Furiously chewing breath mint gum, she'd throw shout-outs at whichever people she noticed were not paying sufficient attention to her ministries. She'd mock them as they scrambled for fallen food that either she dropped, or that she may have thrown at them. It could have been performance art mimicking the abuse that homeless people regularly get, but it wasn't. I saw it, once just ten feet away, shrinking backwards into the crowd of onlookers, media included, their cameras whirring, note pads burning. Often, she was the talking head behind the panoramic, a terrible scene, the evening's news, a human-interest story for sure, Gabby was prolific, a personal liaison to many great stories.

~ ~ ~

There was another player too, quite contrary, who started as a stand-in for The Board's founder. Once upon a time, she agreed to meet with Dan, who in turn asked me to join them as well. A few minutes early, I arrived on the corner of east 44th and Lexington Avenue only to see her just arriving herself. Either because of her strident anger, or her many forced "Hollywood" selfie-smiles, her muted disdain for those who proved impervious to her practiced charms is difficult for her to hide. Anyway, there she was on that corner. Dan had called to tell me he'd be a few minutes late, that we should meet him at the Oyster Bar in Grand Central Terminal's basement where he was finishing his lunch. I explained this to her as I formally introduced myself, hand outstretched. Apparently under internal pressure, she didn't notice my hand. In short, she left me hanging. She could not bring herself to even look at me. Her face turned dark red. Rage red. She blurted out "NO WAY!" No way what? "Is this a set-up?" Is what a set up? "Is Dan coming or not? Where's Dan? No, no, no, no, no. I am not having this. I am not meeting with one of his underlings. Where is Dan? WHERE IS HE?" Hey...not to worry, I said, we can wait until he gets here to talk substance. He just called me. He's coming but he's held up at a luncheon. We can go meet him, it's only a couple of blocks away. My hand was still out there, hanging. I kept it there to make point. "No, I wanted to speak with Dan. NOBODY ELSE! Where is he eating his lunch? Where is he? WHERE IS HE? I am out of here, OUT! This is a setup. A SET UP!" What was being set up? Lunch? Passersby were straining at the neck for an explanation of the kerfuffle. Was I hurting her? I kept my hand out, now partially to show the onlookers my lack of aggression. I was staring her down, praying that she'd relent. Soon, she literally turned and started fast-walking crosstown just short of a run. I turned and tried to follow her though ultimately, I couldn't keep up. I mean I wasn't going to literally chase her; if I gave full chase while she was yelling at me "Leave me alone" over her shoulder, I think someone would start dialing 911 with my description. She was too fast for me anyway. I couldn't even keep track of her after a block or two. She just kept going. We never again did speak. Not ever, though I did see her do some on camera stand-ins ranting about how bad we were. I could never engage her or find out why she'd been so reactive. Again, guess we never should have gotten all those people indoors.

Important to pause here. Time to read Stephen Crane's *Men in the Storm* which puts a solid check in the box next to "perspective." I mean, who is suffering here? Is it you Ms. Contrary?

It can certainly be a bad career move to take The Board on. Its members hold the patent on a three or four decades-old mindset, any challenge to which will lessen you and yours in the world they've created around it, the world you've really no choice but to be in. No, that's not exactly true, you can act out at least until you're taken down. True enough though, the team of conductors on the fiction-as-fact freight train will name names all the time, that's their bailiwick, but when it's your name, if you were to make the effort to expunge your culpability instead of snapping to, you may very well be labeled *part of the problem.* Broad-brush strokes only, and the train bears down.

Here's an example as to how it worked in the media oh so many times, one of many stories for which we were not contacted by the writer. Remember Peter Smith? The guy who demanded all our social services money, "or there'll be hell to pay?" Now keeping good on that threat, his friendship with a certain reporter most helpful, he accused us of "making homeless people sit in chairs." One city daily, then two. Fake news. "They should be finding people homes instead of making them sit in chairs," Peter's voice blasted all over the stories. And to illustrate, in one there was a picture that showed a man in a wooden desk chair sitting slumped, looking totally exhausted, numerous bags all around him, his bushy hair silhouetted by the ceiling's fluorescents. That was the initial story, and lording over it, its headline, a quote from Peter, "They Make Them Sleep in Chairs." They might as well have shown someone exhaling: "The Homeless Need Oxygen, But Instead, After Inhaling, The Business District Requires Them to Breathe Out."

On most any night, except the most frigid ones where people are literally forced indoors by the police, about 95% of all homeless people in the city are sitting on the edge of any one of the city's many thousands of shelter beds, not on a friend's sofa, an important distinction. For those 5% who did not have any place to go but who did not want to go to a shelter, the city opened what they called drop-in-centers. Half of them went there, the rest remaining on the street. While policies varied, some of the drop-ins took people over 55 years old, or women only, or only those who were mentally ill; ours was an open-door policy for anybody over 18 years old. Each of the city's nine or so drop-ins were places where such people could walk in off the streets unannounced, 24/7. There'd be food served, showers available, case managers, referrals to other places for treatment, and of course the city expected the staff to make a pitch for each person to consider taking a bed in the city shelter system. However, one could decide to stay in a drop-in-center permanently. By city design, drop-in-centers did not have beds, a policy decision by the city to mesh with local zoning laws, but also to steer people towards where the city wanted them to be – into shelter beds. At the centers, no beds, people were in the chairs because they didn't want to be in a shelter bed. Whether they were in the pursuit of assistance or respite, wanting to be under-the-radar or just left alone, they were allowed to sit all through the night, every night, no problem. Having 150 to 200 people sitting with us through the night was not uncommon; and there'd be up to

300-400 people in and out all-day long. Come on Peter, you knew that. Come on reporter man, you could have found all this out. No beds here but we do not "make" them sleep in chairs.

Was it intentional misdirection meant to be damaging or was the reporter just being lazy? Maybe, but we cannot consider the reporter an "innocent." Publishing a poorly researched article educates no one. It is a form of fraud, the public misled.

Psychiatrist Robert Jay Lifton's article, *Eight Criteria for Thought Control*, might explain what is going on here. Number six on his list, "thought-terminating clichés." Loaded language designed to avoid rational discussion.

George Orwell, in *Down and Out in Paris and London*, said that while the "fall" is the worse part of homelessness, once you've hit bottom having survived the descent, there's a feeling of relief – no more impending doom, and now, relative comfort.

Fifteen

W hy were we so successful in our outreach efforts? Why should our success have so significantly bothered others?

~ ~ ~

Three-quarters of a million people come into and around Grand Central Terminal every day, then as now, activity that in the late 80's and early 90's swirled around several-hundred homeless people who were there night and day, including another several hundred that each day come and go. Overall, one could tell who was who by watching for movement, that is, who was standing relatively still and who seemed frozen in place? Compounding this massive human traffic epicenter was a newly established freestanding food line, the city's largest, freestanding as in "no chairs," under the open sky, eating "rough." Two blocks long. Dinner time. On stage for all to see, hundreds waiting for the appearance of a food truck, a station wagon, with paper bags partly filled with we-hope-you'll-stay-put-so-we-can-see-you-tomorrow food. This was on Vanderbilt Avenue, which ran alongside the terminal's west side. It was doing its bit to add people, static, into the moving mix.

For the owners of the buildings and their renters, retailers, and residents both, besides or because of all this "negative" activity in and around the terminal, leases were being broken right in two. Occupancy rates plummeted. Was there a tipping point? Was this it? A few hundred-extra people on a line on just one of the many blocks surrounding the great big terminal disrupting the hundreds of thousands of others? Could it be? The commuters saw the homeless around them as a drag and just didn't feel as safe as they wanted to feel. Talk about feelings, the property owners and their managers felt that these homeless people gave cover to something much worse. In fact, what they called "quality of life crimes," such as bag hustling, pickpocketing, and very aggressive panhandling near Grand Central terminal, increased upon the establishment of the food line. Bad guys were taking advantage of the chaos that the line contributed to on top of the natural chaos of a transportation terminal's life, trying to blend in with the hustle and the bustle of the crowd. Graffiti appeared everywhere, inside the terminal and out. Tourism was down and property values were taking a hit. Did the homeless threaten the future of their real estate portfolios? One thing for sure, they didn't hold on to their fortunes nor expand their holdings by manifesting passivity. Proactive responses to "business-inhibiting" problems such as the food line got them to where they were, they believed, and clearly, they were not going to just sit back and watch.

One may not have expected it, I didn't, but the business improvement district managers were open to trying new things, especially if they saw a direct line between action and profit. Instead of trying to get everyone to leave, an outcome they dreamed of pulling off, no way, they hired me and let me create a program that ironically added to the number of "regulars," and for it to work right, it had to be nearby, that is, smack in the middle of their very own neighborhood!

We found a place only two blocks away from the food line, a former high school. We built up a fully equipped kitchen with a cafeteria big enough to hold half of just about everybody, bathrooms and showers and storage too, plus space throughout to meet with social services professionals, a medical clinic, a movie room, several sitting rooms, and so forth. Talk about "flip," The Board began flipping out. What really riled them up was that before we did any of this or that, we talked to just about everybody, polling them right there on the streets. Trying to give them what they wanted. Populism.

It was to the chagrin of The Board that we made a monumental discovery. That most every homeless person on the food line, man, and woman alike, saw employment as their best way out. Even better, they seemed to know that it'd be up to them.

March 31, 1989. A mild, rainy, a late afternoon start that lasted well into the night. There came together a group of 30 residents from the local community, community board leaders included, a Columbia University epidemiologist, along with another sociologist from her department, and several Drop-in-Center staff. What would we learn? We assigned pairs of these interviewers to specific geographic "zones" in which they would seek to interview each homeless person they came across. Thirty minutes each. They they'd pay the person for their time with a free meal coupon made good by a local delicatessen.

Weeks later, I stood in front of the 50+ person team of business improvement district directors in full attendance, the midtown property owners of the Grand Central Partnership Business Improvement District, plus a few others. An opening joke – I immediately announced that for about 2 billion dollars I could solve the problem of midtown homelessness within two to three months. Laughter. It did not seem to faze that crowd, a few even joked back by patting their pockets in search for their checkbook. Then it all took a turn for the serious, my reason for being there.

~   ~   ~

"Since day one of the Vanderbilt Food Line, its operators have been telling us that the people on their line are homeless because of greedy landlords. Maybe so. Perhaps we can reduce this whole problem to greed, but I assure you, that finding would not be limited to landlords. More to the point, by doing something very few seemed to be doing, that is by talking with these homeless people, what we found out was for the purposes of helping them, spectacular. As it turned out, the people on that line did not see things the same way that the food line organizers did. They disagreed with their own advocates! For example, as for who was to blame for their homelessness, only 2% of the 200 or so people we spoke with blamed their last landlord or their employer. Again, clearly in the know, by and large, they were not blaming greedy landlords. In fact, over 70% blamed themselves for the mess they were in. 70%. Now, we know that self-blame has a practical psychological purpose, and self-reflection can result in overreach, but here, our acknowledgment of their perspective could possibly help us chart a different course. Their perspective. Our biases aside, believing them would likely further free them up from feeling helpless. It would have its own benefits, but overall, to understand how they see things is all-important in reaching them; it's the "reach" in outreach. What good does our resistance to their perspective do for them? Instead of engaging in a battle of wills or waiting on them to see the light, we need to begin by accepting their self-diagnosis and their treatment plan. Our work is to support them."

~   ~   ~

That the homeless disagreed with their own advocates on the central issue of what was causing their homelessness was bigger than life. It's the kind of reality that puts the "out" in outreach, okay? For those of us who wanted to figure how to bring them indoors, this was huge. To paraphrase Mary Rose McGeady, interviewed in a book I co-wrote, *Beyond Homelessness*, she is the long-time executive director of Covenant House, it was emblematic of the difference between advocating *for* instead of *with* someone. *For* is about power and control, *with* is restorative and enabling. Interesting, the people on the food line also seemed to see things differently than the social workers working to get them indoors. When the social worker looks at these homeless people, they see traits to treat, substance abusing behaviors, untreated mental illness, and above all else, both denial and resistance, which many times are read as indicators of personal problems and personality disorders, again, things they could try to treat. Street homelessness though, has come to epitomize resistance to their treatment approach. The principal purpose of outreach then, for these social workers and their agencies, was to overcome this resistance. While the social workers may be on to something regarding how many of them need treatment, it is not what these people who are living outdoors are looking for and offering it will not be what brings them indoors. It is going to take something else."

"The best news of all: 90% of the people interviewed said that what they wanted, as much a place to live, was a job. That was what they saw as their ticket out. Amazing, right? Two things. They blamed themselves, and they wanted a job, both of which represent mainstream American values. They take full responsibility for fixing their condition and they want to work themselves out of the mess they are in. All during the outbreak of this terrible social problem has been this lost chance to view them as unemployed and disconnected, looking for work and in need of a connection. This was how they viewed themselves rather than what to us may have seemed more pressing, the idea instead that they were merely homeless and looking for a home or that they are sick and once treated, will get back on their feet. I will say this, that the former is way more practical to attend to than the latter." Getting right to the point, I said, "There are two approaches we could take."

"The first approach is the safe approach. We could use our annual budget of $250,000 to give out grants to help sustain current outreach efforts. Through our funding, we'd encourage the social services agencies to work together, which they do not do a lot of, to increase the number of real options they can present to people on the streets, in effect, to help them "up" their game. They'd want this help too. We could put into place a financial reward system keyed to evidence-based outcomes that meet a set of goals, which we'd regularly review. Each year's results could then be presented in an annual conference. For the homeless people themselves, it will, again, over time, bring benefits large and small to some. Improvements to delivered services, rewarding success and all, infusing these dollars into their programs, would be popular within the field, and over time, improve the situation out there on Vanderbilt Avenue and to this whole area. I will say, however, that this safe approach would likely make more permanent the fact of the food line, and to a degree, the static nature of midtown homelessness. We'd be saying what is true, that the people on this line are hungry and can't be ignored. Afterall, they do need the help being offered. So then, we could lobby right alongside the service providers, our statistics used as tools to prod the powerful in New York, Albany, and Washington D.C. Here's the ironic part. To be most effective given their approach, given this approach we'd be supporting, current outreach agencies would be looking for the people living on midtown streets to stay put, until that one day comes that they'd be able to "reach them," and that then they'd be agreeable to accepting help. Food and clothing would be used as rewards. This lengthy approach would give the outreach workers more of chance to "break through." However, this slow approach, regardless of its merits, would seem to further endanger them, no? It would keep them in place, waiting for the next handout that takes them nowhere. Still, they wait for either housing or employment. Not resistant to other ideas, just not interested." My speech was about halfway done.

I continued. Big breath. "As for the less safe approach, less safe because it's untried, but also because it would possibly undermine current approaches out there on Vanderbilt and throughout this district. Here it is. We could do the work ourselves. And our approach would be not trait-centered, that is, based on what we perceive as their diagnosis, but social status-centered based on where they perceive themselves among their peers and the rest of society. That's why we would focus on employment. Our very first hires would be formerly homeless people, men and women who had succeeded in overcoming their homelessness. They would form our outreach team – talking to their peers, speaking about what worked for them, and it would be extremely compelling."

"We'd develop a number of programming start-ups, small efforts, each of which would be further pursued if proven successful. If successful, it'd be attractive to outside funders and if not, it could be dropped on the spot and replaced with another start-up that would."

To drive my points home and to arouse their enthusiasm, as this was my preferred choice, I offered up a working metaphor, that midtown homelessness was caused by a very basic marketing problem. People were not being sold the products for which they were shopping. That was why they were not "buying." They are the customers shopping for one thing, jobs, while the salespeople were persisting in trying to sell them something else, treatment. Here's the short version of the rest of my presentation, not too far off from how it really went. Dan only gave me "seven and one-half minutes" to present. Thank goodness for that extra one-half minute for I had used up most all my allotted time. Still, I pressed forward, basically ignoring Dan's fidgeting. I'd be done in just two and one-half minutes more, I promised myself with a hidden smirk.

"One. We work with St. Agnes church to get full use of their school building. Currently it is a 12-hour per day program. We need it to be a 24-hour per day year-round facility instead. I think there is some room to negotiate there. The Monsignor wants to see a successful program and is very disappointed over how things have been going. Right now, by day, their school building is half-empty so, the students that are there could maybe go to another of their schools, also half-empty."

"Two. We get more beds. Right now, the Center gets 30-50 beds to fill each night. They are laid out in church and synagogue and mosque locations, abort 15 beds at each place. They're overseen by volunteers, most being available about nine months out of the year. We would work with the agency running the program under contract with the city now, the Partnership for the Homeless. Together, we'd approach five new churches. Not hard to do – we already have three locations agreeing to participate. We run the first one well, and the others will follow. Funding should not be too difficult to find.

~ ~ ~

"Three. We start an employment-training program that would copy successful programs already in place around the city. Roughly speaking, most of the people who'd be coming into our Center are receiving monthly public assistance payments through the Department of Welfare. The Department lets people who are receiving job training to earn up to $50 per week in stipends without affecting their Welfare assistance. Taken together, Welfare payments plus stipends, temporary housing would be possible. That would give them enough of an income. The training would help them work off their "work rust," pick up some marketable skills, update their resumes, and upon their graduation, we'd help them find work. That's how these programs work. Usually, trainees are assigned to food services or maintenance, but we could add several other opportunities. It would be much more difficult, running the center with so many trainee/helpers...they'd need a lot of supervision, so it would be costly, but the training would go a long way to help them in ways they want to be helped. It would help them heal in front of their peers, or as we say, their community of peers. And it would help us in the management of the center in that so many people would be invested in the program. The program's value would be palpable, felt by all who came to stay. A heart beating for them. Their self-esteem would be subject to what could be called a "mender bender," a healing arc that could in no other way be attained. Here, I want to refer you to read sociologist Elliot Liebow's article *The Terrible Knowledge That You're Not Needed*, a copy of which is in your folders in front of you, in which he extols the preventive power of employment. It is more than just a social anchor, in this culture of ours, it is essential to mental health and to socially acceptable adaptation."

"Four. Crisis-loans. To help people out of an immediate crisis, or to help get business-for-self ideas off the ground, we could start a crisis-loan program, let's say, up to $500, that would, of course, charge zero-interest. These micro-loans could go to individual homeless people, who could then be partnered with mentors from the local resident or corporate community. Later, they could pay these loans back to us by volunteering at our Center, by helping us help their less successful peers."

"Five: Research. Given that by way of our expansive survey, we already have launched a research and study effort on the social problem of homelessness in midtown, we can move over time to establish a social problems research library and learning center. Through conferencing and joint projects, we could bring together several perspectives. We could put together a great library that included every study we could get our hands on, and we could conduct survey research of our own to stay one step ahead of the people we serve."

They chose that second option, the one with the five elements, that of establishing their own programming, that's right, the riskier hands-on plan, and they went for all five except the last. They said the research could wait. Very exciting. But they were circumspect. Dr. Dumpson said something like: "Our taking steps like these will be read as if we are outing them on their failures. If we begin to be successful, they will like us even less than they do now. They are going to act out. So, if we are going to do this, our best bet is to keep track of our outcomes – they can't take away the facts." Oh yes, they can.

Later, they offered me a position as their Vice-President of Social Services. At first, I somewhat jokingly cited Bob Dylan as never "allowing" me to take such a job, certainly not to quit my job and come on board full-time with them, the super-wealthy, corporate, property management community. How about we take it slowly? Could I start part time, and take it from there? I loved my work at Presbyterian Hospital, and had an excellent experience working with Herb Pardes, Fred Kass, and Paula Eagle, my supervisors who ran the department of psychiatry at Presbyterian Hospital at the time. I thought I could hold both jobs – great work, an additional $10-15k a year, what could be better? They agreed, and I did that for about half a year. Eventually though, the work in midtown took over. In August of 1989, one year later, I left the massive hospital and its scores of busy corridors for those of midtown, where people move around more in a maze…

To the casual observer, now years after we were forced out, midtown looks a little bit like we were never there. In some ways, this story hurts everyone's credibility.

Sixteen

New York's mayor Bill DeBlasio inherited what? Badly run and packed wall-to-wall shelters that were so dangerous he had to bring in the police department to make them safer, all of it, now on him. 1986 all over again? No, it still is 1986, few lessons learned. The shelters are unsafe, and very few people are being placed into housing of their own, about 1 in 50 if you count the people regularly staying in shelters, more like 1 in 100 or more if you include the turnover in a year, plus all the people on the streets as well as those who show up for emergency housing in family shelters. Add drop-in-centers, short-term street level detoxification and treatment programs, and up to 20% of the people coming out of public mental health institutions or jails etc. and these ratios get even worse; it's as unlikely as ever that housing will ever show up for them any more than it has for the general needy public, the many of us who live in housing above our means. It won't prove to be the solution not because people don't need affordable housing, but because so many people do, and for most everybody it just won't happen, not can't, but won't. For example, one of the most influential ad hoc members of The Board, The Son, named that because of whose son he is and the powerful positions they've held, past tense, announced a year or so into his second term in office what he hailed as a major initiative to house the homeless. "1200 new units of housing," he declared. By the way, once completed, a few years down the road, that would bring the number down from 100,000 to about 98,800, but that's only if those numbers hold, and they won't. He also says he will set up a commission to study the problem further. No joke, by far, it is not his first homeless study group. Don't we know already its findings?

~ ~ ~

That person is on the streets because she is an alcoholic, look, you can smell the alcohol. She even says that she loves to drink, "It's all I've got," she says. It's real. So, you bring in an alcohol expert to talk to her to get her into treatment. If rebuffed in the effort, which happens most of the time, the expert will pull back and wait for her to want treatment enough. "She hasn't hit bottom," they'll say. Yet, if being on the street in a box and drunk doesn't constitute hitting bottom for this person, how long should we wait? In most instances, the alcoholism expert is going to be correct about people needing to want treatment before it can be effective. Until she wants to stop drinking enough, her addiction will pervade wet or dry, dry being infinitely better. Dry allows for more function, which is the goal. Function. Truth is, in our larger society, the one whose standards we hold them up against, 25% of people with jobs drink alcohol during the workaday. 8% use alcohol heavily. Yet, only about 25% of alcoholics enter formal treatment. That's right, alcoholics have jobs and, what's more, their alcoholism is not addressed during the interview process. That is not allowed unless the alcoholic brings it up either directly or indirectly, by putting in on display. From a regulation standpoint, their personal problems are seen as separate from their need for employment. For them, employment-first is a right? They have a drinking problem, yet not only are they viewed as employable, but they are also employed, and going forward, the law will protect them from being fired simply because they are alcoholics. But if we look at the person living on the street, we say that even though she has already hit bottom, she doesn't want treatment for her drinking. Not now. At least, not yet. Okay, maybe not ever. Can we accept that she might be one of those people who, given a chance, can manage to function while still drinking and if not, will always insist on trying? Look, there should be nothing peculiar about an outreach worker asking someone who appears to have an alcohol use disorder if they want help for it. If she or he says that they do not, simply put, should we refuse to work with her, to in effect hold that against her? Or maybe we should find another way to reach her? What does she want? A job? Hmm...

What our job becomes is to help her find work on one of her "good" days. If not that, then what? She must stay outdoors and be considered "resistant to treatment" until that day comes that will accept treatment on our terms? Their way, upon graduating a treatment program (that they can't get her into because she does not want to go), she will then have concrete proof of her "disability" and be instantly eligible for supported housing, no employment. But even if she is lucky enough to be that one in fifty or so, "Housing-First" fixing her one problem, not having a home, at the expense of the other, her ongoing disability of alcoholism. A disabled person can't work. If they could, they would no longer be considered disabled and they would lose their housing eligibility. Then, it's back on the street. Housing-First is a platitude, and when it does "work," often the person is no closer, even further, from their desired end, which is employment (and independence). Maybe we need to ask each person right up front what do they want? We can call it the "anything-first" approach. What will it take for you to come indoors?

You do not need a master's degree for this kind of outreach. You need an outreach worker with the type of credibility that "specialty experts" don't have. Outreach is a sales effort, not a treatment session. Outreach products must speak to the person. Can it be that simple? No, it's the hardest thing of all to teach. Many "experts" are averse to even trying. See, "The Hindrance of Theory in Clinical Work," by Carl Whitaker. In short, their schooling gets in the way. They think they know what the person needs. They forget that the person in front of them is a scientist too, making his or her own calculations, deciding when to buy-in. Instead, the professional often gets caught up in thinking the person is "in denial" if he wants anything but the treatment being offered. If he turns them down, it's him being "resistant" to the treatment he needs. This is the most damaging aspect of the labeling process. The attitude is, hands palm up and out, "Why listen? It just feeds them a fantasy world. Let's be realistic here. They need treatment." But just then, they are interrupted by a chant, "Housing, housing, housing," and suddenly, the *Stepford Wives* button has been pressed. The experts give up their dreams of treating the person. Just like that. They know what's expected of them. They bow their heads, no problem. In these ways and more, trait-centered outreach is ineffective. We can begin to understand why. Right?

Most alcoholics are not homeless. However, people who are homeless are Outsiders, and if we want to help an outsider who is also an alcoholic, maybe we should look at how the Insider is handled in such cases where they are unemployed but wish to work. If an Insider is an alcoholic, unmotivated to go into treatment but most interested in work, what he can do is apply for a job during his most sober moments. Once he gets that job, if he can get past the probation period, if his drinking problem becomes apparent to his employers, being that he now has a job he wants to keep, he is likely to be that much more motivated to get help, and he can most likely get treatment, in confidence, as we said, through his Employee Assistance Program, which would refer him to a qualified private professional or program. Here, he would make a great effort to complete the course of treatment as that would be his ticket to a return to work. And there we go. That's typically the way it works for Insiders. Because of connections to people and places that can be turned to, unlike people living on the street, "Insiders" are more able to avoid the worst. This is because their social networks include people who are stable and upwardly mobile, who not only would want to help them but who have the resources to do so. They might be alcoholics whose drinking will forever hold them back from their potential. Or, they might have a panic disorder or be taking medication for what had once been paralyzing anxiety, but which then became a prescription drug problem. They could have some long-term sadness, even depression, or a mood-disorder, all of which are terrible in terms of the extreme discomfort they cause. But here's the thing: Usually none of this is taken as the full measure of their lives, which when we consider future possibilities is most fortunate.

Preventing Connection   Encouraging Connection

- the label "homeless"
- addressing the disconnect through employment
- trait-centered outreach
- status-centered outreach
- the lack of consumer rights
- consumer rights – free choice
- shelters and treatment centers
- upwardly mobile peers
- over-professionalization of services extensive use of paraprofessionals
- the wait for housing
- industry jobs goes to consumers
- power-driven leadership
- replacing The Board with humanists

The lack of affordable housing is a widespread problem, but when reliable and safe housing is obtained, even if unaffordable, it can serve as a broad solution for that person's economic woes. However, there are about 100 million people in the USA living in housing that is well beyond 30% of their income, the affordability measurement. Half of these people are in situations where 50% of more of their income is needed to cover rent or mortgage payments. Needing housing that is affordable is what our shelter residents have in common with the general population. Sadly, instead of helping these homeless residents find the employment they need to escape shelter life, we ask them to sit tight in wait for that rare gift in hand, affordable housing. That's a good reason why it's unfair to refer to them as "homeless." Better to refer to them as "on hold."

Thinking of them as being sufficiently disconnected as to be unable to pay for housing, if it indicts them, it indicts us. We are connectors or not. A tech writer, Gideon Rosenblatt, describes it this way:

> One way to think of connections is as a kind of handshake between two parties. Both parties must extend a hand to make contact. The connection has a beginning and an end, and these are usually close to each other in time. In the early stages of a relationship, the connection can frequently involve some sort of exchange, even if it may take a little creativity to see what's being swapped. In this sense, connections can be said to be transactional.

There needs to be a radical shift that moves us away from focusing on the one need we barely can do anything about, their housing, to the one we can directly affect, their disconnection. Their unemployment.

Is it necessary to further emphasize the drama? Standing outside of the entire housing market, the people labeled homeless are being counted, their census taken. In New York City alone, the latest point-in-time count was 63,000. Nationwide, it's about 700,000 people. That's how many people do not have enough money to pay for a roof over their head. They are contained within an overflowing "pool" of people three times larger, the extremely poor. The market refuses them – its rents are not low enough, and there is no real estate to sell to them.

Some people have so much housing, they live in one place while they rent out their other one, that is, without having to "give it up." No wonder that in New York City for example, there's about a 1% vacancy rate. Rents being what they are, people are squeezed out of the market only to be sent further to the city's periphery and beyond. Commuting times and costs grow. For them, these hurdles can render day to day living more troublesome. Yet, for people without the necessary income to live even at that level, for those that are in the shelter system, the city's vacancy rate is as good as 0%. That's bad.

New York has set up homeless shelters, which essentially are emergency camps for economic refugees unable to make rent. 95% of homeless people live in such shelters, the larger of which produce quite difficult conditions to endure. They proliferate despair and inaction. Speaking of despair, the other 5% of NYC's homeless people live on the streets.

In that we continue to maintain and expand this very shelter system, by neglecting its central failings, it is on us.

~　　~　　~

The Board's ineffectiveness, and its "pernicious rigidity" towards staying on course despite the evidence, work hand in hand. They give us all the proof we need of a conspiracy most silent. The kindest take on their approach, which requests desperate people to sit and wait, is that it is as cold as ice. They advocate for something with such poor outcomes that one can only conclude they are inhabitants in center-city, Vhadra hell, Alan Ginsberg's "place" for people who are so f'd up they don't even know it.

Seventeen

We are talking here about people who sit against our buildings or lay on our sidewalks at our feet. Anything but invisible. Oh, by the way, they see us too. We see each other, neither of us sufficiently motivated to speak – about what? It is evident, the disconnection between us two, for both of us, this is a textbook breeding ground for stigma and misconception.

~   ~   ~

The passerby passes by, going back to his own people among whom he has multiple connections that sustain and promote him. The guy on the ground is going nowhere. As the passersby pass by, he may feel further demoted. At best, he's leveled off, on lock-down, kept alive by his nearby "buddies" who he can barely trust. At worst, he is downwardly mobile still, a little bit more alone, increasingly disconnected. Is there no bottom? Apparently, the mainstream is an exclusive group.

~   ~   ~

Songwriters, Jerome Kern and Dorothy Fields: "Nothing's impossible I have found, for when my chin is on the ground, I pick myself up, dust myself off, start all over again."

~   ~   ~

Think Neil Young's *The Needle and The Damage Done* as metaphor. With its ability to distract from pain and discomfort, our source for pleasure when taken in the right dose is our network of others. What facilitates our personal survival in what can be a fast-paced somewhat forbidding world of others, is our self-centric, micro-community, the world as seen through our eyes even as we further invent it. The Psychology of Perception, 101. Not always soft and fuzzy, our relationships are formal, informal, and tangential, six degrees of each. We don't need social medias for all this, yet we understand that in today's era, when we meet someone and talk to them even for a minute, we may have just stepped into one of their circles, and for all they know, they've stepped into ours. Very possibly born again during these moments, our communication initiatives amplify layers of social webbing. It is not always going to be our relative dollars and cents wealth that will save us in times of need; often more quick acting are the various elements of this network of ours. A measuring stick of mental health, this, a hundred years before the internet, was what Alfred Adler referred to an individual's level of *social interest*. Circles circling circles. Listen to the Irish rapper, Kate Tempest's working-class tune, *Circles*. Think of the concept of equifinality. As sociologist Peter Rossi saw it, the size and quality of a person's network of kith and kin is often an indicator for homelessness, which can be experienced as the ultimate personal disgrace. Downward mobility, right down to rock-bottom. And at the bottom, in New York City alone, are about 5% of the homeless, those not in the shelters. Thus, they live in a political petri dish, profiled by their advocates, diagnosed by their caregivers, and categorized by governmental funding streams. They are typically unemployed and to many, unemployable; if working, they are typically underemployed and underpaid. No one is coming to their rescue. Even the media is largely unquestioning, its perceptual fields molded by their base need for readership. Inevitability is not a myth, yet its power is expressed by way of impending destiny. It is, however, something which can be interrupted by action. On the other hand, what did Marshal McLuhan say? "I've always been careful never to predict anything that had not already happened."

Some seventeen years after we started, the consistent efforts to eliminate our programming was nearing completion. Yet, there was just a little more work to do. That last push started with the placement of a certain member of The Board directly into our lives. He took over a high place within the city's Department of Homeless Services and began to officially "monitor" us. Call him "The Intern." Before his promotion, when he was a law school intern for one of The Board's mainstay programs, he was considered one of the little people. Everyone starts off that way, it's only fair. Promotions will come later if deserved. The Greatest Happiness Principle turned upside down. Your methods are good if it makes the leadership happy. One day, to make himself happy then, he contacted us to say that in its present form, our multi-services center was too difficult to measure, or to compare with the city's other drop-in-centers. It was too dissimilar to be allowed to continue as is. Apples to apples, he said. We had to be like them, regardless of their outcomes, not them like us, regardless of ours. Boom.

The Intern invented issues which would keep us in a perpetual state of establishing "corrective" actions with dates that required follow-up, less doing and more following-up. "We saw a large fish tank in the hallway outside your office," he wrote. "We do not allow city funds to purchase such items. Please investigate and return to us your corrective action to include discipline of the relevant staff. This is not the first time we have questioned expenses at your agency. If these matters are not cleared up, we may be forced to reconsider assignment of your contract." Truth was, it was a fish tank that I brought in from home. I brought everything in with it – the gravel, filter, light, heater, and fish too. Corrective action? Discipline?

Another time, he informed us that he was upset to see that we purchased a $5,000 conference table plus thousands of dollars' worth of leather chairs, eight of them. He stated: "This is in direct violation of policy. We never approved any such purchases. Therefore, you must immediately submit your plan to correct such misspending going forward, to enforce purchase controls, and to maintain records of all money spent." The volunteer chair of our board of directors, we found out later, coerced by her under-the-table work as a consultant for the city, insisted that we not fight back. What? She wrote that we would stay within budget and would put purchase controls in place. That we would redouble our effort to maintain meticulous records. Get it? I was sure to provide a copy of the purchase receipt, that the conference table under discussion was a scuffed-up floor model, costing us only $500 and that the chairs, which came with the table at no extra cost, were not leather. Apparently, pleather works. $500 in total. Delivery was free. Okay. But what was with our board chair. What was she up to?

Our Center was not wholly reliant on city funds. This allowed for more flexibility in our programming, but instead of enhancing our relationship with the city, it made for tension, as they grew increasingly focused on the fact that they had less control over us than they would have liked. We were complicated. In some sense, our success was an embarrassment to them. Sometimes, their other programs were looked at in terms of our accomplishments. We challenged the natural order by not being such a pushover for them all to deal with. Ultimately, our success led to our program's demise.

The city's negative momentum against us eventually led to a change in the Business District's leadership itself. Dan was out. A soap-opera mentality was afoot. A central casting's castoff was inserted to replace him, an actor no longer in search of a part, this one paying him a quarter of a million dollars in a recurring role as a political appointee. Finally, the city could have at us. Our doors were swung open to a new wave of surprise audits, but always, the "real" evidence against us was written in invisible ink.

From the start of the start, there were a whole lot of many who were proprietarily concerned with the social order of the homeless industry. The fact that the super-wealthy were getting involved made things all the worse. How dare they? How dare we? That we got everybody off the streets and made more housing and employment placements than any of the other programs meant little in the face of these issues; what mattered was their face. Someone decided that ranking above success in outreach was conformity to their model; uniform approaches were deemed essential. Better for statistical purposes, easier to study outcome, they said. Apples to apples, said a very sincere Mayor Bloomberg, part of what DeBlasio was to inherit. Flatlands. All valleys, no peaks. Good looking out for the city Mr. Mayor. Now, who was it we were supposed to be helping? The Board or the homeless people?

Eighteen

There should not be even one homeless person suffering at our feet. For example, nobody should be living outside on the sidewalks of New York City – not just because of the lack of privacy and hygiene, but because its concrete is just too unforgiving; no wonder the mortality rate – 40% higher than the norm. Yet the fact is so plain – people will come inside only when they want to. The goal then is to get them to want to. Exactly perhaps what a department store might do to attract new customers. The merchandise, the price, the store's ambience, the attitude of the salespeople, the service, all of it counts. The reciprocity is in the sale, which squares things up between the customer and the store. They are even. The shopper compensates the store for its work in bringing the product to him or her and after paying, he gets to leave with the product. That system works. Its wisdom is somewhat absent in our interactions with people who are homeless. Trying to get someone housed who has been actively homeless may be most humane, that is, if it is available. Problem is, either way, it may work against the homeless survivor's need for reciprocity and self-sufficiency, which is heightened by the concrete reality of outdoor life, double meaning. Anyway, let's be real, the housing is not there.

~   ~   ~

Is society a web of patterned interactions? C. Wright Mills. W.E.B. DuBois. The homeless are not seen as "ready" for the one thing that from the start they really do want, which would resolve nearly all their issues, which as we've said is employment. But because they are not seen as ready, just by asking for it, they are seen as "in denial" and those that offer such help "unrealistic" or "feeding a false reality." Given this process alone, we can say that most homeless people have no chance.

Nineteen

Network Fairs, and we ran over a hundred of them, are essentially social services, breakfast, sales meetings to which people that we discovered that same morning sleeping in public places at 5am, are invited by way of a printed invitation, which we handed them on the spot. They were the consumers whose needs we wanted to address.

~ ~ ~

COME TO A VERY IMPORTANT MEETING

Make some changes?

On your terms.

Your decision.

You can stop letting other people choose for you.

If you come to this breakfast meeting a few blocks away, about three hours from now, you will be offered:

1. Free breakfast.
2. Dozens of social service agencies to choose from. Make appointments.
3. Help with first month's rent if you find a place within six months. Pick up the paperwork.
4. Five dollars ($5) travel stipend at the end of the event.

~ ~ ~

The presenters were our sales force: Formerly homeless men and women who succeeded in getting themselves off the streets and out of the shelters. Along with them, staff from a variety of programs around New York City get together over breakfast, to make impassioned motivation and educational commentary.

At the end of the three-hour event, it was hoped that the attendee would be so moved as to pick at least one agency presenting that day from which they'd like to receive help and they could exit with appointments in hand. At the very least, if they didn't want to do that, though nearly all did, at least they will have left better educated, with a new understanding of the many possibilities at hand.

This is an outreach alternative that tries to deal with whole group structures, pre-existing relationships among people living on the street on the one hand, and between them and their potential service providers on the other. We get rid of the "sick" model for the person living on the street and the "healer" model for the therapist; instead, they're more like collaborators. For both, there is an interaction between a "consumer" and a "salesperson." This allows for a liberating process of redefinition, one which will interrupt what the ethno-methodologist Harold Garfinkle called the "routine grounds of everyday life." Relationships between street peers, layered by multiple interdependent routines, which may be perpetuating disconnection from the mainstream, now allows the consumers to experience highly personal "pivot points." Sounds small, these "little" decisions, but it's not. They can be monumental, momentous occasions. Suddenly, it's not too late. The person becomes able to "know" and to "be known" by his peers differently. The goal here is that later, because of his growing network and through their shared experiences, he will be able to delineate from among his larger peer group those with whom he has most in common. In effect then, he begins to better understand himself.

Our goals:

1. To attract people who live outdoors to come inside for programming for "anything from a cup of coffee to a social services referral."

2. To connect the neediest homeless people, that is, those on the streets, to social service agencies of their choosing.

3. To create an organizational structure that encourages cooperation and engenders new channels of interagency cooperation among organizations that serve homeless people.

4. To test and model effective techniques, which can be added to the mix of service possibilities.

Outcome-based measurements. Ethical considerations prevented us from randomly assigning some people to Network Fairs while offering others no such opportunity at all. For that reason, we considered the "experimental" group as consisting of all those invited. On an individual basis, our decisions as to who to invite were random insofar as we did not typically have advance demographic information about our subjects. Christopher Jencks, author of *The Homeless,* found that single adult homeless people who slept outdoors did so in parks, on the streets, in doorways, abandoned buildings and public building, so there's no rocket science here, just us setting our sights, bias-free.

On 28 different mornings, that is, prior to each day's Network Fair, there were 979 people found sleeping in or near one of the following eight locations. They comprised our "experimental" group:

A. PATH Trains Entrance at 33rd Street
B. Herald/Greeley Sq.
C. St. Francis Church - 31st Street side
D. Macy's Dept. Store loading docks
E. One Penn Plaza
F. 30th to 35th Streets - B'way to 8th Avenues
G. 44th Street - 2nd to 3rd Avenues
H. 40th to 46th Streets - 1st Avenue to East River Drive

To avoid drawing people either onto the streets or into the vicinity, given the benefits of the "experiment," advance notice was not given for the dates of Network Fairs. Because it was important that the site of the Network Fair be convenient for the Subjects to walk to, from the sleeping places listed above, the event was held in one of two locations, based on the availability of date, both of which were between one and a dozen or so blocks away.

We held the Fairs either in the dayroom of the St. Francis Church, located at 129 West 31st street, NYC, or at the Church of the Covenant dayroom, located at 310 East 42nd street. Program managers from a variety of programs around the city were contacted several days prior to each Network Fair. Variety was the key. The goal was to enlist the attendance of, at minimum, five different agencies, which we did most every time. They were eager to attend. Good breakfast. Interacting with their professional peers. Opportunities to bring in some new clients, which'd help them meet their contractual needs, and so on.

Between March 11, 1992 and February 24, 1994, as we said, 28 Network Fairs were held to engage all those seen to be sleeping at 5:00am in the locations specified above. Peer outreach teams, comprised of three to five formerly homeless people, all of whom we employed at a living wage and who had become housed "on their own," approached people who were seen to be sleeping on the street. The peer outreach workers distributed the invitations to whichever street people they found in the areas assigned. They handed each person a flier, along with an encouraging "sales" pitch such as: "You should come to this breakfast," or "Try to come, you will get a great meal and it might really help you just like it helped me," or "It's worth it, the food's good, and you'll get $5.00 for just a little time." Conversations were kept to a minimum for practical reasons: The people being approached were just waking up and could not be expected to react favorably to extended conversation.

The target population was expected to arrive at approximately 8:30 in the morning and, as if driven by consumer incentives, arrive they did. Black Friday? Members of the peer outreach met the invitees at the intake table where they were asked to present their invitation flyer, which had been marked by the location of where it had been handed out. They signed-in and were given a folder and two pencils. The folder contained the following:

- Print-out of participating "Network" agencies with contact information
- Menu of agencies and the services they offered
- Appointment sheet for each attending agency
- Network Fair activities chart
- Survey

Upon filling out the survey, they'd receive a receipt, their ticket to eat. Then, they went up to the breakfast counter run by the workers and trainees who had prepared the meal, their peers. They received an all-you-can-eat breakfast tray, which they'd proceed to fill with standard buffet items, eggs, breakfast meats, pancakes, potatoes, toast, juice, tea, coffee, etc. The social service agency representatives, arriving at the same time as the homeless invitees, were also greeted at the intake table, and asked to sign-in. They were then shown their seating assignments and offered breakfast as well. After co-mingling with a group of their peers informally during the thirty-minute or so breakfast, the Invitees, our Subjects, turned their attention to the presentations. The host then delivered a short speech welcoming everybody, outlining the goals of the Network Fair, and challenging everyone to make the most of the event.

During the next segment, there were several short motivation speeches delivered by formerly homeless people who have been helped by previous Network Fairs. For the next hour, the host introduced various staff members of attending social service agencies, each of which made five to ten-minute presentations. The job of the host was to introduce each speaker and facilitate the questions which invariably followed. To choose and to make appointments with some of the presenting agencies, the Subjects were then instructed to move around the room as if at a sales meeting. The host, along with other staff, moved from table to table helping where needed. At the exit table, our Subjects showed their completed appointment sheet, which indicated which agencies with whom they made appointments, were asked to sign-out, and then were given their payment of five dollars for attending the Fair.

~ ~ ~

Follow-Up. In the days, which followed the event, visits were repeatedly made to the areas where we first found our Subjects. This time, outreach was driven by specifics, that is, based on the names of the subjects and their program choices, as well as with our outreach worker's personal familiarity with each of the attendees. Additionally, calls were made to each of the attending agencies during the days following the Fair to determine whether appointments were kept or not. Anecdotally, three out of four appointments were indeed kept. Anecdotal, because in the cases of these phone calls, given the rules of confidentially, information could not usually be obtained. Often, our inquiries were limited to the general observations of the Program Directors. "Oh yeah, they've been here." Or "We can only say that we have met with the person in question again." Or "Yes, things worked out very nicely." Also, "No, we haven't seen him yet." Or "He came here only once." As well, monthly follow-up meetings, open to all agencies participating in Network Fairs, were held prior to, on the day of, the next Network Fair. During these meetings, besides a sharing of relevant information, program philosophies and strategies for intervention were contrasted. While many agency representatives were reluctant in that space to share the names of their clients, they'd provide us with information relevant to the numbers of Fair attendees who kept subsequent appointments with them. Turns out, so they said, that most of the consumers visited and revisited their program of choice several times afterwards. One time, we set up a reimbursement program whereby each agency would report subsequent visits to their programs by Fair attendees to obtain $15 per day, per client visit. We saw this as an incentive, like Medicaid's pay rate, more for the agency's paperwork chores than for anything else. The results mirrored the anecdotal information. After the Network Fair, participating agencies put in reimbursement requests for 164 days of service for 44 different clients. By the way, when the Peer Outreach Team met any of those of our Subjects who had attended the Fair, they urged them to go to the programs they had chosen, and offered themselves as escorts or mentors, trying to further assist the person as well. For the purposes of this study, the formal follow-up period for each of the Network Fairs lasted for a period of one week following the Fair itself.

An average of seven social services agencies and other organizations, drawn from a pool of sixty-two, attended each of the twenty-eight Network Fairs over the course of a two-year period. Participating organizations offered a variety of services such as housing, employment training, drug and alcohol treatment, mental health diagnosis and treatment, education, legal, and health care. 979 people were invited. 825 people attended. That's 84%. Of those who attended, 627 people, 65% of the invitees, immediately selected agencies, making on-the-spot appointments for follow-up services. During follow-up, only 15% of those who attended these Fairs were seen again on the same streets during that two-year period. No doubt, this approach consistently brought in an unusually high rate of people for "at least a cup of coffee" and often right to the desk of a social worker. Everybody ate, heard about programs they had never heard of before, and could no longer claim they were uneducated.

As Rossi points out, in cases where the participants in a program are volunteers, the problem of "uncontrolled selection is almost inevitable." In that sense, to truly support our findings, we'd have to look to understand what would have occurred were the intervention of Network Fairs not offered. We could look at the norm, at the outreach results citywide, that is, wherever this approach is not offered, as in "just about everywhere else." Could it be? The results indicate that success of our status-centered outreach occurred at much higher rates than would have occurred without them. As Rossi said, "determining impact requires comparing," and our rates were comparably very high.

Because we worked without a control group, we lacked formal experimental design. However, our model had demonstrable impact. The type and fact of attention paid to our subjects mattered. Its application produced the intended effect. Were we to extend our practical thinking, related to the consumerism model, we may speculate that those 13% who did not come had competing things on their agenda on the day they were invited to the fair. Absent of the intention to get help that day, they came for the breakfast, maybe some information, and the $5. It is also possible they had higher degrees of consumer skepticism than their peers; perhaps they cynically believed it sounded too good to be true. In either case, or in other possibilities, they were unconvinced that they should "shop" that day in our "store." They were our toughest hard-to-please customers. One caveat, however, is the possibility that during the 24-month period, the number of different people who attended constituted everybody at least once. That is, the "no-show" at one Network Fair came to one that followed.

When they arrived, they were not greeted as needy persons who might need to be social worked, but with relative "disinterest" as to their traits. Instead, they were welcomed much the way an owner of a retail store will greet his potential customers, at worst with enlightened self-interest, at best with an air of hope and expectation.

In Rossi's *Evaluation, A Systematic Approach,* he writes that the critical issue in impact evaluation is whether a program produces desired levels of effects over and above what would have occurred with or without the intervention or with an alternative intervention. 1). We were able to motivate and educate an otherwise difficult-to-reach population. 2). We accomplished this without long periods of waiting for what we might have labeled as trust to develop. 3). We accomplished this by arousing the will of people often thought of as reticent, even lazy, i.e., they responded of their own volition. Even if they were back on the street the next evening, we can take comfort in their improved positions having multiplied their knowledge of relevant information. Hail to the consumer. From JFK's 1962 speech on Consumer Rights in front of Congress to the doorstep of today's homeless shelter. Hey, why not?

Twenty

It started late 1989 and it lasted about 17 years. In midtown Manhattan. A perfect storm of street level programming. First and foremost was an outreach effort whose success led to the running of what became the largest program of its kind in the country – the homeless made that possible. Consumer power. They made our Center the largest by continuously showing up, day after day.

~ ~ ~

Conceptually, our new program was an exception for sure. It treated the homeless as consumers and perspective customers both, the streets being seen as a marketplace of sorts where outreach workers were trying to sell their products. With this perspective, you can no more indict the homeless as "resistant" and "in denial" any more than Macy's can label their shoppers that way for browsing instead of buying.

~ ~ ~

From the start, more than half of our Center's staff was drawn from the homeless themselves. They started at a living wage and quickly became formerly homeless.

~ ~ ~

Our organizing idea was that the people we served were our customer base. We knew if we didn't listen, and weren't real in how we responded, if they couldn't feel our respect for them, we'd have no chance. That is, we wanted them to belong to our club. We wanted them to be members, to shop in our store. The positive outcomes were theirs for the taking, what exactly did they want? We asked that of them every day, which is why our agency came to be involved in so many diverse projects. A lunch-time comedy club, an organic garden market, a self-help center, a writers' group, a soccer program, a newspaper, a video-resume program, a public phone-cleaning program, a recycling program, a corporate basketball program, a training program, a mural-painting arts program...

We knew they were on the constant look-out for a bounce-back moment, a type of edge-of-the-seat vigilance attributable to their lifelong struggles. Entrepreneurial then, "out there" more than most, on their own for too long to just drop it, their idiosyncratic, living-in-the-moment street survival strategy, always, in these ways, highly conscious and aware. Their operating mission was to find a way in. We knew that. They wanted respectability. They wanted a real job. And they wanted to be able to keep that job. Makes sense.

Regardless, as you'll see later, we were told to shut it all down. Get this: To accomplish our demise, so much energy, they spent six years accusing us and about a half of a year investigating us. Because even they could not deny the number of our success stories, before they took us down, they were "forced" to acknowledge that our agency's work was "unparalleled in the nation for its success in housing and employment." That's an actual quote. Yet, unbelievably, they went on to say that because we were not managed in a way that would have better defended us against what it called "fanciful" charges, that is, false allegations made by them, we needed to end our outreach program and have the rest of our operation completely taken over by, you guessed it, them. Them. There was no other way, that is, if we wanted to be "run right." Guess we needed to avoid the management mistakes of our exceptional and unparalleled success. Dry, bitter humor. Oh yeah, that food line showed what they were capable of, and boom, with a snap of the fingers, they did it. They took us over. A visit to the current program, what it became after they "ended" us, or a brief tour of today's midtown streets is all that it takes to see just how they've successfully transformed it all to one big package that doesn't work. Just look in and around Grand Central Terminal. Back to the future. In midtown's case, the homeless have started to live outdoors again, but at least the people that were running that Center, that'd be us, are no longer a problem. It leaves the outreach to the "professionals," which leaves many more of the homeless on the streets. It leaves the homeless without their consumer rights once again, with little to no choice, sitting in their drop-in-center chairs, trapped by their survivalist mindset, trapped alongside their peers, trapped by their sparkling new management. Is it true that hell is other people? Feels that way. Jean Paul Sartre. No Exit. No exception.

Twenty-one

We entered the troubled social services world, went out-of-the-box, and fast became successful. We drew funding from competing sources. Ooooh. Out of the box? Amazing, isn't it, that all we were really doing here was enabling self-help? Walking our talk, we were filling more than half of the jobs at our agency with the very people coming to us for help, with their "disabilities" and all their many "disadvantages." Typically, if they got through our training program, which meant they had shown up on time over a four-month-straight period and wanted to work for us, and we had an opening, which was typically the case though not guaranteed – how could it be? - we'd hire them and commit to try helping them hold onto their jobs despite whatever other problems they might be having.

~   ~   ~

Obviously, if they had come into a treatment clinic and asked to be seen, we would assume that they wanted help with something. If they were to make such a request for professional intervention and then resist it, their resistance might become an important part of the story. Symbolic-experiential approach. The here and now. Intuition, not theory. Carl Whitaker. If they didn't ask for treatment and we offered it anyway and they rejected our overtures, it was not seen as resistance. We'd ask again, maybe at another time, maybe with a different grouping of our outreach team. Their being on the street was not a specific request for help, even if we did see it as some sort of cry-out. That's something different. Outside, looking at them over there on the sidewalk, of course it looks like they are in a bad place and that they need help. But their eyes might be seeing a better place than where they've just been. Of course, we believed they could be in a better place still; that's what always drove us. We'd offer help up front...Hi, we're here to see if anybody needs any help. If not you, are you aware of anyone who might be in need? To take the spotlight off them while connecting, pretentiously, we needed to base our work on whatever it was they reporting needing to get themselves up and off the streets, how else? But it had to be what we'd call a "deliverable." Homeless? Sorry, the evidence is in, your housing will likely not come. You'll have to find it yourself. Want a job?

With time always working against them, we had the idea that to help people living rough, as the British say, "rough-sleepers," we should enlist their own peers to help them. They would do the outreach. Whether homeless in a program, or formerly homeless and on-the-job, or previously doing much worse and now doing much better, any of these scenarios made for some powerful outreach work. Quickly relatable, further along the path of recovery from the severe disconnection that is homelessness themselves, they'd bring the credibility and trust necessary for outreach to be effective. They had the proper sensitivity too. Speaking personally, they'd present through a certain kind of humanity that we figured would out-perform more "professional" social services agencies. And it did.

Professionals could not get the job done; the job being getting people indoors to safety. So, what then? That's the question that moved us to try something else, maybe to start with a look at outreach as the exchange it is, a sales interaction. A salesperson trying to close a deal. A large sales force trying to close a lot of deals. Take the treatment dynamic out of outreach. Of course, if someone on the street could not relate, if they had a medical emergency, a need for immediate treatment, or more likely, a request for it to happen immediately, we'd offer transport to our

Center for professional help. However, if they did not wish to come to our Center but wanted to see a professional nonetheless, we'd call on our professional staff for some assistance out there on the street. They'd come out with the team and speak to this or that person, rarely needed, but always available. We could take them to the hospital as well if necessary. We could also call 911. But usually, nearly always, they'd talk to us, obtain whatever information they needed to make an informed decision, and walk with us to the Center, or agree to come by later their own. We'd give them a membership card to our Center and tell them we'd stamp it "official" when they finally came by. That would entice them for a visit. Later, inevitably, there they'd be, at our Center's door, checking us out. They wanted in. They wanted to belong. Surprise, surprise.

My father had a clothing store across from the main public library, Fifth Avenue. Dressed like the people who shopped there wanted to dress, in a suit or a sport jacket/slacks combo, button down collar, colorful tie, etc., he was eminently affable, interested always in what they had to say. Trying to see their visit to his clothing store through their eyes. It might be a shopping trip. It might be a trip just to look. Maybe they wanted help in figuring out what they should purchase. Maybe they wanted to do it on their own. Either way, they were there, and he was happy about that. His interest in them had to be real. No problem for him, for he believed that there was always something about each person, up front and center, that was likeable. That was his strategy, to showcase his interest and respect for each person. That might mean a simple "hello," or it could mean a longer conversation. He didn't care, for what he wanted more than anything, was for the person to be a regular – for the person to want to come back. Exactly.

~   ~   ~

With the person on the corner, seemingly homeless, what about them would be likeable? We are not talking here of expressing our love for humanity through them, but of their personal qualities. Was it something they said? Their receptivity? The location in which they chose to hang-out? The way they looked off in thought when speaking? Their intensity? Their sense of humor? Their skepticism? That's it. We respect you for turning us down. You are deservedly circumspect. On the street, it is smart to be skeptical, no doubt.

Well, in my father's case, his location was a clothing store. He wore what sold in his store. His customers liked the way he dressed. They could dress that way too. He was highly relatable. The clothing was what it was, but his sales were psychological in nature and very personal. It wasn't going to be him doing all the work, nor was it ever about faulting his "resistant" consumer, instead, their decision to buy would have to be organic. The person, having worked themselves into a state of "readiness," was there at the store imagining themselves in this or that article of clothing, looking for something to buy. Their imagination. He just had to get out of their way, and it'd happen, or not. Simple, they wanted to improve their wardrobe. Why else were they there but to shop for themselves (male customers) or for others (women customers)? Perhaps to dream? To buy or not to buy, the move was theirs to make, no pressure. Do it now or take months. It's okay.

In *Selling as a Dyadic Relationship*, Franklin Evans wrote "The more alike the salesman and his prospect are, the greater the probability that a sale will occur. This is true for physical characteristics (like age and height), as well as economic and demographic characteristics." Now, even as this might disrupt our modern sensibilities, it has been shown to be true, and the goal here is to get them indoors, right? So, we ask, is that a middle-aged woman leaning against that building over there? Hmm...the cardboard square that she's clutching to her chest says her kid is staying at a friend's house for a few dollars per day, but that she is running out of money fast. We talk to her. Turns out, she does not want to go to a family shelter. No way, she says. First thing we do is we ask ourselves if we have an outreach worker who is a middle-aged woman with children? Oh, look, is that a kid in his late teens? Let's get someone who's been in that very same position. Let's get them together...they can talk about what might or might not work. Wow, an 82-year-old man who has been out there forever. He doesn't want to talk to us. Let's see if one of our elderly outreach workers who only recently came off the streets can come out to talk with him. Can we make that sale?

Research shows that satisfied customer reviews have a high impact on purchasing decisions. In substance abuse treatment, for example, when success is achieved, it comes about more predominantly from the input of people further along in recovery, that is, ex-addicts and paraprofessionals. A satisfied customer review, in vivo. They are helping themselves as they help each other. That's a big part of the AA model as well. Big brothers, role models, and mentors, all of them are referral agents. During times like these, when responding to his peers on the outreach team, the target person is going to feel much more self-directed, his sense of being a protagonist aroused. This is necessary for recovery, something that needs to remain intact for that person to properly recover. That's what working towards employment can do for a person. The sense of personal achievement, of acquiring the job, or of successfully working to keep it, can self-perpetuate. Good treatment is self-referential and can put a life on track. Bad treatment derails.

Let's put all this together: If we want to resolve disconnection and enhance self-agency, we are pointed towards employment based, social-networking approaches. Outreach is performed by relatable formerly homeless peers who, satisfied with their most recent personal achievements, share their own success stories. To their peers they embody progress. If they talk themselves up, that is, share their story, a story that they weave, in effect, selling their truth as something relatable and accessible, they can serve as a magnet, literally drawing the person indoors by his or her own bootstraps. We found that this process also helped the outreach worker whose confidence would grow from each instance of relating to a peer, in the telling of his story. His oral history.

Sad and so true, our approach left us open for attacks. The angle was that we had "untrained and unprofessional" outreach workers out there. Yes, by certain standards, we did, but no, not for the actual job-at-hand. For that, they've been training for years. Okay, but we did a lot of process work every step along every way. Adult-learning 101. That's why what we did worked so well. Yes, you want to say that our outreach workers were less "sophisticated" than yours, okay, our best outreach workers did not have your college degrees, yet they succeeded where to this day, you still don't. Can't say it enough. Ironic. That's probably also the reason we got taken down, something that didn't really have to happen. Free market forces?

Because our outreach program operated successfully not only in public spaces but also on private property, it brought heightened attention to our work. Nobody else performed outreach on private property – that was always reserved for security guards. Perhaps then, it was no wonder that cognitive dissonance "prevented" people from seeing us differently, regardless of what was real. Like other programs, our employment training efforts included paying a stipend to people receiving welfare. Yet, we were brought in front of a judge, the one and only Sonia Sotomayor, because we paid stipends and that judge told us we should have applied for a minimum wage exemption and because we didn't, "Sorry fellas." On the upside, she also said that given the benefits of our program, Congress might want to take a looksee at creative approaches such as ours. Nice. In the end though, she also ruled the way she ruled. Was she implying that had we applied for a minimum wage exemption for our training program, she'd have ruled differently? But for our not filling out certain forms, our helpful "one-of-a-kind program," her words, could have kept helping people? Would we not have still lost our one-day hearing in front of her, this future Supreme Court Justice? Did Ms. Sonya understand how she was played by The Board? Wow, she was so lied to. Did she appreciate the negativity of their power? Was it her job to care? Sure, the BID's staff attorney or his colleagues never even thought to ask if paying stipends had a legal basis. I never asked them to investigate it either. None of us ever thought to apply for an exemption, you see, we were copying other programs none of which had done so either. They were the lawyers, so okay, that was their "bad," however, I was the executive director, and I didn't ask them to look into it either, which was my "bad." Oh well, they got us on this technicality. Guess there's got to be a first. First us, then the others, right? No, not at all. To this day, they have done nothing about the many other agencies who still pay stipends. If they had decided we should be first in a new campaign to "free" the homeless from such abuse, why then did they stop with us? Guess that helping the homeless was not their goal. All those programs are still doing today what we were admonished legally for doing yesterday.

~   ~   ~

Stopping us was the whole point, wasn't it?

~   ~   ~

But if to the judge our filing an application was all that should have happened, this being a hearing and not a trial, such an application could have been required of us by that judge, on the spot, so to speak. Judge Sotomayor, yes that Sotomayor, could have made us apply for that exemption and could have made us pay whatever fine was applicable, end of problem, and the homeless could have continued to receive the exact type of help even she seemed to think they might very well need. End of the problem? No. It was not her job to end the problem. It was an opportunity though that she chose not to take. But, by now exasperated, we asked then as now, is putting an end to this problem anyone's job?

~   ~   ~

Private property owners were using security forces and security dogs. We replaced all that with teams comprised of trainees and staff. The guards and the dogs stood down. The homeless came in for help, finally. Did anyone see that?

~   ~   ~

Because each day we reported our outcomes to our funders, private property owners, The Board insisted that meant that we were a security company ourselves. Security, not outreach. What? And, because of how little we charged the banks for our outreach services, and because it costs less than what their security operation cost them, we were just "cheaper security" who "undercut" our security competitors. What? Zero sum analysis, that's what. But we were a non-profit – we didn't charge the extra needed to generate profit. What? Wait a minute. The property owners still had their security guards. They were failing to reduce homelessness in their ATMs, so they tried us. When our approach "worked," security was redeployed because they were ineffective, not because we were less expensive. They didn't fire any security guards, just hired us in addition to them. Wasn't it a good thing that these private property owners tried something else? Wasn't that more hopeful than just kicking them out, which is what they are allowed to do and were doing, it being their private property, their ATM vestibules, or their tiny parks in front of their buildings, off-hours? What they did was chase them off by way of fear, a possible dog bite or the possibility of an arrest; they'd ignore every need the homeless person had for shelter, "not our problem." Here, we were doing something better, no? Okay, stop. We don't have to ask. Yes, we were doing something better.

Here's what had happened. Five banks came together having called a meeting with half-a-dozen social service agencies. They were looking for a solution that would reduce homelessness in their ATM vestibules as what they were trying had been failing. We were invited. They asked around the table if any of us thought we could effectively reach out to the people living on their properties. Representatives from each of the other agencies were reluctant to commit to the project. They expressed concern that the banks would cut their funding once their "homeless problem" was solved, that it would prove to be an unstable situation for their staff. Also, they were worried that if they failed, their funding might be cut. They said that outreach was too complicated, that it took time, and they were not convinced the banks would be in it for the long haul. When it was our turn, we said that we'd be happy to try. That it would be a great opportunity for the people in their vestibules that we'd be there instead of security. We lauded the banks for reaching out to us. We'd tell our outreach workers upfront that this would be a time-limited contractual program, a temp job, and that their work in any one location might be temporary as well. With a dash of sardonic cynicism, we said they were used to "temporary" solutions. We said that their security efforts were failing because it was not a security problem, that the people in their ATMs were not the bad guys. The banks thanked us all, and we left. The following week, they asked us to send them a proposal. They offered us a 90-day contract. Initially, the banks kept their security presence in full force even after we proved successful. As we were able to consistently bring people indoors and out of their ATMs, some of the banks went ahead and cut back on the size of their security forces. Ironic to some perhaps, but a humane outreach program costs less than impersonal security efforts.

Doesn't matter. Case closed. Gavel down. Time for some uninspired decision-making. The judge expressed the kind of thinking that works to keep the security dogs barking. Another way that the homeless have no chance.

Dear Judge: If you just leaned forward and squinted, maybe turned a few more pages, you would have seen past our book cover.

During our training sessions, we asked our outreach team to stick to the script of whatever it was that had worked for them, whichever friend, job, or treatment program that helped them get off the streets, could they "use" that experience in their work with us. We asked, could they talk about what they did to overcome their own situations? They'd practice doing that in our training sessions; we'd roleplay outreach scenarios. Always reiterate, we'd say, that a person's options included coming indoors for something other than to receive "help." Just to use our showers or eat a meal, to use our self-help center, for example, or just to sit for a spell? Fine. But you can also tell them we had a hospital medical clinic on site, St. Vincent's Hospital, that we had professionals they could talk to for a referral somewhere else if that's what they wanted? Remind them that we were co-ed. Let them know we were air-conditioned. That we had a big screen television. Great food too.

My own experiences, right from the start, my bias then, having spent almost three years in a protracted fieldwork project as a graduate student in the Bowery, and working in the field ever since, and especially following my training in family therapy, led me to shy away from a doctor-patient dynamic and its trait-centered approach. The participant-observation project in the Bowery taught me the nature of their suffering. I remember thinking that I'd be letting them down if I took a structurally superior position like with a list of prepared questions or a prescribed approach, they, "the patient," me, "the social scientist," they, "the troubled," me, "the healer" there to analyze them, they, "one down," me, however unintentionally, "rubbing it in." It.

Wait a minute, we asked ourselves, did they come to us for this help or was it that we went to them? Not to forget, so many of the people we'd be approaching when performing outreach are at their worst, traumatized at that moment or in post-trauma, exhausted from worry and lack of sleep, despairing from their lack of options, and stressed by their downwardly mobile equally despairing peers with whom they were bunched up with, overcrowded, and what's worse, from their total inability to produce, i.e., to be productive. Bob Dylan's line: "If my hands are tied, who tied them and why and where was I at the time?" So much self-blame. Too much? Maybe it's time to listen to Kendrick Lamar's The Blacker the Berry. "They may say I suffer from schizophrenia or something. But homie, you made me."

That's right, taking responsibility is essential, but they are already doing that. They blame themselves for the mess they're in. Like any of us would, they experience themselves as owners of their situations and like us they want to be the one to fix it/them. They want to work, and across society, of course there is the prestige and increased social status that goes to the person who can get off welfare through employment; who's situation doesn't have to be fixed by their better situated "superiors." Oh yeah. They want that too. Ask them. Nowhere to go. Jean-Paul Sartre's *Nausea.* "I want to leave, to go somewhere where I should be really in my place, where I would fit in . . . but my place is nowhere; I am unwanted." Sartre was talking about all of us. We are talking specifically about them, they who live it in spades. It.

After the Bowery, I went to a three-year post-graduate training institute in family therapy. This was life changing; for the first time, I was struck with the concept of circular causality. Rather than committing to a blinders-on search for the A that caused the B I wanted to understand, I learned to look at the function of B, what did it cause; was there secondary gain? How might it be mediating a relationship between A and C or D each of which perpetuated the other forward and back, and soon there's a set of interdependent interactions, a societal family dance. Circular cause. A caused B to cause C, which caused more of A, and then there was D, which affected each and so forth, a non-stop series of circularity. That informed me. I was going to pull back from looking for causative factors, even from the idea that knowing what they were would even help, other than for the discussions it might bring forth; no doubt the old process was fun but to what end except my own? I stopped trying to determine what caused purple, whether it was red or blue? Interestingly, in family theory, once you could "see" the circle, you could start your work anywhere along its perimeter or within, and still end up getting to the issues. Equifinality. The mistake would come if instead you picked on something static to explain something fluid or limit your examination and discussion simply to your favorite variable, which is the easiest route of them all. And it's done all the time.

Before I ever got to midtown with this story one day to tell, I must acknowledge a smidgen of romance in my career choice, a condescending quality to be sure but one which I admittedly don't struggle against; I appreciate them for their outsider status, just as one would prefer outsider art for its concrete, organic essence; somehow it grows more on its own than not. I preferred spending a few hours in a Bowery pub or a shelter dayroom to almost any other social setting. There was a real life-based liveliness to the crowd. If they were so disconnected as to be alone, that sad fact overrode anything else and gave them a leg up on my respecting them, just as you might feel towards anyone you meet who is mid-trauma. They needed my help. So, in my own defense, I was trying to bridge a gap, not operate from the distance offered by a certain attitude of superiority of position or status, i.e., with furrowed brow. The analyst. The expert. As much as I liked to talk, I was intensely interested in their stories, again, admittedly sometimes with a voyeuristic attitude, but only sometimes. The capacity people must survive certain things can be overwhelmingly impressive, and no matter how strongly you're leaning forward, when you really see what they are going through, it can set you back on your heels. It was just as we were instructed by Dr. Rayna Rapp, who was our anthropology professor at The New School, now at NYU, that each person deserved to be understood like any of us, to be recognized not only as members of a class or community, but as individuals, one-by-one.

~ ~ ~

In midtown, we wanted to improve their standing among their own peers. That's where it mattered the most, in the building of their self-esteem, planting with the seeds of self-motivation, in total, to increase social connectedness. They were the only ones who could lift each other up, we knew that, whether it occurred competitively, or so that they may be further seen by their peers as competent, or to impress new friends and loved ones. Membership. Social networking. A Self-Help Center. Choices. Social services jobs. Business-for-self opportunities. Inclusion. We'd figure it out, one person at a time, a certain kind of hard work that the social service worker herself often found liberating for its absence of pre-determination.

~ ~ ~

An accolade: One person at the center said she felt that we "put the 'art' back in heart." Corny, but to this day I remember that; sweet. She was a hyper-grateful, middle-aged woman who had earlier left her apartment because she had been depressed, having been abandoned by her husband who also took her dog, abandoned, and more alone than ever, who came to our Center after what she called a series of "date-rape" scenarios she had undergone while trying to live on the street. Refer here to Meryl Streep in the film *Ironweed*. With us, she started just with wanting a meal and a shower. She relaxed for a few weeks like that. Then, one day she sauntered into our Self-Help Center on the second floor, the first of many mornings like that. She would take a coffee and sit at a computer – teaching herself to conduct on-line searches. She got a jewelry-making business going. Then, taking a room in Brooklyn, she became an at-home jewelry-maker. Imagine that, a so-called homeless person becoming an at-home businesswoman. She was a person who faced a crisis and, spiraling downward, relatively untethered, she became so disconnected as to hit the streets. Approached by a team of our outreach workers, a team from which emerged, yup, a middle-aged woman who too had been abandoned by her family. A connection was made and boom, she came indoors to use our showers. Upon finding our Center then, she became a woman who, though now living alone in her new apartment, was not so disconnected, relatively speaking, at all.

In the Bowery, formed by our anthropological experiences, my research partner Benedict Giamo took to American Studies teaching and I went towards hands-on practice inspired by Alfred Adler, and Carl Whitaker who, believing it took about five family generations to "create" a schizophrenic, used to hospitalize the schizophrenic's whole family. And there was Salvador Minuchin who used to arrange lunches with an anorexic's whole family ever so slowly changing their "mealtime dynamics." I began calling what I was doing "social-networking therapy." Sociotherapy.

Twenty-two

There was a blur and a flash as Dan burst through my open office doorway. Sitting at my desk, looking up, I'm all eyes. May 2003. I was staring up at the president of the city's most prominent BID who was very excited by something he had just read. He was clutching in his fist the Village Voice, saying: "This is great." He held out the paper and offered it to me as he waited for my response during ten or fifteen seconds of silence as I read. Horrified at what I saw, I asked, "What are you talking about?" "What am I talking about, don't you see, they hate us... they wrote that we are terrible. This is great. We made it. If they hate us, that's proof we're doing great work." "What? The Village Voice? I love the Village Voice." "Look at this, they said we're running vigilante squads and that we're beating the homeless. We've made it. We're helping so many people it's literally blowing their minds. They're concocting all sorts of stories. They want to say that we've been using homeless vigilantes to secretly beat up other homeless people for years now; that we've sent scores of victims to the hospital? This is such bullshit. Fuck them. This is great." He left the room as fast as he could walk, which is how he always walked, leaning forward, like he's fighting to win a race, his shoes worn down by the toes. Wow. The Village Voice. Weird that they never reached out to us, apparently uninterested in what we'd have to say.

Another day. Yet another story – this one, even bigger, a cover story in a major magazine. *Food Fight*, Late Summer 1995, yet another reporter in a deadline panic showed up on our doorstep. He wanted to bring clarity to a running dispute between The Board and the Business District over that food line. His starting point was what happened when we opened our 24-hour facility with its extra-large cafeteria. The food line was reduced to a relative few. Okay, that makes sense, so what then, the article seemed to ask, were we all feuding about?

To satisfy his "time crunch," four weeks was the plan, it was taken down to two, he lined up a bunch of last-minute phone calls to some of The Board's lowest. They said that our outreach program was wrongheaded; that it was not professional enough (our outreach workers were formerly homeless), and that as it was "attached" to a BID whose true goal was to sanitize midtown to make it more attractive to tourists, it was not designed to help anybody. As for me, he concluded that compared to others in the social services field, my belief that homeless people can work made me sound like a holdout for cold fusion. He wrote that he could not find anyone who agreed with my premise.

The idea, (i), that homeless people can work, (W), is at least metaphorically equal to believing in the concept of cold fusion, (CF). Reduced to the formula iW=iCF. The nuclear effect. Hey...the experiments are real. It is possible. Check it out. Postscript: This reporter did not interview any of the hundred or so formerly homeless people working or training in our Center. He could have asked them if they agreed with the work premise.

Another one of the points which the article dwelled upon was the apparent outrage among the heads of various social service agencies that our outreach workers "coordinated" with police or security personnel working in the same area. The reporter said that the goals of a good outreach worker did not align with those of the police. We should not be working with them even though this was happening on their private property, where their private approach to homelessness otherwise goes unchecked. They are allowed to charge people with trespassing. He reported that our critics said that on private property, once we were hired, private security "steps back," which means we are acting on their behalf, that we were aligned with them over the idea that the homeless don't belong on their property. Okay. I get it. This was about my working with the BID. In that same way, here, once again, I'm letting private property owners hire me to help homeless people. Private property owners who are, again, the enemy.

In our outreach efforts, being real with each homeless person we met, we did inform them, in case they did not know, that they were on private property. We told them that the owners hired us because we had explained to them that this was not a security problem. That it was a homelessness-related problem. That if they dropped their batons and extra-long flashlights and leashed their dogs, we'd approach each person who was living on their property and examine what their options were. However, our critics said that by telling them they were on private property, we "became" security. To them, this meant we were forcing people indoors. What? You think that the homeless person doesn't understand the difference? Infantilize them why don't you? Belittle them by thinking that, why don't you? Undeterred, our critics said that we should not be telling them they are on private property. Just walk away, they said. Don't tell them. Wait a minute, you want us to believe that informed decision-making is a bad thing? You mean they are so fragile that helping them get out of harm's way was too harmful? Helping them identify the jam they were in and offering them whatever help they wanted was bad, better to keep them in the dark? If it were us, wouldn't we want that head's up? After all, we could not change the fact that they were on somebody else's land. Was it not a reasonable expectation that the owner might protest? "'F' the owner," they replied. Oh yeah, that's what this was about. Much more than wanting to help any homeless person, they were angry at the owners. Endgame.

If he had dug, he would have found his article's talking heads hypocritical to a fault. The Board. Then, as now, and to this day, they work in tangent with both private security and police, for example in Port Authority or in the subway system. Ever hear, "End of the Line, everybody off?"

The bigger problem was the goon squad charges. Peter, the chair of the Grand Central Partnership, hoping to deal a deathblow to that story, made up, that his BID ran a goon squad that beat up homeless people to beautify midtown, already disproven, he decided to reach out to his nemesis, that's right, The Board itself. A brilliant move or classic desperation? No, it was not a brilliant move, even if it was embraced by an internationally prominent, ADHD impaired, gray-haired lady. No, wait a minute...that's giving her too much credit. ADHD is no excuse. The frontal lobe still functions, and the pre-frontal cortex, smaller perhaps, nonetheless continues to operate, even if sometimes in staccato. There were just too many times the facts could have gotten in the way, instead getting lost on the way, a case for intention from on high, many times over. If not ADHD, myopia then? Fishing wrap in the hands of The Board? The way Peter was having it, it was going to be up to the latter to investigate us, the former to report on it. Together, working on their own, peaking at each other's work, no proctor to call them on the fact that they came up with the exact same fabricated answer, they'd spark the final dismantling of our success.

Why yes, The Board was in live action form, hired by Peter to investigate the veracity of the accusations they had launched. What was happening? Dan and his boss, the chairman of the BID, Peter, had heard from someone who had heard from someone that there was split, that some members of The Board were disgruntled with how their minions were handling matters in midtown now. Wait a minute, could that be true, some of members of The Board might be thinking that the BID did a few good things after all? Wishful thinking, or auditory delusions? "We are an open book," Peter declared. Forever deft, The Board's founder said he would help the BID but only if the business district promised to accept his findings and follow whatever he recommended. Wow. And, what happened next? Peter said yes.

The Board's investigative findings? Well, after a three-weeks of "looking into matters," two weeks short of what had been planned, this was becoming a pattern, "to beat them to it," the lead investigator called me. I said that I thought they were the "them." He said, "No really, a lot of people are calling for your head and frankly we were looking for a way. But, after our investigations, we see you did nothing at all that would be worthy of that. We were impressed with what you've been able to accomplish. You are one of the good guys...but we do have to find something that we can point to or else they would just say we rolled over."

Very revealing. Who was "they," and what did he mean, "they would say we rolled over?" He went on to say even more. That he had decided to say how badly managed the business district's social services department was. How we had been hung out to dry by the Business Improvement District. Ah, ha. Full circle. For example, he said, there should have been more social services experts on their oversight committee, experts who would have had the credibility needed to defend us against the goon squad allegations. Huh? What? We did nothing wrong, that's right, no goon squad, but that we were unable to sufficiently defend ourselves against false charges, was the problem? Shame on the business community for succeeding without enough social service experts.

To some fanfare, his investigative report came out. In its opening statement, it said our work was…well, by now it's been said enough, you know…unparalleled and all. Then, it cast our successes aside for what apparently was the more important issue, the scandal itself. A field of play. They found the goon squads charges, that we had a plan to beat up homeless people to make them come inside for help or else they should scram, to be "fanciful."

Imagine that. One word. All of it, the lies, the bad press, the lost funding, the pointed fingers, and the scores of personal attacks, brushed aside with just one word. No culpability. No further elaboration. None. Fanciful. Was that it? Given that we were unable to fend off fanciful charges, we were guilty of "poor management." Bam. Our unparalleled success was done wrong.

Basically, we needed to be run by more credible defenders than the bunch of "muckity-mucks" of which the business district was made. Guess who these credible defenders might be?

Here is where Peter's decision to follow all The Board's recommendations came home to roost. Some of The Board's more well-placed members, in local government, academia, and media, sprang into action in some of the same ways the Democratic National Committee acted to "handle" Bernie Sanders. No trouble here manufacturing the consent necessary to take us down, thank you for the lexeme, Noam Chomsky.

"Let the dismantling began," they charged. Our success? Fake news. Goon squads? How dare we? Take our funding. Get it. Got it? Glow and radiate. Be "fanciful." We shrieked, in a whisper of course, for loud voices might prove get us into further trouble.

The engine thrust of our programming was going to be cut down to a throttled neutral, our outreach and employment programs dismantled.

Twenty-three

For about seven years, from mid-1988 until mid-1995, we brimmed most everyday with unbridled focus and relief; call it professional joy. Then we were bridled.

Sister Rosemary McGeady, the head of Covenant House for runaway youth, during her interview for our book *Beyond Homelessness*, warned us that for this employment approach, we might rub some people the wrong way. You see, she said, we were doing "with" rather than "for." That's employment for you.

An observation: Down at the bottom, disconnected, one increasingly has good reasons for bad decisions. In a world of decreasing choice with willpower draining at every turn, practicality rules the day. One person, for example, even with carfare in hand, might make the risky move of jumping over the subway turnstile without paying. Why would he do that? Maybe, because he needed his last dollar for something else? Maybe, he owes someone money who he's afraid to run into with empty pockets? Maybe, his judgement is impaired by his very badly aching feet? Still, of course, he could get a ticket for "theft of services" if he were caught by the transit police.

For another person, a bad decision could mean passing up on the slight possibility he'll get hired at the next day's employment open house to wait on a more-surer thing, for example, an acquaintance of his who owes him five-dollars and is expected to be in the neighborhood the same day. Or, for example, there's logic to not taking your prescribed medication when sleeping in a congregate setting such as a shelter. This, to avoid sleeping so deeply as to "invite" the advances of a predatory neighbor from a nearby bed, is a decision made even though not taking the meds will likely lead to another hospitalization.

It could run even deeper. For example, to avoid meaningful relationships, the obligations of which might be difficult to keep up with. Better to keep to yourself in an on-the-move survival strategy, than it would be to join forces with another, better to become proficient at the emotional cut and run. What's the downside? Tremendous loneliness. What is the flipside? You might decide not to take an outreach worker's offer to go indoors to a shelter if to do so meant parting from your partner. This is yet another case for rethinking how to best help disconnected people who are homeless, perhaps as part of a couple? Can it be that we should encourage close friends or lovers to separate from one another?

For singles, the homeless shelter is there for you if you are willing to be among hundreds of downwardly mobile peers, desperate and alone too. A man alone, among hundreds of other men, everybody alone. A woman alone, among hundreds of other women, everybody alone. Yet can't we say that people really don't want to be so all alone? John Donne.

If you are on the street with whatever few belongings you have left, belongings which the shelter would not allow you to take inside and store, it could be that you would prioritize having access to a storage facility over a bed to lay in.

Imagine being told you are going to have to give up your dog or cat if you want to go inside to one of these shelters. You might decide to stay where you are, to hold out for a better offer; just another consumer making a well-reasoned decision, nevertheless likely to be judged as self-destructive. But what of that one remaining bond, otherwise 100% disconnected and alone? Pet owner and pet. Man's best friend, or not? Is it self-destructive? Can't we accommodate them? Don't ask.

On the streets, there's but one degree of separation. You are as down as you are out.

Perspective. I remember sitting at a round table in the center of our cafeteria with a man and woman who were recently married after meeting in our Self-Help Center upstairs. Each had fulltime living-wage jobs at the Center, one in maintenance, the other in our clothing room, living together now in a Queens apartment. They were eating lunch, which only cost them one dollar, a staff benefit, and were aggressively challenging me, "Tell us even one thing you've done for us. We've had to do everything for ourselves. You never helped us." "What do you mean? Look at you, look at us, look at all of this. Can't you say we've at least done a few things…how about that we tried?" They smirked, looked down and said, "Look, it's a mind trap, you understand? This is the kind of stuff they said while they were recruiting us for their lawsuit. They said we haven't been helped. That you should have paid us more when we were in training two years ago; that you paid us a stipend instead of a salary. Said they can get us some serious money if we sue you and win back pay, maybe even as much as a thousand dollars. We signed up. Hope you don't mind, but we are suing you." His look turned a little sheepish. "Yeah," repeated the guy almost to himself, "we're suing you. Oh, could you pass the salt, please?" "Sure, here you go." Wow. And that's how I heard about that one...more to come.

~ ~ ~

Preventive strikes. Secondary strikes too. Funnily enough, through an unlikely inversion of happenstance, "property managers as grass roots organizers," of monumental sociological significance, to The Board, we were a Trojan horse. But they acted first. They established a food line. Choosing its location carefully, they entered the geography of the business district with purpose. Now, the business district was entering theirs. At first, the people on the line were used to make a political statement. Now, they were making their own statement. Voting with their feet, they came into our programs very quickly. Ironic, but that decision, made by the homeless for whom they advocated, reenergized The Board's concept of us as the enemy. Hold on. Read on. The process of emnification was not yet complete.

Not enough experts working on behalf of the business improvement district's intent to help the homeless people in midtown? Some facts. Early on, before anything started, to get it right, they had recruited people like the former New York City Welfare Commissioner, Dr. James Dumpson, who worked right up until his recent death at the age of 103. Another person who helped with the business district's start-up, more subdued, was Paul Gibson, another lifetime social worker who had served in the Abraham Beame administration as Deputy Mayor for

Planning. He had been the chairperson of the NAACP's Housing Committee and former vice-president of American Airlines. An amazing combination of experiences. An out-of-the-box move by the business district placed a famous restaurateur who owned and ran Four Seasons, The Oyster Bar, and Gallagher's Steak House, and who owned a luxury yacht in the Mediterranean Sea, and an upstate New York thoroughbred horse farm on the start-up committee too. He was the mercurial president of the New York Democrats Club as well. Jerry Brody. Always tanned, impeccably dressed, no room for doubt, direct and decisive. He's got your back. He'll stay true – and he did. Years later, when the good squad charges came out, personally and most secretly, he personally trailed our outreach team several times late night and early morning. He said he found them to be "laid back and wonderful." Impressive. And then, also came Mary Holloway, the super-bright and forthright shoot-from-the-hip President of the Association for a Better New York, the irrepressible lady in the hat, different ones each time; I remember one with a two-foot plume, like a peacock. She was super smart and blunt. She liked you if you deserved it, no other reason. In fact, these four people and over fifty others who volunteered for the Grand Central Partnership business improvement district, the BID, were an amazing amalgam of endeavor and accomplishment, mixed motives and drive, wealth, and belief-in-self too. This last trait was shared by all – could that be translated to help in the case of midtowns homeless? That was one of the more important questions that needed to be answered.

Those midtown years were truly great ones, filled with rewards for a collective job well done, adulations for our numerous programs, read on, from the press, newspapers, and magazines, and on radio and television, more importantly, from among the many thousands of disconnected people we helped, truly felt handshakes and hugs, lots of tears and gales of laughter, our shared moments. Is why we ran into a brick wall an iatrogenic experience personified, a most repugnant example of suppression, or what?

Twenty-four

Unfortunately, the old gray lady's blue paper assigned a certain reporter to our story, who was beyond vainglorious, Mr. Wolfe, who could have chosen to reveal any of the three big stories that were happening. Instead, he made one up, and may I add, what's worse, not out of thin air, no, it was from air thick as any. Was there any way he made this decision on his own? Come on, look at his body of work. No way. No. He was sent, and it doesn't matter by whom, but it does have "The Board" written all over it. Wolfe was thinking "Pulitzer," and why not? He could have written a story titled: Property Owners as Grassroots Organizers. That would have been a social services story of the nineties and beyond. Just imagine the social nerve it would have pinched. Or, he could have written about our unexpected success, having eliminated an omnipresent food line, its former attendees now available for interviews, think Michael Herr's *Dispatches*, just pull up a chair in our cafeteria, cup of coffee in hand. Or okay, maybe he could have written about how we inspired The Board to fulfill its more negative competencies. They were actively working to stop our success story, which they saw as slowly unraveling theirs. The attack of the straw man. Their mission "for the homeless" became transmuted into "not for the homeless." Or, on a different scale, Wolfe could have gone for all positives, and focused on the apolitical story of the city's, indeed the country's, largest drop-in-center for adults and its unique hiring of the homeless to help run the place, its consumerism approach, its use of membership to address self-esteem issues, or its focus on self-help and employment. What about on its huge number of housing placements? These were all stories waiting to be plucked from the vine, always giving. But Wolfe just had to go some other way, didn't he? It was just another example of bending of the truth to make it fit, the blue paper was known for that, just don't go up against them: "Business Group Hires Goons to Beat the Homeless."

Property Managers as Grassroots Organizers. Now, that's a headline which could have been all in "caps," exclamation points at the end, front page; or is it just me? Well, no it isn't in fact, it's not even my line but somebody else's, the late Professor Winick from City University Graduate Center's department of sociology. The whole story coulda and shoulda been the blue paper's story to run with. But to be able to hide behind talent, you must have it in the first place, like for example, in Christian Parenti's case. Even with the wrong story in one hand and cognitive dissonance in the other, rare for him, and with very little time, always, he tells it so well you want to read it through, but not here. Take the wrong person's word for something because "it just makes so much sense," anecdotes thrown into the mix, anger, and sadness both...and boom, fake news? Bottom line. Any reporter could have asked any or all the hundreds of people visiting us each day how they came to be there? They chose not to.

One day, no notice, Mr. Wolfe showed up at our Center to ask me, "Is it true that you are running a goon squad? Is it true that your outreach workers engage in roughhouse tactics to get people to move?" What?? "Excuse me. What did you say?" His follow up question, rehearsed as a setup, was "Isn't it true that one of your managers has a crack house in the Bronx? And, that Frank, your head of Outreach, meets there secretly to plot activities with the goon squad?" Catching my breath, not yet catching on, I say emphatically, "That is complete fiction."

Not only that Mr. Wolfe, but you should know that we have a hundred people around the clock doing outreach. We are one big team. We all work closely together, dissecting problems, fine tuning the operation all the time. As our agency's executive managers, we were very involved but still, obviously, we couldn't know everything that was always happening. We had a formal structure that required us to record and investigate every complaint or rumor that we heard so...what are you talking about? You believe we are beating people, roughing them up? Nobody could get away with that kind of behavior around here. We must be very positive. Tell me what you've heard. I will investigate it. "No."

Wolfe would not walk around and talk to the people there. Strange. Maybe he thought that they were "our" homeless, that they'd be loyal to us, that they would lie to help us, or maybe that they'd be too scared to talk up. I egged him on. Still, he wouldn't. I suggested he go meet with our outreach workers. "If you sit with them and talk to them, you will see that there is no goony-ness, no goons, no goon squads." Wolfe seemed taken aback by our openness. I thought-hoped that he would take me up on my invite. He leaned back to allow his crooked mouth to drop open. It was obvious he was gasping for air, the level of deviousness on which he operated was exhausting him, but nevertheless, no choice really, he agreed. Only other thing he could have done was leave. Anyway, in a room made up of a few desks and tables spread throughout, lockers along two of the walls, bulletin boards big and small hanging it seemed everywhere jammed with notices, a massive wall map of midtown with our outreach locations indicated on it, which for the sake of supervision was sectioned off, the statistics from each listed, including the names of people we'd outreached, and hanging by a hook on the wall next to the map, announcements, reminders, people's phone numbers, etc., a very big clock above, all of it, making up our outreach department. The people too.

Sitting there was a Wolfe in lamb's clothing, unarmed with questions, his note cards empty. Remaining quite silent, sitting with eighteen of our workers. I counted twelve men and six women, all but two or three were African American. Their ages ranged from 25-60. Everyone themselves from the streets, a few of them now shift supervisors and managers. I introduced him. With rapt attention, every head turned towards Wolfe, some more readily than others. This was all happening to them "out of nowhere." He did not ask them if they were goons. He did not ask them if they ever engaged in roughhouse tactics, nothing about the crack house. He just sat there and looked at them and they looked back. One of the workers softly asked, "How can we help you?" A few laughed, enjoying the moment. One woman: "Seriously, what do you want? Where are you from again?"

Wolfe's passivity was palpable. I had to step up. I asked the workers to explain how they performed outreach. Six or seven spoke about trying to be persistent, others about the use of humor, the need to sometimes wait out a person's decision-making process, showing up repeatedly throughout the night, night after night, showing concern, returning to talk, then the conversation came full circle back to persistence. One talked about the "easy sell" because we were co-ed, we had great food, plus we had a color television, and we were air-conditioned. Turning to Mr. Wolfe, "We came off of the streets ourselves and you can see we're doing pretty well."

Oh no, is that it? He's going to just let the meeting run its course and then bolt? Well, if he wasn't going to bring it up, I was. I interrupted the next round of silence and asked them to discuss what the wolf had asked me – if there was any kind of activity that involved fighting or intimidating homeless people to get them to come indoors. Had they heard of it, or did they believe there was a goon squad amongst us that were beating the homeless? Were they or anyone else involved in a goon squad? They responded with guffaws. "What the 'f' are you saying? That we beat up people who won't accept help? What? And what, that we win every fight? And that none of us ever spoke up about it? Man, you don't win fights on the street. You don't even try cause there's always tomorrow, you know, if you punch on somebody to bring them in, how you going to be in the same building with that guy the next day and the next? At some point you're going to have to turn your back. It just doesn't make any sense at all. None." "How you going to get somebody to come inside to a place they don't even have to be at by beating on them?" "You survive by getting along." "Hey, if they don't want to come indoors, then they don't. That's that. Who cares? Think about it. See you tomorrow. Nobody's in that much of a rush." "Persistence wears down resistance." One person, one of the supervisors, off the streets herself only some months earlier, explained it something like this: "Sometimes when you're doing outreach, you might catch a person at the wrong time. You know, they could be wasted, for example, or they could be groggy or in a bad mood, even hallucinating, and sometimes the outreach worker does get barked at, but we know where that comes from. We brush it off, or if we are momentarily frightened maybe we get defensive, maybe we bark back for a minute. These are what we call 'training moments.' We know what they're going through. We've been there." From across the room, our oldest worker, he turned 72 years old only a week earlier, spoke out too. "It ain't that hard to bring people indoors. Most people want to come inside, especially the more vulnerable ones, people with mental health problems and so forth. They are on the street mainly because they do not know what their true options are besides getting medicated or hospitalized. They are the quickest to come in. You just have to approach them right." Guess what? Mr. Wolfe didn't write down a single word. He had his pad out, its pages unfurled. In his other hand, index cards face up, empty. All along, his pencil stayed in his ear. Was he moved at all by what he had heard?

Wolfe left the room with a very quiet "thank you," and he never even mentioned having met with them in his subsequent articles, the first coming out a week or so later, caps and all, front page, Second Section. "BUSINESS GROUP HIRES GOON SQUADS TO BEAT THE HOMELESS." And, on the day after they ran their article, the paper had an opinion, which someone thought was fit to print, Op-Ed style, that upon being asked if any of the outreach workers may have engaged in roughhouse tactics, Grunberg said "That is fiction." No. I only said that the goon squad and the crack house story was fiction. As to whether our outreach workers used roughhouse tactics, I said much more. Guess I fell for a reporter-trick – ask a crazy question followed by a sane one and then use the response to the crazy as the response to the sane. "He said it, didn't he?" Juxtaposition.

The Wolf lied. The Wolf omitted. The Wolf's supervisors and editors at the paper went with it. What was the motive? They allowed for weak premises without backup to be repeated several times throughout the article – guess that's to show the reader how extensive their reporting was; the length of the article was all? They assume most people won't read the whole article, especially not if it's "continued on page….," but the average reader will note the article's length, at least subliminally, which gets directly related to the amount of credibility granted. There must be something there goes the thinking, what with all the smoke and fire and all, you know, there's so much it needed to be continued on another page.

So, what was the worst part for me? Was it sitting in front of the city council chambers on public trial? Unable to answer the questions completely without hearing the committee's chair scream: "Just answer the questions as they are put to you. I will not allow digression. Just answer the question." Oh? You speculate, but I can't digress? Digression was my specialty, and here I wasn't allowed to practice it? When I worked at Columbia Presbyterian, digression was virtually required, was proof that you knew what you were talking about, that you could round out an explanation, present the whole story. There was a lot at stake here. They seemed to want to shut down our outreach program. That could cost a hundred plus jobs for the homeless, another seventy training spots, and then what of all the homeless that would be left outdoors, unattended to? This was advocacy running rampant. The more homeless on the street, the bigger the prize? Play ball!

Steven DiBrienza would be a relative unknown no longer, chairing what was typically an unspectacular social services subcommittee of the New York City Council. But now he had the spotlight with political kudos his to take, so many. He was about to paste one on the big old Grand Central Partnership, the city's largest business improvement district. He despised the premise it was foisted upon, that because government was not doing enough, the private sector needed to step up.

For a relative unknown committee chairperson like him, a defining moment such as this was something a city councilman might wait years for. And here it was, his bandwagon, long overdue. He was about to be front and center in a running story in the city's most illustrious very blue paper, yes, them again. And the details were tailor-made for the oldest scenario in town, one never too far from the truth: The poor have not, and the haves care not. Those goddamn, wealthy, property-owning, Grand Central Partnership, business district punks. We got to stick it to 'em, he chortled. As for us, we all tried many ways to say "No, it did not happen," none of which worked.

~   ~   ~

Despite there being a most obvious con at work, no evidence, the accusers were the heroes. The "goons" sitting there in ill-fitting suits taken right off the rack in the back of the "prop" room were the victims. Think of it, if what they claimed was true, why should they be exonerated? If true, they beat up a hell of a lot of weak and vulnerable people. Yet, that quickly, it was decided charges against them should be dropped in exchange for their testimony. By whom? Isn't that a criminal justice system decision? What would their victims say? What? No victims? Oh well, reading from a script handed them as they walked to the table, they "admitted" to everything. Shouldn't they have been asked who prepared their testimony for them? Oh boy, can you believe it, the brave admissions of the goon squad won applause. It was clear to everyone there that they were courageous heroes, so wrong, and we were to be charged and, no guarantees, released in our own sorry recognizance. They timed it perfectly. They didn't let us on the stand until nearly all the cameras had gone away, the entire photographer's pool, dissipated. Half of the councilmen had left as well. There was virtually no one left to listen. The hearing had started at 9am, but there, with us taking the stand at noon, there was but one lone photographer and she was having trouble with her equipment and was more focused on that than our testimony. Most of the reporters had gone away too, their deadlines to meet. Guess they had their story already. IT WAS SO FRUSTRATING AND UNFAIR, I screamed silently to myself.

~   ~   ~

Just one reporter, Jonathan Goodyear, from yes, that same paper, talked to me, but alas, came up with what would be called in his industry, a "balanced and fair" article. He included our rebuttal, true, and that's good, but in much less detail and only after providing a ton of detail offered up by our attackers, the Board. This meant our "side" came across as what it always was, defensive. Too bad for us, but that's the advantage that accusers earn. It's the prize that comes to those who strike first.

What would the public say if they learned what our secret was? That it was our very outreach efforts with its emphasis on consumerism, on choices and incentives, on jobs, on decision-making, that attracted homeless people to midtown from all over the city? That was it. Our secret. Everyone everywhere claimed that it was very difficult to bring homeless people indoors. We showed that it was much easier than people believed. Our effort was so counter-intuitive as to not even come up on some of New York's most prominent radar screens.

How to reduce street homelessness? Make your programs attractive and accessible by choice and have relatable and credible salespeople sell them. Offer jobs. Yes, it will attract homeless people from everywhere, but the good news is they will be seeking your address so that they can come indoors. Their goal will be to come inside, to be a part of something. If that is what your program offers, they'd rather be in it than lying on the sidewalk, or living doubled-up, in the way of a friend or family member, sleeping curled up on a makeshift sofa in a tiny, overcrowded, New York City apartment. And their attraction to your program will be infectious. That's a good thing. Your neighborhood's static street homelessness would end up giving way to pedestrian traffic; they're up and moving about, no longer unnoticed, and invisible. Weird, but if you get up and blend in, that's right, you are no longer invisible. If you can turn the homeless person laying down into a pedestrian with somewhere to go, your outreach has worked. Remember the commercial that showed a groundswell of people running, literally from every direction, with the narrator saying, "everyone's rushing for cocoa marsh"?

Here's an example of how one of the worst of the charges leveled our way went down, that we assaulted a sleeping man who was laying deep in the snow, and then chased him away: It was reported by The Board that members of one of their watch-groups, their cameras and notepads in hand, had been following some of our outreach workers during their late-night shift when they saw "horrific abuse." They said that they observed our team trying to wake a man who was bundled inside a combination of blankets and cardboard deep in a snowbank on the corner of 42nd and 1st Avenue, 7pm, on a Saturday evening. They said they saw a couple of different outreach workers prodding the man to get a response. Didn't work. They kept prodding, they said, this time while yelling at him. Didn't work. They kept prodding. Suddenly, the homeless man jumped up, screamed, and ran into the street to get away. The outreach workers, they said, then got into a van and drove away. The watch group then called the police to report the "horrific abuse." They also said that their subsequent tailing of us two weeks later showed that we changed the license plates of our van. They said it was obviously a cover up. Of what? An in-house investigation by our former NYPD two-star police chief who was looking for evidence to back up their accusations, or the lack of it, to either back up our denials, or not, found the following: The outreach logs found no mention of that interaction on that evening. It did mention however, in an entry two weeks earlier, an incident that seemed similar. The investigators tracked down the people who were on duty that night. What had happened apparently was that following a bad snowstorm, remembering that the body of a homeless man had been found on the east side, near First Avenue, midtown, some months before that, dead in the snow, caused them concern as they were about to pass through that same area. They were talking about it as they crossed the intersection of 42nd street and Second Avenue, "Oh my God, look!" They shouted at the driver to stop. In their logs later that night, they would enter that they saw a person laying in a corner on 42nd and Second Avenues. That they pulled over to check on him. They shouted as they exited the van, "Hey... you okay?" No answer. Was he alive? They continued trying to shout him awake as they neared the large snow-lump. He was unresponsive, not moving. They peeked under a piece of cardboard covering his head. They reported that while trying to check on the man, just as they lifted the cardboard, four people, two men and two women, approached them from half a block away, now in a run, yelling at them to leave the man alone. "Let him be, he has a right to be there," they shouted. "Hey, we're just doing our job. Back off." Apparently, though he had been unresponsive, he woke up to the conflict and the noise. He screamed something unintelligible, got up, and ran away. The team saw, obviously, that he was not as they feared, dead, so even while the students were still yelling at them, "Look what you've done." They outreach workers climbed into the outreach van and took off, continuing to make their rounds. During their investigation, the former police chief's detectives spoke to the doormen of the buildings right across the street from where the watch-group had said all of this had happened. They reported that on the date that the watch-group reported, there were no homeless people sleeping across from their buildings. One said he had earlier that evening shoveled the area and didn't see anyone there. So, no snowbank, and no homeless person laying in the snow on 42nd and 2nd on the weekend that was reported in phone call by the watch-group. Then a curious fact – the phone call to the police to report the abuse they claimed to have witnessed that night was made from a phone booth in Queens at a location an hour's drive away. As regards the license plate change – it happened three months earlier, in the year before the incident in question.

Over a seven-year period, we had engaged over twelve hundred different outreach workers, all formerly homeless. Twelve hundred. Either they worked for us at two dollars above minimum wage with benefits, or they trained with us in our pathway-to-employment training program, PTE, which offered a $50 weekly training stipend, the maximum amount allowed by the Welfare department before they'd reduce a person's benefits. Ironic, but had we paid the minimum wage, it would have been less than what they got with the stipend plus welfare, which together was enough to help them get housed. Guess there's a reason why several homeless programs all over the city were offering weekly stipends – We got the idea from Volunteers of America, one of the city's largest nonprofits, whose program was called Project Break Through, PBT, where people were being trained and, receiving that same stipend, were getting themselves housed, and earning job references, and gaining workaday skills, still with a few dollars left over. Side note: We were being sued for paying stipends because we were violating minimum wage. Okay, I get it. Stipends are less than the minimum wage. Less. But as one trainee once told me, "Sometimes, less is more."

Almost as innocuous as masking tape being found over the stairwell door locks in the Watergate Hotel, one of our outreach staff drove off with our vehicle after his shift. He called us a few hours later and made a ransom demand, "…if you want to see your car again…" He needed money quickly, he said. We gave him two hours to bring the car back or else we'd have to call the police. He did that, so we didn't have to make the call, but we did suspend him. He understood, he said, even if he left our building angry. "I brought it back, didn't I?" He went straight to The Board. Suffice it to say, this disgruntled complainant was quickly named "chief of the goons." Yes sir. Turned out, according to news reports, he was running the entire "goon" operation. The chief.

Faced with such a "confession" of assault on such a large scale, did The Board call the police? No. Well okay, what did they do? Did they ask him to document his crimes, get him a lawyer so he could properly turn himself over to the police? Seek out his victims to see if they were okay? No. Quickly, they ushered him off to The Scion who ran the blue paper of record and who put dear Mr. Wolfe on the case. Too bad, his poor craftsmanship, coupled with a most basic inability to properly investigate, didn't work out so well for him in the end, his "premise" having been discovered to be a fantasy, and not just his alone. That itself would have been a great story – Pulitzer? And after the dust settled, and the story was fully dead, though The Scion kept it to himself, it seems that Wolfe, sans Pulitzer, was banished to a desk in Queens, an outer borough, as in "way-out." In other words, he was never heard from again. Interesting isn't it, the incidents at the heart of the story were witnessed by two bogus advocacy groups. Bogus? Instead of sharing the humanity that our outreach workers and trainees brought to the job of reaching out to their troubled peers, they promoted a story that asked people to view the homeless as goons. What kind of advocacy was that? They said there are hundreds of victims all of whom are "out there but afraid to come forward." How do you know that? Did they come forward to you? Do you have their information, their names? Where are they? Who are they? Did any file a police report? Did any need to be seen at a hospital? Any records of this? "No, but we know it's been happening. We know. Trust us." Have you met with these victims? "No, we don't know who they are." Wait a minute, you're saying that with twelve hundred different workers involved in seventy thousand interactions, not only didn't our goon squad ever lose a fight, but what, we suffered no injuries either? And all of them successfully conspired to keep it all a secret? Come on Mr. Wolfe, we ran a goon squad of such great skill as to never lose a battle, injuring our targets without leaving so much as a mark on them or even one clue that would lead back to us? Really? The homeless were frightened by our prowess, our effort rivaled only by the similarly impenetrable Japanese Ninja. With this kind of success, we should have been lauded as running one of the best-trained, best supervised squads of any kind ever? Hah, that's no joke.

Apparently, we were accused of running a perfect goon squad but of being bad at everything else. In every program we attempted, save for the "criminal" side of our outreach program, we were supposedly very bad. We didn't offer "real" training, they said. We had inadequate supervisory methods with little accountability, they said. We were misguided in how we provided social services, they said. We were just bad at the whole thing, but we were able to put together a perfectly selected, hundred-plus squad of formerly homeless outreach workers, each of whom could fight undefeated, without injury, able to scare hundreds of their peers who they forced to come to our Center in silence? Where were the "whistleblowers?" Amazing that we were able to operate undetected for so long. It's like the child's parable about the blind man stumbling over the invisible log that wasn't there.

They were beating up their peers, literally chasing them into our Center for home-cooked, excellent food, air-conditioning, big television screens, bathrooms, and showers, and storage facilities? The goon squad "forced" them into our metal-detected, safe, roomy Center, where they could choose between self-help or professional help, or just sit and rest, even get referred to a bed for the night if they wanted? We forced them into a highly desirable geographical location, which hired and housed them? Oh, did I mention it was also co-ed? Lots of questions here none of which a single professional reporter asked.

~   ~   ~

Of the 1500 to 2000 different people that came into the Center each month, upwards of 6,000 people annually, repeats aside, lots of turnover, once forced in, wouldn't someone had been heard screaming from one of the Center's many street-facing windows, let's say, by a passerby, "Please, let me out of here!" Maybe a sign dropped from a ledge, unfurled to read, "HELP!" Maybe a note passed on in a late-night hand-off let's say to one of our volunteers, "Help me. They forced me in here and now they won't let me leave." All this drama was taking place or not taking place, in an open-door, 24-hour facility, with people, many of them already anonymous enough, able to come and go as they pleased.

~   ~   ~

Maybe the worst part was sitting between two detectives from the district attorney's office. They sat far enough apart that I couldn't fit them both in my gaze. I had to turn my head to look at either one of them, their ruse. They each had a profile shot of me as I answered such questions as, "Are you aware of any incidents of violence, which were ignored?" The interview was my second with them, and it lasted several hours; the first had been at my desk, more informal. Anyway, this time I was back out on the street by lunchtime. I could have fallen to my knees thanking the heavens above that I had nothing to hide. Those bastards, I thought, they get to make up a story, then they bask in the media glow they've created for themselves as advocates for all the homeless. Bask, to the point of sunburn, third-degree. Three conclusions, and you know to whom we point: 1) The Board was not comprised of even one real coalition for the homeless. 2) Throughout the entire ordeal, there was no urban justice. 3) There was for the homeless no pathway to housing. Unreal.

~   ~   ~

On a personal level, the worst moments were either one of two: One was riding home on the Metro-North train scanning the AM radio dial only to hear Bob Grant, conservative champion of the right, a talk-radio hero, as always, hooking his claws into one of the left's causes, this time, "homelessness." Of course, his constant sleight-of-hand usually didn't work for the good of logic, not for anyone but his Fox News type of followers, some subset of the Republican and Libertarian "base" plus rubberneckers, mainly, on most matters, he was a train wreck of anger and discontent. I was one of those rubberneckers. I liked the way he moderated his voice for the sake of drama. I liked how he put forth his arguments – he could lay one down between commercial breaks like no one else. Though his show really was a misuse of talent and intelligence, I was on the train that day, listening, and there he was, finishing up. He was interviewing one of our ex-outreach workers, now an informant for The Board, "Bubba." He was talking about how he beat up homeless people everywhere. "They told me they hired me because I was good with my hands. That's right. My left hook got me my job." Grant responded with a full dramatic deep-voiced pause and what a great voice he had. "I see that in the blue paper, Grunberg is reported to have said the charges that his workers rough-housed the homeless are fiction," he said, and then, drawing out the 'I' from his highest voice to his lowest, very low, "but I believe Bubba." Yeah, okay Bob Grant. What do they like to say, that you can always get up and turn the dial? Done.

The other bad moment, number two, came when I was sitting at Dan's desk, the soon-to-be outgoing president of the business district, an indirect casualty of this all. The speakerphone was on. We were waiting for Peter to come to the phone. Regarding my job security, I was at that moment quite nervous. The scandal years had begun. Would I be scapegoated? No matter how closely I had worked with nearly a hundred property owners by that time, I never really believed they'd be loyal to me in any kind of pinch. And this despite seven straight years of my always receiving their support or at least their pats on my back, all this worry then, as much my predisposition as anything else. Truth was, I was probably someone they feared a little in that they might have been worrying what I knew and what would I do with what I knew. What if there was a goon squad and I knew all about it? Was I keeping certain facts to myself? No, and no, but still, did they really know that? I certainly knew a lot about them, right? Did they fear that? Of course, there were a few days, the first ones right after the charges were made, when I wasn't completely sure about anything myself. I mean, could it be that despite my being so close to the operation, that I was so poorly plugged in I knew nothing about a five-year long goon squad? No way, but...

Twenty-five

Things that happen in New York aren't much of a secret. Worthy of notoriety or not, New York's initiatives, its policies, incidents, accidents, and hits and misses often have influence elsewhere as in, "Look what happened in New York."

~   ~   ~

Wouldn't you know it, in most matters related to homelessness, there are a handful of people, New Yorkers mainly, whose influence has been disproportionate to their success. Their approach has gone national. It's gone international. Coming together in the early 1980s, these service magnets, the founders, signed on to a doctrine, which drew themselves into a tight circle of support. Ever ready to expand, their way spells *the* way. Some forty years after those seeds were planted, they still have what they initially wanted; nearly the entire industry marching to their tune of a "Housing First" approach. Even if it is a primary solution that has delivered for so few, it does have secondary gain. It organizes everybody. It helps an industry of providers know their place. It allows for a certain kind of apples-to-apples scrutiny. This is what you are to do, now go do it. Don't get distracted. "Go get them housing first" seems to have an irrefutable logic, but for most homeless people, it doesn't get beyond face value.

~   ~   ~

Homelessness is worthy of emergency action. Very few homeless people get housed by anybody. Housing-First may work as a clarion call, but that's as far as it goes – how far can it go without the housing? 70% of homeless shelter residents end up leaving shelters on their own, maybe even before they are "ready" to, before they had their own housing to move into, maybe before they have a place to live. At one point, as the numbers of people sitting inside the shelter system grew, the percentage of those not turning over grew. Large numbers of people who never even leave the shelter for a few minutes. They stay indoors in the shelter 24/7 for months at time. Ask them, and they'll tell you they want to work. Clearly, they'd need skilled support, but... they'd get out and they'd connect with others, and they'd earn their rent money, and they'd feel whole. Social service workers everywhere already have the skills. Employers have the need. Jobs can be found. Action, not immobility.

The Board had to develop a new category. Brilliant. Shelters suck. Staying in one for a long period of time is disabling in and of itself. Therefore, "chronic homelessness" should qualify a person as "functionally disabled." And so, it did. "Homeless" for two years or more with a twelve-month episode became the criteria. Shelterization. Now, sitting tight, going nowhere, not working, was advantageous. Tuck in your shirts and behave. Sit still and trust the staff. Housing-First behavior control.

Scrambling for power and influence, they used to have to work hard to win over the media; now, thanks to that hard work, they don't have to do this anymore. They picked the label, framed its causes and its treatment, blamed, sued, defamed, and lobbied their way towards an empire of sorts, where billions of government and foundation dollars flow each year to fund their efforts and then some. They push for the unreachable, a grandiose vision, housing for everybody, which gives them, among other things, careers set in stone. In the UK, this would be referred to as a brilliant scheme. As watchdog groups, they essentially make their life's work biting the hand that feeds them, all of it, by design, I think by now, the fake rebel yell.

Making names for themselves, traveling as imprimatur, at the turn of a doorknob, the well-placed members of The Board often go on to become commissioners or executive directors. Upon application. They are the keynote speakers at whichever conference they choose. At meetings, they get the floor merely by taking it, and when they send a letter to the editor, it is published upon receipt. There really are people like this, several dozen, a few more perhaps. When they put in for a grant, it's theirs, when the media has a story to run, they are the go-to talking heads. Since the early Eighties, this is how it has gone, a little social order going a long way. They are the experts seen on the television set and heard on the radio, consultants to all. Yet having invented the establishment they now run, their lack of success makes them imposters, posers really. That's cynical, but for close to forty years now, there's been little change. Outcome has become less important than sentiment, something they can deliver 24/7.

Their ideas and advice have fueled a response that is succeeding in the smallest number of ways. They've got hundreds of thousands of people under shelter roofs throughout the country yet, in the basket of an industry of governmental agencies and foundations whose promise to fix the homeless problem is, apparently, eternally renewable, The Board's thought-leadership comprises all their eggs. Is that all they can do for all the people who cross over their thresholds? Is it that the aura of altruism is enough? Alas, it is a migraine's aura, coming from a hurricane's eye, the anguish of others, this "problem of homelessness" that they define. Pain extended into the future unknown. Knowing better, we read their power as oligarchical, their arrogance as concrete. At this point however, anything but discouraged, governments seem to think they have little choice but to continue the same "correct" path. Amazingly ironic, along with the homeless themselves, everyone is literally in a box.

~ ~ ~

The most profound reason for membership on The Board and for others who comply with its thought-leadership is career profitability, not just for the well-off but for the line-worker too, the little people, the real heroes with great bedside manner. They've been hung out to dry. They can hardly speak up. Hey, you want to keep your job? Housing-First.

~ ~ ~

The Board's initial work aside, for its founder was gifted with $1 million-plus he used to get things up and running, for their top tier, the founding members and beyond, this has meant quite a few of personal breakthroughs in their not-for-profit salary ceilings. Still, this is the non-profit world. They make what they can without drawing a rebuke from their board or attention from the IRS, but that's not all that is "earned." Besides super salaries, having been launched into rarified air, they profit not just from the cash but the cachet, which yes, can lead to more cash, but the point here is the cachet, unique to this line of work, so very deeply satisfying. From the start came the business of impression management, a necessary creep. They find themselves on "I help-the-homeless" stage in a massive auditorium. Honored by the deserved applause, their inner grin spreading the night wide open, a social skyrocket, is way more than simple personal folly. Beware, it can be dangerous to the cause. Read Max Weber. It serves to maintain the status quo. The adulation creates a charisma that reduces the likelihood they'll ever be challenged. Perpetual motion, an endless zip-line into perfect storms of authentic self-satisfaction, that's right, we must call for a homeless services climate change or there will be no revolution. That's the work of charisma; it chokes out critical analysis. The interaction seems to be the thing. Social media aside, sometimes one-on-one does rule, but at other times mass movement is where it's at. Problem is, given who is in charge, these interactions are tasked with reductionism, just making the long wait for housing, housing, and housing easier. Godot? Okay, well at least there's more food, more warm clothing, never enough of each. Then there's the other side of the equation, to wit, what about the effects of these interactions on the people-in-need? The constant receipt of help is necessary but is often delivered in a way that may be detrimental to the target population. The eventual reliance on it, the one-down aspect built into the process, the help in and of itself is so important but in that it occurs in such large and impersonal waiting rooms, they come to be possibilities squandered, hopes dashed, lifestyles insulated. Disconnection.

Misconception, plus a little money, plus heaps of personal praise tie these very social circles together. Momentum. Everybody moves in sync, like escapees from a prison farm chained at the waist, weaving figure eights, a certain kind of patterned infinity. In short, bad guys can be complex people. All bad? Who's that? Think about Jack Nicholson in *The Shining*, in character, frozen in place, in a maze of misdirection gone evil. He was just trying to expunge something apparently eternal, but he was an innocent man once too, right? Then he was infiltrated. Welcome to the power of leadership, its grip real enough, it cuts, carves, and slices just so. Just so.

Twenty-six

Bad methodology, poor research skills, overlooked footnotes, discounted cross-references, or worse, denied findings, any of it can produce false conclusions. This is a problem that cannot self-correct. What did Margaret Mead answer to my question as to whether as a researcher I needed to spend overnights in Bowery flophouses? "How else are you going to know what the roaches are doing?" Some said that it would take a certain amount of intellectual courage to go there, that we'd need it to overcome our fears. It wasn't always easy.

Mayor, mayor, mayors everywhere, change your approach. Yes, housing is central to our homeless lives. Get more affordability into our hands, please. Build it, buy it, convert it, and renovate it. Did we say please? But please don't confuse any of that with programs that would more completely help us, your disconnected shelter-dwellers, who continue to live with the thud of the diagnostic hammer. Instead, do you not get it, with just a few enhancements, the devices of the workplace will absolutely get the job done? Pun intended. Rhetorical. Emphatic, not inquisitive. Hire us. We'll show you.

~   ~   ~

Cognitive dissonance, a type of linear thinking, facilitates an uncomplicated transition from preconception to misconception, where facts, not getting in the way, are forcibly knocked aside. In a flash comes distortion and with it, oddly enough, a further strengthening of personal conviction, the type of confidence best reserved for the truly knowledgeable. Ay, that's the rub, oh well, they can grow their beards and put on half-sized "professor" glasses, look down on the rest of us as we try to humanize the situation. Okay then, Boom! A certain type of advocate is born, indeed having entered an honorable profession, the helping profession, an achievement with social meaning. Curriculum vitae relevance. They "network," but on a one-way street, not networking really. They'll let the homeless meet them, but not the other way around. Going with the flow, when they do choose to become executive directors, professors, public policy lawyers, assistant commissioners, elected or appointed officials, or members of any sort of media, their influence grows. They speak as authorities on the topic of homelessness, their listeners allured by their clarity of vision, as addictive a feedback loop as any. The "gee whiz" factor is drawn from a melding of armchair experiences and allows for shallow-thinking-with-conviction. If it's treated as an endpoint instead of a beginning, it can deliver, very dangerous, a laser beam of false awareness. New Age. It is a tree, one tree at a time, but those are the trees that fall in the silent forest. That's the sound of "gee whiz." Read Peter Rossi. Facts get drawn and quartered by simplistic formulation, that's why we call it "misconception," the universe being missed for one of its parts, a type of disconnectedness that goes beyond housing, housing, and housing.

May the numbers of those who are weeds diminish and may the numbers of those who will weed them outgrow.

Twenty-seven

It is assumed by The Board that you are homeless due to your incompetence. Yes, they blame the landlord and the politics that allows for wealth inequality. But that the system of benefits is too complicated for you to manage alone, or that, being a victim, you are too vulnerable to manage alone. How else to cope with not getting housing first? When you enter a shelter, you are assigned to a person who will take over the management of your "case," your case manager. Manufacturing consent? You are assigned to this one person, a conduit of sorts, to whom you must answer and report, a person you did not choose and typically cannot change without great rancor among the case management staff itself. Try, and there will come a few case notes in your chart, your "adjustment issues" dutifully noted. Fortunately, most every social service professional cares about the people they are helping and do all they can to soften the edges. However, despite all that is at stake, the valuable days, weeks, and months that can and will swiftly and somewhat fiercely tick away, you may only consult them or their supervisor – there is often no team of specialists to work with, there is no opportunity for second or third opinions, take it or...

From an employment perspective, there is a worst-case scenario, which is a most common housing strategy. You are told that to facilitate being housed, you need to qualify as "disabled." That you can then be "placed" in a sort of ongoing housing probation program called "supportive housing." You are supported, but you are also limited "for your own good." In one sense, this is the easiest type of housing to get into, the most often accessed too. During the lengthy application process for approval by the Social Security Disability office, which is necessary to be considered disabled, you will be told that it's best that you do not look for work as it might reverse your eligibility. You are told that a job search is an indication that you might not come across as disabled. You are either disabled or not. Your case manager will not want to "confuse" the Office of Disability. They use as their main evidence of your disability the fact that you are chronically homeless. That you have been not held a job in some time. That you're in no position to even look for work; your application rooted in your case manager's belief that you cannot at this time be successfully employed. This is something she will need to prove. She is just being honest. She could never recommend you as being "job-ready" and she can't imagine an employer hiring you, and if he or she does, not finding a reason to fire you very soon after. Looking at your chart, she can see that in your past you've held several jobs, all of them short-term. Stable employment hasn't happened yet, and while this is not necessarily uncommon in any 23-year-old, based on that fact, your case manager will be able to prove that your "disability" has been holding you back. Good intentions all around, no doubt. So, rather than encourage you to keep looking for work in futility, she asks that you not "go there." For now, in her words, "you are unemployable." And you must stay unemployable. Right to the top, the case manager's team leader herself firmly believes that continued failure in this arena could damage you. You don't need another failure, she insists. "You are a disabled young man." Or, she says, "You are disabled, young man." Or "You are disabled young, man." Man, oh man.

Annually, upon approval, the treatment team to which your case manager belongs will need to rebuild the case to the funders who would pay for your housing, typically HPD, Housing Preservation and Development, that you are indeed (still) disabled and cannot work. Year-by-year, as a resident in supported housing, you will live under the auspices of this process of proving and re-proving your disability. You prove it, and you keep your apartment. You don't, and you're out. Makes sense. You are now in housing earmarked for disabled people. Typically, a part-time psychiatrist will interview you each year and will put his snapshot of your moving picture to paper, linking his analysis to previous diagnoses you may have received, or that your biography in your chart upholds, and render a diagnosis that "works" for your continued placement. You may qualify because you've been homeless for 12 consecutive months or intermittently homeless for 24 months. That's a new wrinkle in the process. Only six months homeless? Wait six more months and you are eligible. And, given your inactivity and growing disconnection, and given that you are residing in a shelter, which typically contributes to your dependence on your case manager and your lessening independence as a proactive adult, you may very well be disabled. A new verse for Alanis Morissette's song *Ironic* is coming up, isn't it? By being offered "housing first," you end up sitting in the shelter for a long time, which "proves" that you are disabled and can't work. That's how you get your housing? Bingo – your situation delivers its own solution. You now qualify for supportive housing. Simple, right? No, not so simple, and not to be discounted, to the contrary, there is a lot of pain and suffering in those 12 consecutive months, maybe more so in those 24 intermittent months. Isn't that ironic?

If you ever did get a job, and your earnings reached a certain rate, about $15 per hour, not bad, you would lose your housing subsidy and with it your housing, so should you, or shouldn't you? What if, after your third month at that earning rate, that point when the system begins to push you out of your housing, you lost your job? Start again? Back to the shelter? Herbert Gans' typology. The deprived and the trapped.

Rich Hall, comedian: When you go to work in the morning, if your name is on the front of the building, you are upper class; if your name is on your desk, you are middle class; and if your name is on your shirt, you're working class.

~   ~   ~

Your designation as "disabled" frees up further funding for your social services agency of record, which guarantees your rent subsidy and an "end to your homelessness." Trapped and somewhat imprisoned by your own trappings, disabled or not, you are now a success of theirs. And so, your case manager can now "close out" your chart, that is, they can forward it to your new case manager in the basement of your new residence. You are the evidence of some solid problem-solving and change-making? Guess so, or guess not?

~   ~   ~

99 out of 100 do not get housed by the shelter's social services team. They are said to be people needing a home – but are told to "sit over there please," and they are expected to comply. This keeps people on the edge of their seats going nowhere. In time, a steadfast form of complacency ensues. That is how "survival" works. Soon, they'll be wincing over their chair-sores. Silently wincing. But wait, even if crazed by disconnection, weakened to a point by the process itself, isn't a person still and always "ready" for housing? Yes of course, it was a belief served up in partnership with the "housing first" approach. It was meant to undercut how otherwise a person might languish in wait as his or her case manager got them "ready." But if only 1 in 100 are going to be housed, what does this say about all those years fighting over the term "readiness"? And what happens to the remaining 99? They come and they go. Come again?

When in that month, for that group of 100 shelter residents, that 1 apartment opening comes, the housing staff will look over their collective caseloads to determine the winner. Who is most easily proven "disabled?" Typically, it's the one with the most positives, or is it the most negatives? Hey, nothing wrong with that, except that this placement is not a fulfillment of any kind of housing-first approach, it is more of an indictment of it, or of the other 99 people deemed to have "less positives." It puts the winds of funding behind very few homeless individuals. They could say, okay, there's no housing for you so we better work the other end. Your income. Let's get you a job. But no. What they say is, you'll have to wait over there. Either it's "we're not ready" or "you're not ready." Either way, "please step over there." In the end, they are still getting screened out. If only they could have been the one, they plead to their case manager. Well, maybe with more treatment, you'll develop more negatives, the case manager replies. They'll certainly have to promise not to drink or drug, because if you do, even it means you do have more negatives, it will in most cases render you as ineligible for supportive housing. Huh? It's a course being taught at social services schools, titled "How to break a man or a woman down, 101." The course requirement? Application for membership on The Board.

For most, "Housing First" is more than an eternally unfulfilled pledge. It's a rewording of the initial mantra, "housing, housing, and housing," simplistic, reductive, and in that it negates, abusive as well. But it works, they say. They have proof. People who get housed this way stay housed longer, they can demonstrate, which means they've been saved from being further destabilized, and in important ways they are correct. He's using the emergency room less. He's taking his meds more consistently. He's no longer in the shelter, instead in a much less expensive support system. Housing-First works. See? Yes, I see. Those things are good, much better than street or shelter life, in some ways better than his life before his skid. Of course, though, it does not reduce his financial dependence; stripped down to the basics, he's as dependent as a child, still being sheltered by others. Still and again, it is much better than being on the street, or in a shelter. As true, is that if he wants more for himself, he is in an extremely vulnerable position. What's happening is that he is languishing in a shelter for a very long time and then if he wins lottery, he gets housing. That's not a system, and that's not achievement, that's just his good luck. He's not going to own that victory. Turns out, "housing-first" is a platitude, a stanza worthy of John Lennon's brilliant homage to dreaming: *Imagine*. Emergency shelter beds help. Offering someone a chair helps. Neither compared to a private room. So, where efforts can be made to help the neediest into safe and reliable settings, they should be made. That means one thing – employment. When the money you've earned goes to pay your rent, you own it.

Unfortunately, there's no end in sight. And so, Alanis Morissette sings again, "Isn't it ironic." Because of the collective failure at resolving homelessness, as the urgency grows, the desire to help grows too. Rest assured, not to worry, if they keep on failing, they'll continue to get funding for their tireless effort. It's a type of tenure one dreads, their repeated failure is not just their success, it is ours too. "We just can't give up," they say and to prove it, they don't. Social services money, mainly for the respect it brings, is the best kind of money.

Twenty-eight

When I was at The New School for Social Research doing graduate fieldwork down in the Bowery, 1977-1979, Leon Festinger taught there. When I first heard him speak, it was about his most famous topic, self-esteem. He said that self-esteem comes from what you think your peers think of you. Self-esteem calibrates your sense of self, he said. It provides, in ethnomethodologist Harold Garfinkel's parlance, the groundwork necessary for positive expression to be possible, for personal improvement or growth to happen.

~　　~　　~

First off, everybody who came in through the doors was automatically registered as a member. They'd receive a white membership card that was renewable monthly. The most basic membership, it was the "no help" pathway, and they could stay on it. It guaranteed entrance, so at the end of the day they'd have that, and if they were still there when it was time to renew the card, it gave staff yet another chance to reintroduce programming options. They could choose not to move beyond white card membership, and we wouldn't want them to change it until they had convinced themselves they needed to. Staying at white card meant they could use our facility from 4pm, just before dinner, until 8am the next day, right after breakfast. During that time, they could take meals, showers, and rest up. Not wanting more than a white card we took as a legitimate decision, maybe even the best one. They understand the pressures on their own shoulders, the competing priorities, better than anyone else. For sure, having a white card meant that they had gone through an orientation meeting, during which our services and their potential benefits were described, that they had gone through a five-minute interview, and ten-fifteen-minute assessment of goals and best strategies for reaching them, and that they had decided on a white card membership. If they were just using our place to pivot, a momentary respite, we knew they'd likely leave after that first orientation but before their assessment. In fact, making both the introductory interview and the orientation was seen as an indication that they wanted slightly more of an intervention. If not, then not. As a white card member, they could also visit our Self-help Center during the day by making an appointment, since they were "out" during the day, or from 4pm-7pm without an appointment. It had a manned information desk, tables and chairs, telephones, computers, access to resource information, mailboxes, message center, voicemail, coffee, and tea. If our visitors wanted to get help from a professional, unless it was driven by an emergency, it would be upon request. As well they could at any time turn in their white card membership for a yellow one.

The yellow card membership was for people who wanted to be in a social services program, to meet with our professional team for any number of reasons, between 8am to 4pm, less crowded. Further, the "most prestigious" blue card membership came if they chose to join our pathway to employment or pathway to housing programs, which were then again more intensive services, again, open to anyone who wanted to step up. They got to this by attending three additional informational meetings spread out over a two-week period, again, attendance as a measure of interest, the start of the "buy-in" period. Real enough, sometimes we'd hear in the hallway one-member chiding another for their relatively "lower" aspirations, as in, "You're only a white card," or back, "I swear, I am going to get a blue card soon, I promise." Or, to the contrary, "That's right, I'm a white card. I'm not playing your game." But as indicated, we understood that people can have very good reasons for not asking for certain kinds of help. On the other hand, this membership system meant that staff did not have to face being turned down either; no need for them to be defensive. They would only have to try to help those who asked for it. They could also offer services to anyone, their right. However, if a person's card was white, they'd be "left alone" by social work staff even if subject to incentivized offerings all the time to participate further, lots of aspirational signage posted, but also by their peers who'd pressure them too. They could identify like-minded peers like the rest of us do, finally, in their social circles, among their peers, as one person put it to rhyme, "You can start anew if you want to." Quarterly, like semesters at college, membership cards would expire, and we'd have to run a registration period. People had to move around our center to different registration "stations" where they could re-determine their type of membership and their path. Though, on any day they could change their membership to any color/level they wanted. This was more of a quarterly wake-up call, a check to keep us all balanced. Everybody was now subjected to social pressure along with the demands that came with their choices. Always at the hands of their peers. Self-esteem. Social-Networking therapy.

Twenty-nine

None of our success would have happened had that food line not been placed where it was. Put another way, there are over 1000 business improvement districts nationwide – imagine.

~ ~ ~

Within a year of opening, by the winter of 1990, there was virtually no one left living outdoors in the sixty or so square block area surrounding us. If we came across anyone on the street, it seemed to be only because they hadn't heard of our Center. There had not been so few people on the streets since perhaps 10 years earlier, late 1970s, when the Bowery was still up and running, intact.

~ ~ ~

Five years after our start, August 1995, near the peak of its campaign to end our program, the founder of The Board was back on the scene. By then, multiple investigations had run their course. There was nothing hidden and nothing to hide. Deep breaths. Next step? Peter and Dan figured that the icing on the growing cake of exoneration would come if The Board itself would declare the innocence of the business improvement district. At times sounding like a bad remake of The Wizard of Oz, if innocence was indeed declared, they believed it just could prove to be the endgame for which they yearned. Yes, Peter and Dan, battle-fatigued, ultimately got out of it what they wanted, which was to get out of it.

~ ~ ~

The bottom-line, the holy grail of the business community, was that we had found a way to bring the homeless indoors, hundreds of success stories to follow. Midtown could be revitalized after all. And it was.

Everyone could see the real results of our outreach work. After all, the homeless were indoors. The BID could have held a press conference with fifty outreach workers to hold up the truth. We wanted that. We begged them to just bring the homeless up to the microphone. Let them take questions. They'll tell their stories. They'll explain the circumstances that brought them inside with us. But...they were afraid of what the homeless *might* say. What? Further, they had paid huge dollars to the biggest public relations man in town, the late great Howard Rubenstein. He'd advise them. And his advice was to not let our homeless outreach workers have their press conference. And if any homeless individual wanted to speak up, they'd put them through an interview and a media training session and then, after all that, no media would want them anyway.

So many untold tales. Here's one. A prominent member of The Board, oddly enough, she was also a self-proclaimed Dylanophile, though it's hard to see how one can be both. Her name was Samantha Barres, and she was the middle-aged daughter of the owner of Sam's Club, the giant retail outfit. Impressive. A chip off the old block, no wonder her closest friends called her Sam-Sam, but she didn't rest on those laurels. She had risen through The Board's ranks – now running a large homeless service agency. Housing-first was her invention, or one she claimed to be hers. "They need many things, but there are three things they need more than anything else. They need housing, housing, and housing." Well put.

A side note. Sam-Sam suffered from severe curvature of the spine and therefore was thought to be a somewhat brave woman. Understandable, as it forced her to walk bent at the waist, in the shape of an upside-down L, her upper body parallel to the ground. Well, one night, as she rushed to the train station for a long, overdue, weekend getaway, at the invitation of the Board's Founder, now our principle investigator, her close friend too, she was asked to stop into our drop-in-center to evaluate the efficiency of our programming. How could she even begin to do that? But in she walked, Ms. Sam-Sam Barres did, to pay a surprise visit to our center. Sounds like a Dr. Seuss tale, but no, there was nothing madcap about it. It was pouring outside, and her flowing hair, stringy and tangled, scrapped along the ground, causing little puddles whenever she stopped ambulating. From what we were told, Sam-Sam spoke for fifteen minutes to a total of two people, a social services clerical worker, a very nice and capable woman, just hired, and the other, one of our graduate student interns. That's it. And when the final investigative report came out, there was an addendum attached to it, written by none other than Ms. Sam-Sam. She wrote that her research showed her that our team approach simply didn't work. "Too fragmented." "Not structured enough." "Too many second chances." "The employment approach was unrealistic." "You can't work in teams. Homeless people are too vulnerable for that. They need to work one-on-one with an assigned professional." Her minutes of research put down years of ours, basically, that there was only one way to do it right. Ignore the accomplishments of our approach, why don't you? "Don't mind if I do," she must have said. An aside: With the passage of time, her posture got way worse. This was just after the newspapers ran stories about how she had been discovered to have been lining her executive pockets to twice her salary with money which came from redirected federal grants meant to cover the rent for some of her agency's poorest tenants. No problem, it did not cost her so much as a polite rebuke from The Board. No pun intended, but they had her back. When I did see her some months later, the change in her appearance was more than obvious. Her head had continued its momentum downward, something to do with a rupture of her moral backbone. It had become permanently stuck way up her... well, leave it to say that her look now formed more like a backwards "P." Now what? Guess whoever it is that loves her the most is wishing for her to go to back to L.

~   ~   ~

Scene change: Now, we are talking about a scion from a very well-known NY family who, having inherited so many things such as his lucrative career path, now worked for one of the world's most famous gray-haired ladies. What is black and white and read all over? Like his father before him, he was a media giant. Unethical for a person in his position to be anything more than an honorary member of The Board, that was only how it needed to look on paper. Hey, if the rest of the story fits, it'll be printed, get it? Anyway, corporations being people and all, the paper was a very wealthy property manager to boot. In fact, The Scion was an influential member of his own group of building-owning peers, and they all hoped to form their own Business Improvement District, funnily enough, located dead-center midtown NYC too. In short, for the control of this yet to be formed BID, he was more than just an enervated competitor of Peter's and Dan's who too were pursuing that same plot of land. They wanted to add the BID to their expanding portfolio of influence. Peter and Dan went all out, but it was said, by The Scion, that given the size of their growing empire, "they must be stopped," a direct quote. And stopped they were. It was now going to be BID chair versus BID chair, and The Scion would not drop his fists. Here was a case of the war being over even as the battle continued. He took every opportunity to kick Peter and Dan hard, to keep them down, who knows, maybe until they could be counted out? How about a scandal? Peter and Dan would just be the type of people to run a homeless goon squad, now, wouldn't they? That would explain their singular success in homeless services. "The truth is, that within our own geographical area," he proclaimed, "we hired several social service professional groups to address the homeless problem. They couldn't get more than a few homeless people indoors when they tried, so how could Grand Central?" Yep, must have been a squad of goons.

~ ~ ~

For the purposes of comparing outreach methods, the NY Community Trust Foundation chose three outreach agencies, we were one of them, to fund. Each agency picked a different area of the city in which to offer services. After six months, we were the only one who successfully brought in the homeless people in their designated area, all of them, about 40 people, and most were still indoors at that time. The other two agencies brought in several people, barely denting the numbers living outdoors in their assigned areas, about fifty in each. Our funding ended shortly after that because, they said, our work was over. The other two programs completed the trial period with such poor outcomes they were funded for two more years. Really. For our success, no more funding. For their failures, two more years of funding. Two more. We suggested that we join them, so we could help them bring more people indoors in their areas. No thank-you, we were told. "That might confuse the homeless." How? By introducing them to more people, and offering them more choices? Yes. To us, given the scope and dimension of the homeless problem, in this case not an abstract but with real humans involved, it was mind-boggling. To the homeless involved, it was very bad. They have no chance.

Thirty

January 1990. Only a few months into our intended programming, I was standing in a vestibule with two other people, each of us waiting our turn to speak at a Community Board Four meeting, this one to focus on homelessness. One of the speakers waiting with me was Peter Smith, his piece of the social services pie giving him an exclusivity deal with the city to run an emergency-beds program out of churches and synagogues during the winter half of the year, big enough of a deal to make him a mini-emperor, and it paid him well too. Who would have guessed? Years earlier, disbarred and jailed for fraud, he was so afraid for himself. Now drawing on those experiences, he seemed fearless. When he saw that they were about to introduce him, he turned to me and said: "Look, I'm going to say a lot of things out there. A lot of things about you. Remember kid, it's just business." He put a fat cigar in his mouth, patted me on the shoulder, and then went through the doors. He said we don't house anyone and that we had no intentions to do so. He said our outreach program wasn't effective, that we weren't professional enough, that we'd never bring anyone indoors. He urged that the community withdraw their support of our efforts and demanded that our operation be turned over to him so it could be properly run. Just business.

Thirty-one

We tried to help people overcome what in the field are called "employment barriers." Instead of the more traditional approach of, again, waiting, in this case, for the person to overcome these barriers, we decided that we were going to hire people with problems yet unresolved. And when on-the-job, if these problems presented themselves, even if ordinarily they'd be fired for them, instead, we'd offer treatment. If they wanted that, and they hadn't yet accumulated paid vacation days or paid sick leave, they could take "unpaid leave," and in any of these scenarios, have their jobs to come back to afterwards if they completed treatment. They almost always did, complete treatment, that is. They may not have started "job-ready", but they'd end up that way.

~ ~ ~

In professional employment agencies, about four months is generally adhered to as the minimum period that an employment reference could be for if it were to have much value. We decided then, that when we were training someone, their "graduation" could come upon their having earned a four-month-consecutive positive employment reference, for example, with a 90% on-time attendance pattern. Sometimes, that took only four months, but most of the time it took longer, from six to eight months. Often, with our willingness to "suspend" someone into treatment before taking them back, sometimes repeatedly, it could take as much as a calendar year, or more, before they could graduate.

~ ~ ~

It took a lot of supervision, time-management, social services work, record-keeping, crisis-intervention, and plenty of what you'd call "workplace forgiveness." Sometimes, the issues were benign, like a lack of focus or unpracticed self-discipline, which meant for some that it might take a few weeks or months before they could manage a relatively uncomplicated task. For example, everybody likely knows the ingredients and has the know-how to "whip" together a peanut butter and jelly sandwich, that's true. But how easy is it to make four hundred such sandwiches with minimal waste, and proper time management, while maintaining sanitary conditions and workplace wherewithal, enough so that we could withstand a surprise visit from the Health Department, and to package and store everything to maximize freshness, and to properly clean up afterwards, and to do all the attendant paperwork? And to do it all under the watch of your hands-on-supervisor and the gaze of your peers...not so easy. Learned organization, of the personal kind. Self-discipline and regulation, is what it took, but most everybody "made it." They earned a legitimate and current reference, and many hundreds were hired by us or elsewhere, taxes taken out, workman's compensation in place, an actual healthcare benefits package for real, and a living wage. And in this manner, many hundreds accepted treatment for whatever ailed them, while before they worked, having no job to "win" back, they rarely entered treatment, and if they did, often did not complete it. By the way, this is also how unaffordable housing became all that more affordable to them. No longer homeless. Building blocks.

It was not long before we achieved our goal of more than fifty percent of our staff being made up of our training program's graduates; 50 people out of 90 on our staff by our second year were formerly homeless. The good news, at least for the homeless, was that taking the job was "worth it," i.e., that it would furnish them with enough confidence to risk closing their welfare cases. This wouldn't have worked if they did not want to do that. As well, for their buy-in, we had to bring them along with a process – it could not be a handout, that is, the process had to help them earn their jobs in front of their own peers. This way, it could heal the rifts they experienced in their own community, essential to the healing process, essential to the housing process too.

There were hundreds of disconnected people coming to our Center. Most visitors identified work as what they most needed. The budget we had to work with was finite. Our charge? To create a meaningful process that would motivate them from the ground up. And as we saw it, we had to act quickly. They were in crisis. A pathway to employment, the answer.

To launch our training program, we called a meeting at the Center of all homeless people in the area who were interested in working. We invited close to 400 people. 320 people showed up. We told them that of all the people invited, by coming to the meeting they showed more interest in working than anyone who didn't attend. That they were walking the walk, while those who didn't show up for this meeting were, by comparison, all talk. It was all very dramatic. Dynamic energy ripped through the massive gymnasium where the meeting was held. Clearly, a contagious buzz was in the air. We explained that we were going to be a program with a blend of public and private funding. That what we were trying to do was supplement our government grant with as much from the business district as we possibly could. That we wanted to offer them the best food, the safest place, the most jobs, the most housing, whatever, but that it would cost more than most programs. We were going to be totally up-front with them. We told them that we were working with $250,000 as a start-up budget, and that it didn't include my salary of $72,000, which was paid separately. We each stood up, my staff and I, and shared where we had been employed before, our work experiences, and how much we were going to be earning. We brought out a massive blackboard and showed and explained exactly how our budget would be spent, and how much had been approved for our use in a jobs program, at that time about $60,000. We spent time going over the motivation of the BID, that ultimately, they wanted us to figure out a way to bring everyone indoors – because obviously as property-owning businesspeople, that's what they wanted. We explained the importance that our jobs program held for us; that given our survey showing how about 90% said they wanted to work, that it would be some sort of proving ground. Most people, we explained, not only believed that they did not want to work, but also that they couldn't work – too vulnerable, too lazy, etc., but that we believed differently, and that we fought for a jobs program to prove differently. We closed our meeting with a challenge, that anyone interested in further exploring this, we said, and only those people, should come to our next meeting, at 3:15pm the following Tuesday. Tuesday came. From the 320 people who came that first day, 200 people now showed up for this meeting. We offered the same explanations and held similar back and forth conversations. We answered more questions. We explained that among other things, they showed up. This meant that even though the others might have had good reasons for not coming, still, they did not attend and "you did." So then, only that day's attendees were invited to the next meeting – 8am, the following Monday. Monday came, and this time about 130 people showed up. Same thing, more details on how we wanted to climb to the point where 50% of our staff would be drawn from them. Also, that only they would be invited to the next meeting. To that meeting, came 80 people. The next meeting produced 40 attendees, the results of this self-selection process, by elimination, by way of their stamina really.

Finally, it was time. We had "found" the most motivated among them, a self-selection process to be sure, one they earned through consistency of attendance. We explained that we had two choices. One, we could further interview everyone, get resumes, look to see who had the best references, and so forth, and finally pick those four or five people we could afford to hire into entry-level positions, which would pay a living wage, and legitimately free them from welfare. Or, two, we could institute a program whereby all 40 of them would get the maximum weekly stipend allowable by Welfare, which all but two or three were receiving. That taken together, their stipend plus their available welfare allowances, would mathematically constitute a living wage. This meant they'd be able to afford to pay into housing and get out of the shelter system. Our plan, as we said, was that along the way we might hire some of our graduates, no guarantees, and that way, as jobs opened, we could reach a point where half or more than half of our staff positions could be filled this way. Guess what, they chose this second idea. It was unanimous that all 40 would be offered a stipend and a place in one of our departments, food services, maintenance, social services, or outreach to begin their training, to get them back into the habitual day-to-day practices of the world-of-work, and to "grow" and make current their resumes. Once they could show up for training for four straight months, with no less than a 90% attendance rate, we would graduate them towards employment. Their resumes would show off this most recent success. They'd also have a great reference to back it up, from their supervisors, from us. That if they faltered along the way, we'd suspend them into treatment, that is, to their case manager, and take them back again, once they were able to try again for that four-month attendance achievement. Some would be able to achieve this attendance rate in the four minimum months while others might take five or six times that; that was the basic model. Also, going forward, that while many were eligible to apply for these training slots, only those who attended three consecutive introductory meetings would become eligible. PTE would be an attendance-based program.

The Welfare Department allowed people to earn up to $50 per week in stipends if enrolled in an employment training program. That was why quite a few social service agencies had employment training programs, which paid weekly stipends. They were very popular. A person could also earn current references while they worked out whatever workplace issues they had, if any, like in their ability to fall in lockstep with workplace routines, or in accepting critical feedback without putting up a fight, or honing certain basic job-related skills, becoming part of a team, getting in on time, learning out to air a grievance "on-the-job," asking for a raise, etc. and they could do it all without the risk of losing their public assistance benefits while they worked it all out. I got to observe one such program up-close for four years, called PBT, short for "Project Breakthrough," while in a position I held working in an 816-bed shelter as the social services director and later as their mental health program director. They had trainees in each of their departments, social services, food services, maintenance, and outreach. A person would graduate as soon as they could finish several months straight, starting on time without excessive absences; for some this took a year or more, for others it came right away. The good part was that if you did fail, you could try, try, try again. It made so much sense. I was always treatment oriented, and this seemed a great way to get people into treatment. In midtown, some years later, we copied the whole shebang.

Our model worked well enough that, as previously stated, the founder himself, some 15 years after first installing his dreaded food line in the Grand Central area, having demonized us through the newspapers and the courts for years, after studying our operation during his investigation, said our employment and housing successes were unparalleled in the country. Unparalleled. He said this even while continuing to work towards our program's end. What?

We explained to this first group of 40 clients, and again to all the clients in the future, that we'd be looking for 16-20 consecutive weeks of good performance, above 90% attendance, health and hygiene, attitude, work habits, focus, getting along with others, etc. That if problems came up that would normally cost them their jobs, unless it was related to violence or stealing, we would suspend them, and reinstate them once they got a recommendation to return from the social work department. Our joint goal was that they'd be able to string together enough consecutive weeks that they could earn a credible "employment" reference. In some cases, these 16 weeks took many weeks longer, 4, 5, or 6 times that – but we would not give up if they didn't. And many didn't.

First, they filled out forms and made an appointment for an intake interview. Then they'd get a referral to an onsite social worker for a more extensive interview. While sometimes appointments had to be changed, sometimes there were no-shows, staff absences, and so forth, typically this'd be done within a week or two. Then they'd get a referral to our jobs program, a Pathway to Employment meeting, which were held twice weekly. They had to attend three consecutively to be eligible for a PTE slot. Each meeting was about an hour and a half long and run by a professional staff and a paraprofessional staff, who would be a former client of ours who had found his way out of disconnectedness and homelessness. Excellent refreshments would be served. It was lively; everyone participated. The only topic was employment – mostly workplace issues, discussing the impact of the training program, handling the bump up in social status at the Center being that they were going to be involved in a program very visibly, in front of their peers, in front of their significant others and the pressures associated with that. All of this built up to their "eligibility," already an employment related achievement. They were on their way. Once they attended these three consecutive meetings, we would enroll them and place them in one of our various departments. We wanted to go unnoticed, that is, not make any untoward "noise" in the immediate neighborhood. We simply did not want to be that neighborhood where people just walked by someone laying on the ground maybe right in front of our own program! We wanted them to come inside so we could upgrade things for them.

Housing? We approached the local YMCA and asked the manager what his vacancy rate was. When he said 5%, we did the math and were excited to discover that he had a dozen or so vacant rooms each night! We said we could easily fill them. He asked us if we could vouch for our people as tenants. We said no, not exactly, given that we've just met them ourselves, but that in our short-term relationships with them, we could absolutely give some of them positive character references. We explained our lengthy screening process. We said that we believed that were comparable to the YMCA's typical tenants. Give them a chance, we implored. And not to worry, we added, because of the rental assistance they'd be receiving from Welfare, you will get your rent like clockwork, on the first of every month. The YMCA landlord agreed with one stipulation. He wanted to keep the rentals only for short-term periods until, on a case-by-case basis, a track record could be established. They could have their own rooms, but initially just for 28-days at a time because on the 29th they'd earn "tenant rights." So, to people who could show they had an open Welfare case, which'd pay $215 per month, this YMCA began renting rooms to our program participants.

Given their lack of references, the YMCA wanted three or four months to get to know the tenant first. Fair enough. For a three or four-day period then, or until the next 28-day period could start, he'd move them out of their room, and if he could, he would give them another room in his building, technically a "different" address. If not, they'd come back to us for that period, and then in either case, they could return to their old rooms for another 28-day period afterwards and so forth. After a few months, after they'd have laid down a provable track record of rent paid, and if there were no other problems, the landlord would just let them to stay in their rooms, lease, and all. Their market grab had always been as a short-term stay "hotel," but this now established a large number of longer-term "permanent" tenants. There were several cases of people who left public assistance but kept paying the same rent for the same apartment. We arranged this understanding with a dozen different YMCAs and made hundreds of placements. They didn't want to have their welfare cases closed on them. This was a risk that discouraged them from looking for work. Funnily enough, earning their public assistance, rental assistance, medical benefits through Medicaid, and a $50 stipend collectively served them better than a minimum wage job. The only way a job benefited them more was if it were paying a living wage. We now had about 50 formerly homeless people, trainees then, and about 50 formerly homeless staff, all of them out there, housed, with supportive benefits or a living wage or better. In this way among others, our center was teaming with activity and hope. Everybody was energized.

The Board made a move to take our successes down. They sued us for paying training stipends, saying that, because they were "helping" us run the center, we benefited from their work. That because their activities were meaningful to us, because our program involved them doing things that one way or another, we'd have to do to run the center anyway, what they referred to as "meaningful activities" like preparing the meals, or cleaning floors, or even outreaching, we were taking advantage of them. Their legal angle. They put forth some of our ex-trainees, those few who had failed out, typically for refusing treatment regardless of the gain. They were literally trained to say things like: "We didn't know it was a training program." "No one ever talked to us." "There were no meetings." "We didn't know what was going on." "We thought it was a job." "We were shocked when we looked at our paycheck and it wasn't more money." "We were confused and very upset." "We want our back pay. It is only fair." The Board's representatives said to us, "You're creating a fantasy world for them. They are not ready; don't you get it?" No, we didn't. Of course, we argued back. How do you get them ready except by meaningfully training them? Sorry, that's not our problem, they replied. We asked, what about the ten other agencies doing the same thing? Their response was epic. Sorry, not our problem either. We're suing you, not them.

We should have asked them to perform tasks that had no meaning or that served no benefit to the whole? At a center for street people, where are those tasks? Ours was a grand scale social services intervention, more costly and harder to do, recruitment, training, supervising, intervening, treating, and maintaining, than if we simply hired a self-contained, well-referenced, never-have-been-homeless applicant? Not our mission. Compassion by design. We wanted to give them the chance to stabilize through work, to make connections with their peers around work, and we knew that it was not going to be the easy way to manage our operations. But, what an opportunity for them! If we were a for-profit corporation, our very business model would bankrupt us. But with government support, grants, donations, and fee-for-service programs, as a not for profit, we could survive our mission. We ran things patchwork style as we stood by our homeless trainees and formerly homeless staff, and their struggles with consistency, and their desire to grow personal capacity. Social status adjustments. Upward movement. At the Center, with their peers noticing their public efforts; whoever made it, had it made, and at any time there may have been fifty or so people busy with employment related activities trying to get to that point, and another fifty who had already done so.

To properly sue us, The Board approached anyone who had ever been in our training program, telling them they stood a good chance, if they won the lawsuit, to get hundreds of dollars in retroactive pay. That there would be no penalty for signing up, and a chance to get some cool cash. Most signed up. The lawsuit was on! We were going to be sued in the Southern District of New York. It either could have been a jury trial, which we wanted, or it could be a half-day meeting, some statements, some legal arguments, an interview or two, and then a final ruling, which was the business district's choice, presumably, to save time and money. It would be a half-day hearing in front of a judge who would later become Supreme Court Justice, Judge Sonya Sotomayor.

Following several months of taking and giving depositions, there we were, in her courtroom. We were told in advance that we should not bring any of the hundreds of people grateful for the quality-of-life perks that our Center offered to testify for us. That this judge would likely not tolerate outbursts of any sort. "She likes things to be orderly," our source told us. We followed that advice, as third-handed as it was, and we showed up at court without bringing any "work references." That quickly, we discovered our miscalculation. The Board was there with twenty former employment program trainees, most of them still staying with us at the Center. We recognized a number who had walked away from the trainee program because they didn't want to have to deal with our social services department offering them treatment. However, they remained at the Center participating in things other than our employment program. Throughout the hearing, by design, in front of the judge who apparently would tolerate it, they were very boisterous. Booing any comment anyone on "our side" made. Several times while one of us were on the stand, trying to answer questions that Judge Sotomayor put to us as succinctly as possible, we'd be booed, which prompted the judge to comment, "Looks like the homeless don't agree with you." Even though it was clear she had not conducted any research into the matter, Judge Sotomayor referred to the "Goon Squad" charges as evidence of our character.

Her decision, that we were guilty of paying people less than the minimum wage for work that benefited us, that we needed to financially settle, to compensate them by way of a formula for back-pay, to give The Board what they wanted, came after she offered at least some complimentary language as to our program's attempt to help people. She said that while Congress needed to examine creative approaches such as ours to see its value for addressing homelessness, and that perhaps our lawyers could have avoided the whole case had they asked the government for a minimum-wage waiver, until then, in that we were paying stipends and not wages, we were not operating within her understandings of the law. Never mind the amicus brief put forth by our expert witness, William Grinker, former

Welfare Commissioner, who spoke on the commonality of the contested aspects of our program and of the importance of the effort. But, your Honor, there are dozens of agencies that pay stipends. But, your Honor, The Board pays their own workers on their food lines with bologna sandwiches, no wages at all! But, your Honor, there was no Goon Squad. But your Honor...

Ironically, the business improvement district leaders knew in advance that Sotomayor would rule against them. The strategy was to keep it short, a one-day hearing was best, and then to take it to the next more likely favorable court. But later, after the NYT and others spoke about our case in bold headlines such as these, "BID Makes Huge Salaries at Expense of Homeless Says Judge Sotomayor," they changed their mind. They thought that when we did win in that second court, it would be presented in the press as our defeating the homeless – which would be terribly bad press. This worried them more than anything. Their social status, not that of the homeless themselves. Our having to end the all-important life-saving employment program was of much less concern, how about no concern at all? And as we closed our program down, as ordered by the court, we were booed for doing just that, by the hundred or so homeless people at our Center watching us "pack up." We were literally booed in our own hallways. Why are we caving in? Was all that "desire to help" we spoke of just a bunch of bullshit? We tried to explain why the stipend program had to end, why they would not now be able to afford any housing at all. "Why? Because of some bad press?" "Man, oh man, you rich guys are a bunch of weaklings."

We hired five people, our top five performers, for the cost it took to train 50. We were brought to our collective knees three ways, lies, lies, and more lies. Congratulations to them for their high road, their noble path to victory. Now, back to your drop-in-center chairs. No income. No hope. No chance.

Thirty-two

The Board had won control of our programming. They filled our own board with many of their own. They named Slim Chance as the new chairperson. Chance immediately changed the agency's name from the Grand Central Partnership Social Services Program to the dramatically different Grand Central Neighborhood Social Services Program, a swap-out, the word "partnership" for the word "neighborhood." Slam, dunk. They got our money. The Board had made a brand-new acquisition, a new "non-profit" cost center, at the time, about three to four million dollars annually, not bad. More importantly, another enemy to their cause, that would be us, was successfully neutralized. Boom.

~ ~ ~

Slim Chance was a nationally known social service maverick, a cherished member of the social services elite who, first time we met, tore open my office door, no knock. I was at my desk, no idea I was even going to be getting a visitor. In just one long-legged step, covering four or five feet, dressed like Tom Wolfe, white hat and all, Slim Chance was at my desk, his hand outstretched, in my face, he was tall, even taller in his top hat, and said, "You're overpaid, and we're going to find people who do your job better than you." I shouldn't have but I did shake his hand, without thought, mine going up at the sight of his, instinctively. Despite having had nearly twenty years of Kung-Fu training, I could not withdraw it fast enough. He held onto it, and I let him. We locked eyes. I thought of pulling him over my desk. Instead, I said, "Hello to you too." He let go. I let him go. Silence for two seconds. We stared at each other. I noticed how Slim was dressed, a Guys and Dolls approach. Rich social services suede, brown leather shoes, double-thick chinos with leather cuffs, brushed leather vest, gold buttons, and a dark, blue colored button-down with a sparkly white shirt. Always grinning, a sense of his high self-praise ever-present, always looking right at me, but not – interestingly, he would not look me in the eyes, only between them. I tried shifting a few inches to my right, then my left, to look at him head on, but he'd dart his eyes away staring a little bit cross-eyed at that point between my eyebrows. It was absurdly dramatic. He was employing strategy. I was his target? His stare, a laser beam. Was he attempting to break into my frontal lobe, his superpower the ability to perform psychosurgery, leukotomies his specialty, from across the room? He wanted me to be his follower and would tolerate nothing else! Okay, I must work with this guy now, I was thinking. He's our new board chair, after all. He's on a high horse, searching for my compliance. I must level the playing field here. My instincts told me that he wanted me to look into his eyes, but I had too much experience with mentally ill people to take him up on that. I wouldn't, and I noticed by his tiny disdainful smirk, that he hated my lack of compliance, easy to tell. My office was about 10' X 10', not that big, and he was moving throughout it trying to get my head to turn with him. Instead, what I did do, whenever he was in front of me, was look at the corner of one of his eyes. I'd switch back and forth from eye corner to eye corner, based on whether he turned this way or that. This went on for at least thirty or forty seconds and it was tedious. Couldn't he just be real? After one last furious attempt, he gave it up and started looking at me normally. Next meeting and from then on, he'd start like that but then give it up within a few minutes. Progress? What's normal? Maybe he was nervous? No. To the contrary, he was supremely confident.

Slim Chance went all out to hurt me, getting not one, but two board votes on his two different and distinct proposals to fire me. He spent several months working on the second one and on the day of the vote, turned over a six-page handwritten note to the board urging they let me go. "In trying to look for employment opportunities for our homeless clients, Dr. Grunberg is setting them up for failure." "Dr. Grunberg visits programs throughout the city without adopting their practices. Instead, he insists on adapting their ideas to his own program model. We must find a better way to help the people that have been put in our charge." His arguments were so flimsy that they had no choice but to reject them. Yet, apparently from what I was told, the voting was close. They did get what they wanted some years later, but it came too late for Slim Chance to enjoy, for not only had he resigned after that second failed vote, guess he was a one-issue manager, but he soon passed away. To The Board, he was a 90-year-old celebrity, to me, a much-revered bastard.

I remember he wanted to walk down 44th street with me. The street was quiet. We walked past the drop-in-center, what had become, to our knowledge, the busiest and largest one in the country, maybe the world. The one we started. The one I was running. At its busiest time, dinner time, hundreds of people being served, there we were, looking at its serene building front. He turned to me, and with his teeth grinding into each other, and grit to his twisted grin, he said, "I just wish I could find someone who does it better than you. I swear to you I will, and then you'll be gone." I said, "If we can find anyone who does something better than us, we'll copy what we can." He locked his eyes on mine and said, "Fuck you." I was not totally surprised but pleased. Slim Chance to none.

Thirty-three

Intentionally misleading the public about a person may could actually lead him to an untimely death. There was intention here, no doubt, if not to kill, then to wound. Should get the charges bumped up. No charges at all. Murder by advocacy. The Board.

~ ~ ~

Back in the day, in the tv series "Dragnet," Sgt. Joe Friday used to say, "All we want are the facts ma'am." We invoke Sgt. Friday now. The facts: Frank was a colleague, and then we hired him. A previously healthy person, he died at the hands of those who thrust our scandal years upon us. We'd like to think his death inadvertent, but if you send a horde of wasps into a crowd to disperse it, if someone with an allergy is fatally stung, that death was what? At the least, negligent homicide, that's what.

~ ~ ~

The director of our outreach program whose activities have been detailed here, an innocent, Frank was inspirational to many of the homeless we were trying to help. Not only for how hard he worked, but for how creative he was, as well for his impassioned motivational speeches. Many times, he "awakened" people to their potential, to a renewed belief in themselves, literally preparing them for self-help. Before we brought him on board with us, he worked for one of the more unscrupulous examples of social services elitism, Peter Smith. Peter was the ex-lawyer who had blown his cigar smoke at me before telling me, "It's only business," and then going out to trash me. He had been previously imprisoned for embezzlement of escrow accounts and a few other things, like lying under oath. His main claim to fame was that he once had been in Robert F. Kennedy's circles as a speech writer and staff aid. Probably because of this, upon finishing his jail term, spiritually renewed and born-again, Peter got a big second chance. At the time, New York's Mayor Ed Koch had been imploring churches, synagogues, and mosques to get more involved in helping the city's homeless. Literally right out of jail, Peter created a social services agency that answered the mayor's call. He started up an agency that essentially was a "church-bed program." What he'd do was pursue overnight use of community space in various houses of worship, mostly churches and synagogues. These spaces were sitting there empty, so why not? Not a bad idea. He'd ask them if he could set up 8-10 beds which he'd fill each evening by busing people directly from the city's drop-in-centers. He would yellow bus them to whichever facility would have them right after dinner, and then by 6am the next morning, out. He would staff each bed program with volunteers from within their very own congregations. The city's Building Department regulations did not permit the setting up of such beds at the drop-in-centers themselves, but they had no problem with allowing this in church settings. Ten or so beds per church led to hundreds of people on those buses every night, about one-tenth of the drop-in-center homeless population. They had to qualify in certain ways, like being sober, even-tempered, and willing. They'd also have to be willing to leave the Center after dinner to a place that had a 9pm lights-out curfew. Still, the selling point was that they could get out of the drop-in-center chair and into a bed, where they might sleep well, as opposed to being relegated to intermittent snoozing. We were one of those drop-in-centers, and we filled a hundred of these beds every night, which allowed us to invite even more people off the streets. It enabled us to increase our capacity to serve. One of the ways that Peter made this happen was by hiring salespeople like Frank to go and find willing churches, temples, and even some mosques.

When we were setting up our own programs, having met up with Frank at an evening Community Board Five meeting where he was making an impressive pitch for their continued support, we approached him and then, upon his advice, his boss, Peter. We have so many people coming to us, we just had to ask. Were there additional churches that could be developed but for the fact he didn't have enough city funding? "Yes," said Peter. "Could we put a dollar amount to the setting up and running one of these programs?" "Yes," said Peter. Okay then, our proposal was as follows: Given that our drop-in-center needed more beds, what if we could bring on additional churches to get us some more beds for our exclusive use? Upon analysis, we figured that it would cost us about $50,000 per church for start-up, perhaps half of that in the second year, and so forth. We would hire formerly homeless people instead of using volunteers to sit overnight in these makeshift facilities. More jobs. What do you think Peter? "We find the funding and you find the beds." Peter was all in. Very enthusiastic. Very. And, why not? "Yes, let's do that," he said.

A favorite writer of mine, Jerzy Kosinski, once said, "In that moment of feeling fused with articulation, one's very life expands. You can buy and sell and rent everything but that moment." The creation of this expansive church bed program felt like that, an incredible feeling when a one-of-a-kind plan begins to come together. We began immediately working with the business district for its approval, an easy task given the potential impact of having that many more beds to fill each night. They were enthusiastic. First, Peter, then them. We felt like we were on a roll. We went to the Human Resources Administration, the city's department of funding and oversight who funded Peter's agency and about 70% of ours, to inform them of this exciting partnership with Peter and his agency. Uh-oh. Problem in the form of a roadblock. They said we could not proceed. That if they allowed us to fund him for that, then Peter would be double-dipping. As they saw it, they were already paying him to do this work. "If you need more beds, tell us, and we will work with Peter to get him to allocate more beds to you. Peter can't take money from you to do what he is already in contract to do for us. He should know better. He's been in trouble for this kind of thing before," they said.

~   ~   ~

Not knowing anything of his ex-con background at that time, we went full disclosure. There was no easy way to research such things, no internet for me to access, this was 1989. Not knowing what the city meant but now more than just a little curious, we went to Peter directly to share the city's comments. Big mistake. We were being upfront, but with my naiveté` on the display-mode, we suppose it could be said that we were being indelicately honest? Peter face flushed red. Woah. What's up with that? Embarrassed? No. It was pure rage. Guess he was now the one who was fused with articulation. He screamed explosively not at us so much as at the room, his lawyer-like, darkened, leathered-up office. Immediately, perhaps forgetting my presence momentarily, he grabbed for his phone right there on the table, quick to make a few calls, each time slamming the receiver down, very, very dissatisfied. Then he turned to me, "How dare you? HOW DARE YOU!? You will regret this." What?

~   ~   ~

"Peter, we came to you to provide funding for your agency in return for something we really need. We were impressed by your operation. We hit it off, no? We are just telling you what they told us. We don't even know why you're so angry. Is it something maybe that we can work around?" Speaking through gritted teeth, he answered, "No, you are telling me this to try and get those beds for free. I have no idea what the city is talking about. I expect this deal to continue as planned." At his point, he wasn't totally wrong. If we could get them for free, shouldn't we? Yet, we did want those overnight jobs, and these beds had the potential to be year-round rather than seasonal, as the people volunteering to sit in the churches as monitors always took the summer off, which caused his church bed program to all but close. "Okay," we said, "I will go back to the office and discuss this with Dan, the business district's president, my boss. Maybe we can generate a letter of support from him. Meanwhile, you can talk to the city, and we'll see if there is clarification. In a day or two we will compare notes, okay?" "There's nothing to find out," said an insistent Peter. "Now, get out." Get out?

A few days later. "Hello Peter. Anything new?" "We need to proceed," he said. "Peter, I'm sorry to say this, but we can't do this deal unless we can obtain city approval. Not after they told us not to do it. Maybe we shouldn't have even asked them, but what would have happened then? Look, increasing the number of beds is the main thing here. If the city won't let us do it one way, maybe there is another way that they'd be comfortable with. Maybe we can give you a grant to hire another bed-developer like Frank and then our two programs could share those resources? Or maybe we can fund your agency to do something else, maybe something new?" His reply? "Fuck you."

He slammed the receiver down, emphatically hanging up on me. For me, was it to be a lesson? Wait a minute. Did I have to do what the city said? At this point though, of course I realized that I wouldn't be very smart to work with this guy at all. His reaction was mysteriously unsophisticated, what with his well-dressed demeanor, his shiny wooden office, all those law books left and right. For me, it was unexpectedly over the top. Yet, even if I did present a wall that he ran into, could he not have anticipated it?

What kind of peace had he made with his previous life's mistakes? How about none? Apparently, for him, revenge was all. He'd always been a sort of a one-man show, a loner, and clearly now, a loose cannon. Of course, also now, as a full-fledged member of The Board, he could drop the "loner" part, and for his new partners, loose cannon or not, be a brand-new weapon in their apparently ever-expanding arsenal. He'd spearhead a new front in The Board's ongoing effort to derail our operation, the business improvement district's social services operation, which he declared he was now against. Rather quickly, Peter became a highly motivated enemy of ours. Noam Chomsky, I ask you, did I manufacture that?

Inhabiting his new role, an example of perfect typecasting, Peter jumped into action. A few weeks later, he walked into the business improvement district's offices, 6 East 43rd St., right past the receptionist, and right past my office. I heard my phone beeping from the receptionist's attempt to reach me, then I saw him out of nowhere suddenly flashing past my door, theatrically stomping to far reaches of our large, subdivided space. Right into Dan's office he went. He literally pushed his door open, no knock-knock. I ran out of my office just in time to see him doing his thing, just in time to hear the loud thud of the door against the Dan's office wall. Wow. Dan had been in a private meeting with one of his assistants. No more. They both looked up more than a little bit startled. Peter was standing in his doorway, fuming, fists at his side. I could hear him hyperventilating. He was pissed. There was nobody else but him and Dan in the world. Mad-dog intensity. "If you don't want any trouble, you will have to immediately shift your social services funding to my agency. Right now. You hear me? Now. I will take care of whatever homeless problems your district has." Dan was composed, not angry, more amused than anything else, even if he was stern. "Hello Peter." "Don't hello Peter me. Make the change. I will take care of your social service needs. There doesn't have to be any trouble. DO IT NOW!"

A pivotal moment. Dan said that he already had someone in place to run programming. "Why not work with Jeff and find something else we can do together?" "I did not come here to negotiate," Peter replied as he stepped further into the room, Dan's assistant having walked out, and after having closed the door to speak with Dan alone, we could hear only the fact of his raised voice. A half-minute or so later, out came Peter, the door slamming this time against the metal frame behind him, shut closed, and there he stood, looking around. Very red-faced, speaking only to himself now, his words more a cacophony of snorts, his hands flailing, he walked extremely fast out of our offices.

Perhaps the city could have found a way to let it all happen. Peter's outrage was not totally wrong, maybe just misplaced, an important distinction, and a fellow in his position, post prison, needed to pay attention to such distinctions, no? He could have invoked a more-than-one-path-to-victory strategy. Maybe he could have carved out of the whole some more beds for us, I don't know, but if it was just extra funding he wanted, we could have worked that out somehow. Sadly, for him, fantastically for us, the path he chose impacted Frank. He and I had by then struck up an excellent and hopeful relationship. Discouraged by how things had worked out, Frank wanted very much to come on board with us. We worked it out. We hired him away from Peter.

Frank would do exactly as we planned, that is, work with us to develop additional "church beds." Not to further arouse Mr. Smith, we were careful to work only with those churches not currently in his fold. The heartwarming part to this story was that the program once developed, as predicted, really helped. We not only developed those new jobs, but we also specialized in developing beds for the "working homeless," those who were working or had other pressing start-of-the-day appointments to get to. What we did do above all else though, was cause Peter's position to harden like cold steel. He would be our enemy, born-again indeed.

Frank got us those seventy-five beds and we filled them night after night. It cost us about $25k per year per church, in each case getting us 12-15 more beds, and they'd be year-round! Frank was a very hard worker. Great guy. Same upbeat mood every day, a real can-do type of person. He became our assistant director of building operations, ran our church-bed program, and still found time to run motivation workshops. Whatever he tackled he did well at. No surprise, the people in our Center gave him all the credit for his achievement. They loved him. He was seen for what he was, an honest, down to earth guy, always on point, direct, no word play, he was especially straight with them and what with all his mottos, a little bit corny too. He was funny, loved irony, and did very little, small talk. Things were going very smoothly. I started up our outreach program and then pulled him into the project. He worked with me in selling our outreach program to private property managers. Then when it was up and running and growing nicely, Frank took over the outreach program itself. He and I realized that wherever there were homeless people, there was a highly motivated property manager or two or three who would pay for an outreach effort. This was for us a great discovery. These were the abandoned homeless, squatting on private property, efforts to help them not just underfunded, but nonexistent. There they were, having crossed the "private property line," what one of our more cynical outreach workers once, the city's "Mason Dixon line." Those homeless were left to whichever resources the property owner would bring to bear, which ranged from ignoring them to applying the full weight of their private security force. Armed guards. German Shephard dogs.

Private property outreach was ironically approached, a public/private partnership to be sure.
Grassroots from the top down saw self-helping peers, once unemployed, now in the lead.
The true experts in the field, successfully working where others had failed. The police dogs were now gone, their show of power poetically replaced. By Frank.

Having been first approached by New York Savings Bank because they were frustrated by a homeless presence in their three ATMs, we agreed to investigate it. Over the next week, I drove into the city twice to visit the ATMs between 3am and 6am, as we knew for sure that if anyone were living in them, they'd be "home" at that hour. I returned the next day to the office with news that we would have to notify New York Savings that they don't really have much of a problem. Only one of their three ATMs had someone sleeping in it. We'd have to withdraw our planned programming. Dan said: "What? Are you kidding me? That's a one in three chance that an ATM customer might encounter a sleeping homeless person. That's horrible." And so, it was. And so, our program was born. Frank came to run it, beautifully, for five years. No complaints. Lots of attention. Very positive press. Awards and accolades. Reporters, in the know, followed our workers around. Met with them. Discussed their success, their personal trials, and tribulations. But then, along came the good squad allegations. Frank was named as its leader. And in more than a few ways, like those outlined here, that did not sit well with him. The press was told by the worst of them that he wore dark sunglasses and drove in a large limousine just behind his outreach workers, urging them to "do what you gotta do." Of course, they implied "mob." He was after all, an Italian man. And he was that; he was also living in a real-life suburban community where prior, among his peers, he had social standing. He was more than devastated. He was traumatized. From it all, there was just one person, that's Frank, who ended up dead. Dead. No joke. Frank died. March 2000. Was healthy, then died. A young family man, a wonderful person. He died as a direct result of their intentional lies. He went from one week where he was running a beautiful outreach program to profoundly worrying about defending his integrity. He took two lie detector tests and passed them both, spoke up whenever he could, researched every accusation, went through reams of paperwork, thinking on it, working on clearing his name around the clock. Like us all, he struggled to disprove a negative while his hands were tied. Everything we wanted to say had to go through first our lawyer and then our publicist. Everything had to be rehearsed. How would it look if we said this or did that? What would their response be? Okay, then what would you do? What about after that? Funny, but I always felt that all we had to do at any point was ask them to talk to the homeless in our geographic area or right there, in our program. The BID hired Howard Rubenstein, the fixer's fixer. He said "No, you never know what the homeless would say." They'll say the truth Howard – THAT IT NEVER HAPPENED IN ANY WAY SHAPE OR FORM, that's what. Okay, maybe they will shout it out with a rough, un-presidential like attitude, but it'll be the truth. "We better not," said Howard, ever cautiously. "Don't go there."

Meanwhile, our accusers said that the homeless were too

vulnerable to be questioned. They were too troubled to "understand" all of this anyway. If all of them were incapable, what about your pretend informants? No, The Board knew it was best to keep the press away from the homeless themselves. They knew it would blow up the position they were taking against us.

How to respond? Oh yeah, from the top of our totem pole came the marching orders – they signed on with Bruce Cohen, the publicist, a genuinely nice person whose experience was mostly to enhance public awareness of our achievement and Howard Rubenstein, the fixer, a legend. They called the shots – no talking with reporters, nothing proactive without their approval. We all knew the charges were bullshit. We just weren't sure how to prove it. Obviously, with the newspapers declaring that our outreach workers were part of a goon squad affected Frank differently than most of the rest of us. He was being blamed and the charges were so fantastic as to take on a life of their own. We were all taking hits of course with none of us quite sure as to what lie they'd next put out. The papers were eating it up. They were making dust. Classic obfuscation.

In Frank's case, he had left a sales career to help homeless people. He was personally gratified by his work, his family too so very proud of him. His friends admired him for his career change, and you could see why. He was the guy who would hang motivation signs throughout the workplace to insert positive thinking wherever it might be absent. Day in day out, he'd confront problems with the most supportive of statements. Going through something? Hang with Frank, you'll feel better in minutes. With lots of humor, in constant motion, Frank was tireless in his efforts. We'd talk on the phone all hours when we were off from work too, never off, just absorbed by the mission. How could we do this better? How could we help this or that person better? However, and this was

Frank's bad luck, to disable our outreach effort, they decided to take him down, our director of outreach. Their main move was to play into stereotypes, what with him being Italian, and they pinned the goon squad operation on him. His homeless were apparently people who at his behest would beat up other homeless people. The homeless innocent though and he was the real perpetrator; he held the strings. As the media was told, so they wrote. "He wore dark sunglasses and was said to be emerging from some long dark automobile." So sinister. They quoted unnamed sources. "He was obviously a mobster, we all knew it," said Pinocchio, one of our ex-outreach workers, now one of several self-proclaimed "former goons." Frank's last name, it ends with a vowel, right? Oh boy, as a proud Italian American, Frank felt the stigma deep in his heart. The pain ran through his whole body. Truth was that people were beginning to avoid him within his own community. They were questioning their previously held high opinions of him. All these years, the inferences, had he been pretending to be a good guy while secretly running a goon squad? Frank was crushed. He began noticing problems with the way he was breathing. It felt first like a chest cold. Around-the-clock anxiety was what it was though, but soon, it went beyond that. He was literally having trouble breathing. He told me that his lung capacity seemed diminished. Just stress? He hoped that's what it was. Rapid, shallow breaths was all. It was impossible to clear the airwaves with even one deep breath. What the hell? Lung congestion? Finally, the doctors at Columbia-Presbyterian hospital figured out what the problem was. Frank had developed a type of aggressive arthritis that turns on internal organs, usually seen post trauma, but only after very serious trauma, like when a mother loses a child, the doctor said. Frank couldn't handle even one staircase. He had to sleep downstairs on the sofa. He kept losing lung function. The doctor reported that the arthritis had reduced Frank to 40% of lung function, a situation ripe for a deadly bout of pneumonia. His capacity was sapped. He went from six feet plus tall to, or so it seemed, much less than that as he was almost always bent over coughing, now unable to work. Reduced to his living room chair, his standing in the community was all but gone. It was not long before this previously outstanding and very robust man passed away. Murdered by advocacy.

They turned false confessions into self-confessed false statements to the press. When Frank died, there was no more talk of him, his killers never brought to justice. They were never even accused. That's right, they have never been stood up against any kind of wall. Until now? Well, perhaps they did not plan his death, however, he did die at their hands. Demolition 101. No apologies? No making of amends, no accountability. No caring. What did they do? They plowed into a crowd, and someone "accidentally" died. Think Charlottesville. They left their victim on the side of the road. Frank.

All of it was made up. Was Frank's death just collateral damage? No, they targeted him, probably not with murder on their minds, just his demise. Not their fault? Tell it to the judge. Frank lay there on his living room sofa wilting away, fifty miles away in the quiet New Jersey suburb of Westwood, NY, while oblivious reporters, dazzled by their sure-to-come Pulitzer Prize, toiled away in the big city, speaking of how Frank motioned from his ever-present limousine, following the outreach team in the shadows, giving orders to his goon squad to carry out unspeakable acts. They said that was how we "succeeded," their air quotes, at getting the homeless off the streets, by beating them until they agreed to come to our Center. They said the homeless were too afraid to speak up.

There were no dark sunglasses, no limousines, no "do what you gotta do" shouted out of their driver's window or while standing beside them, none of it. Yet somehow it was "eye witnessed" and reported by four or five ex-employees, none of whose stories stood up to subsequent investigations. They had, all of them, been suspended for various reasons. However, it was Frank who died as a direct result of their "admissions" of criminal actions for which they'd been promised to pay no penalty. Like the death of a person who is stricken by a fatal heart attack when he stumbles upon a burglar – that burglar is seen as responsible and is charged additionally and accordingly, no? Here, we call it as we see it. "Murder by advocacy." The Board had motive and opportunity.

One thing we know we can say, for all his great work, and he was a beautiful person, now buried and unknown, is that the homeless, even "the goons," never had a chance, and neither did Frank.

Thirty-four

If we want to limit someone by way of the labeling process, "homelessness," in this case, you are basing it on the fact that they've got no reliable place to live. Do that, and you are lumping them in, those two million homeless people, with tens of millions of cost-burdened others, including those on the brink, into an apparently unwinnable affordable housing fight, nationwide, small victories aside. It's a housing fight very few win. Most don't and, going by the last forty years of effort and outcome, people who are homeless only get access to a little bit of the little bit. 90% will have to continue to wait for someone else to win their fight against a society of landlords in a country where the quest for ownership and business-for-self entrepreneurial attitudes reigns supreme. Can we say, good luck with that?

There are 10 million Americans who own multiple homes. There are 17 million vacant homes. Okay, given the American ethos, and all the red tape surrounding vacancies, plus the fact that there is nothing inherently wrong or illegal in owning something you keep empty or unused, these numbers are not going to change much. On the new construction end, even if a sufficiently bold, broad, and immense enough initiative were launched by government and builders alike, to provide affordable housing to all those millions of Americans who need it, homeless people included, we would be talking about many, many years down the road for it all to come to fruition. And there are no such initiatives on the housing horizon. What about that guy or gal sitting in that drop-in-center chair or shelter bed right now, today, and for many, many years to come?

Possibility #2: There is no housing for them. So, we do our best to help. We start by enabling the people who have no reliable place to live by attending to their many disconnections. Back to Jon Donne. Segue to Liebow. Employment. Put another way, help them on the income side, that is, to make enough money to buy their way back into unaffordable housing. Cynical? How about practical? This way, they won't have to sit in shelters sweating out their congregate existence as we make the "dream appeal" to landlords and the society that will not have them. Not to forget, they are unemployed. That's not a situation that most landlords are drawn to. For self-esteem, certainly, but for ending homelessness, that's not good. In this America, it will keep you homeless. More simply put: People should not have to rely in on housing-first advocacy, no choice, looking for that one in a hundred landlord. It's right in front of us. Can't we get them the jobs they need? Sure, we can. In many cases, we can be their employers.

If possibility #2 is not chosen, if you've become homeless, be forewarned, the barrier to your success will not be your disability, attitude, or personality diagnosis, none of that; it'll be seen in the power of others. Put another way, the beneficiaries of that first approach are not going to be you, the downtrodden. It will be those to whom you are expected to report. The momentum in this industry is all in their hands. They can be fierce, and so far, they are winning. Bigly.

~ ~ ~

Madame du Barry's comment at the guillotine, "Just a moment, executioner," has morphed into the homeless advocate in the courtroom, "With all due respect, your Honor."

The homeless never had a chance, and in our effort to help them, neither did we. Mainly this is because of the putative conglomerate, The Board. They get off first, fast, and often. The strategy has been to be get and stay in control of the labeling, essential, and then to oversee the public response. It's a vast social problem. There are so many people needing those three hots and a cot, impoverished and disconnected both. Sad it had to come to that, but the broader the definition, the bigger the problem, the bigger The Board grows, the more important they become, the more condescending too, but that's a different story, to wit, their ever-lowering expectations bring about a mindset that stoops down to talk. For the gal or the guy on the shelter bed, it can't get much worse than to have to look up and see all that. "Now, now, let me tuck you in." Get lost.

One of The Board's most influential and powerful ad hoc members, The Son, faced a press pool, a sheaf of blank papers in his hand, which he shook to emphasize his fabrications. "They housed their goons with HUD money," he falsely claimed. Actually, a few years later, after a protracted legal fight to obtain it by way of the FOIA, and they fought furiously against its release, we saw what was in the real report, what they wanted kept under wraps. What? That the investigators concluded quite the opposite of what The Son was saying, him with the American flag in full wave behind him. "Grunberg should have known better than to use such frail and vulnerable people to perform such a complicated task as outreach. These folks wanted better than they got," said The Son, mimicking the sounds of credibility, forever self-grooming for the Presidency. The Son spoke so compellingly as to rise over his own horizon. More importantly, what he said was accepted as a given by the press pool, instantly believed, the homeless, our puppets, and we, the puppet masters. Thankfully, years later, by way of the Freedom of Information Act, we were able to get our hands on that report. It appeared that The Son had never read it.

Most people without affordable housing are not homeless. Most poor people are not homeless either. Very few people earning a living-wage at a full-time job are homeless. They find housing.

Not being able to afford something has at least two sides to it, probably many more. First, the price for housing is being set by market forces, right? No, not really. The USA's current system allows the landlord, except in cases of rent control, which in NYC covers about 1% of its housing, more ways to "skin a cat." Most of today's landlords aren't forced to do much. There's rent stabilization, true, but still, the landlord has more wiggle room than their tenant's tight budget could ever handle. There are so many ways around whatever controls have been put into place, preferential rent-setting for example. Point is, profits don't have to be maximized, that's just our way and, as we said, we should not expect that to change? It's just that landlords know full well that there are plenty of people doing well enough to pay whatever the going rate is, and they set that. In fact, marketplace analysts call it "pain in the market" when rents are "forced" to come down. Most property owners will use comparative sales to inform their own price-setting, true but most of the time, the property managers have ways to impose their will. For example, they might want a certain tenant so badly they renovate the space specifically for them and not for others, or they might offer incentives specifically to attract certain tenants. Sometimes they'll not want certain tenants, so they raise the bar to screen them out. Sometimes this; sometimes that. Point is, except in case of rent control, they are not really forced to set their prices anywhere, and they can pick their tenants. They decide what to do to get the best return on their time and money spent. They call it "market forces," and they say, "Hey, it's out of my hands." In a market-driven system, the clarion call is for the most profit for the least work. Maybe the complicating factor here, is the "least work" part?

If someone has no reliable housing, and for survival, needs that housing but just can't pay for it, doesn't that render a lot of this rental price-setting as price gouging?

Jerzy Kosinski, in *Beyond Homelessness*: "I have great respect for the homeless individual, whom I refuse to see as a victim of society, and I refuse to see as a victim of his or her own self. I see the homeless person as a chance being at the mercy of forces that he or she was not able to figure out or may not be able to figure out. And if he or she cannot figure out the state of homelessness, why should he or she when the state cannot figure it out either?" Insight. The unemployed person is reconnected with society through his work ethic. He is reconsidered then as a self-sufficient person. Ironic. Yet, in survival mode, so much at stake, aren't they among the most self-sufficient?

Besides the individual in full-blown psychosis for whom the outer world has lost significance,

Emerson's notion of self-reliance aside, who among us is truly self-sufficient anyway? Bob Dylan:

"Name me someone that's not a parasite and I'll go out and say a prayer for him." We define self-sufficiency by our relationship to others. We calibrate our sense of independence and self-define through others. However, what the psychotic person has in common with just about anyone entering the shelter system is there's been a final "break." That piece of straw that broke that camel's back. The person shows himself to have been increasingly unable to intervene in the run-up to his own break. The psychotic is increasingly cut-off too, his prodrome phase realized full-time, the decline experienced in real-time. Apparently, mental health researcher Rachel Aviv wrote, it is impossible to predict the precise moment when a person has embarked on a path toward madness. For the person to whom it is happening in real time, it is also difficult to locate the moment in which their descent into insanity began. For this, retrospect is all we've got.

With homelessness, certainly not primarily psychological, it is not so very different. There is a long process of incremental detachment, which we can call the descent into homelessness. The landlord can turn the key overnight, but typically not without a heads-up. Often, there is a protracted run-up, which we will likely read as a decline in person's quality of living, typically, again, related to income. Soon, the disconnection is complete, a storyline partially embedded in what Robert Jay Lipton calls "proteanism." In his book, *The Protean Self: Human Resilience in An Age of Fragmentation*, he said that in the best of situations, modern-day proteanism adds to a person's capacity to handle what has become a multi-dimensional society, successful multi-tasking that does not result in loss of self. In those cases, it allows for the integration of a personality's many parts into a cohesive whole. Yet, to a person whose life is more fragmented and downward trending, it may very well have the opposite effect, it may enhance the capacity for their demise. In this sense, a "home" speaks to the idiopathic process of disconnection no better than a pill speaks to the prodromal process of psychosis. Instead of arguing the "cause" of the break, rarely definitive, consider that the break's the thing. And the stress that follows is yet another thing. If it's debilitative, it triggers treatment. Answer: Prevention and recovery are best handled by way of social connectivity.

Employment generates social connectivity in ways unmatched and it can parlay itself mathematically into a future where prevention from the worst, shelter or street life, no choice, is going to be more likely. Containing a certain type of social glue, employment can be gainful too; actually, it must be gainful, or a person would have to forever rely on holding down two jobs, or three, but doesn't that subtract him or her from participation in family life, no choice? The plight of those earning less than a living wage. Market forces? Can't the employer pay him more? Okay, here is where government can step in. The money to enable that employer to pay a living wage can be provided directly or through tax incentives. We can call it "fair work." You see, if he gets less than a living wage, he'll need rental assistance. Food stamps as well. So, the government, can redirect funding already in place. Many of the jobs are already there too. Attrition is real. For example, there are two million federal jobs, 16% of which open annually just through voluntary separations, that is, people quitting, or retiring, etc., the rate being usually about 16%. In 2017, little different, the attrition rate was higher, at 16.7%, where over 450,000 jobs became available, enough to take care of the total number of able-bodied homeless adults, 18-64 years of age, on any given day. Just saying. There are very few places to look for affordable housing, but lots of places to look for jobs that can lead a person to housing affordability.

Some laws and/or rules would have to be changed in favor of a public/private partnership that would bestow consumer rights, for example, the right to choose your program and its direction. People need to be empowered to run from the shelter and the label both, right into newly reconfigured employment hostels, no longer homeless warehouses, that would be about connecting them to people and places, that would be about employability, a quick, direct solution, short term. What of the long term? Can't they be linked to the life-credits division of their local state university? Their near demise, and their struggles to avoid it, could count towards their college degree. It's done all the time. Infusing their past experiences with more value, it would give course credit for their knowledge and experience like it does for those of us never-been-homeless. For their survival to date, give them credit.

A negative competency to be sure, The Board performs as if a complaint department for a major department store. Most of the clocks Macy's sells work perfectly, a few of them, however, do not. "It doesn't keep proper time," say the complaints. Many hundreds are sold; five come back broken and so, quite deservedly, there are five complaints. Instead of putting the five into perspective alongside those many hundreds, The Board holds a press conference to announce that the clocks, which the "all-too-powerful, overpaid, muckity-mucks" at Macy's are selling don't work. "They don't respect their customers!" The press reports the fact of those broken clocks with some powerful headlines, no perspective offered: "Time Stands Still: Macy's Sells Clocks That Don't Work." It cannot be denied.

Labels direct us. For those of us who may wish to help someone, labels guide us. Here, the label "homeless" directs us to help find or create a "home" for this other person, where to help in a way other is to defy the very label itself. Call that a case of "label dysfunction." It has underserved them. There are a lot of other things that they can't afford. "Lacking the ability to afford" is a central problem. The fact that they are relatively disconnected drives that. We want labels that can point us towards corrective, possibly redemptive, action. For most of us there is little reason to over-contemplate that. Understood, given that the homes are not there and not coming, apparently, this term "homeless" helps housing advocates only, not the people themselves. The people affected, are self-defining differently.

There is enough reason to believe that re-labeling might be transformative. For example, the word "homeless" locks out everybody who might want to help but who can't provide that home. It puts limits on a homeless person's chances at making rent. It shapes the conversations around him who is failing and those who are failing him; it limits the caregiver too.

The idea of housing-first is that if housing were available to a person who also needed treatment for a serious personal problem, he or she would be given that housing, later receiving whatever other (treatment) help was needed. This is based on the humane premise that you do not ask someone to wait for that day when they are ready for housing, i.e., people are always ready for a stable roof. But affordable and accessible housing has been increasingly difficult to find since the early 80's. But even when landlords do have something available, they want the most stable people they can find. Ironically, these landlords, since 1990 or so, were usually social service providers themselves. To house their clients, they went into the non-profit housing business. As they scanned their caseloads, the discussion always centered on readiness. Could the person take care of his home and himself without such support? What about with it? What kind of support and how much? Program people started developing trait-centered specialties – wanting specific types of readiness in specific types of people. It was women over 50 with dementia, or veterans in recovery, or elderly people, or kids who aged-out of Foster Care, and so forth. Agencies acquired their own housing, which they needed to keep filled, for solvency's sake, drawn from their specialized cadre of clients. And then, they'd offer on site-treatment, something referred to as "supported housing." Hence, housing-first, when possible, but, since there is little housing, nearly every person in the shelter system, is ostensibly being prepped for that day when a "housing-first" opportunity comes. The Board champions housing-first, indeed, demands it, but that's not usually what happens. Usually, the very system they strive to replace, treatment first if anything, is what happens.

Question. If people can be placed into housing and then supported if needed, why oppose giving someone a supported job, even at your own social services agency? It is an odd question to begin with, and the answer is obvious. We ask it because the housing isn't there, and we know it, but the jobs are.

With a job, they can pay into housing. In most of society, besides surviving a credit check, a person needs housing references to obtain housing, and in many cases, as we have learned, the long-term homeless person would not be able to hold onto the housing without supports. Housing-first short circuits all that. It invents a reality, which did not exist prior and does not exist for the person outside of the invented reality. Okay, go for it, but don't refer to our offering someone a job without employment references, and then offering supports if needed, as not being reality-based? "It doesn't happen in the real world," you say. Yet, given the wide availability and need for the services of employee-assistance programs by the general population, it apparently happens all the time. It is more reality-based than you say. No?

"Rough sleeper." A common use phrase in England referring to people who sleep in the open air, outdoors, as in, I'm homeless, but not in a shelter. In this country, given the state of the shelter system, for most people who are currently labeled "homeless," it is an accurate label that can be applied to people in shelters as well. It speaks this way: "I'm not sleeping in an optimal place. I might be homeless, but not necessarily. I'm sleeping rough, that is, not in a place meant for people to sleep. It's not a place which I command. I'm roughing it." They might need our help with housing, they might not. They might have other problems, they might not. It's innocuous enough, yet it tells the truth about their sleeping conditions, and that's all. Certainly, it doesn't put us somewhere we can't get out of. It's all in the name, "rough." That is, until they come into some money, then better times ahead. Rough sleeping is a modified, active verb that part of a strategic action plan. The person is a protagonist looking to sleep in a better place. Bet you the first question he'll ask is: Got a job?

Usually but not always applied to those living outside, given the conditions of so many of our shelters, and its poor outcomes, the term "rough sleeper" needs to be extended. That's right. In New

York City, they've got 60,000-plus people who are sleeping "rough" all over town and only some of them are outdoors.

Having to sleep rough is the ultimate sign that you need to increase your income. The rough sleeper knows that. Talk to some of them. They'll tell you. They might tell you they're afraid they can't hold a job, but they'll work with you if you promise to work with them. They don't want to rely on someone or something else other than their own two hands. Otherwise, they'll lose time, which snowballs away. Soon they're stuck on several lists, bumper to bumper, for as far as their eyes can see. There's a governmental term, long in-use, now in relative disfavor, out of hearing range yet still widely applied, which is "housing-ready," which they are likely not. But, good news, did you ever hear of our brand-new, aggressively optimistic, "housing-first" approach? If you're not working, you qualify. In fact, please don't even look for a job. Grow, shelter system, grow.

How about this construct? People living in shelters or on the streets are, relative to the whole, isolated, and disconnected. Surrounded by downwardly mobile peers, their collective disconnectedness putting them at a disadvantageous position when social networking. Their situation, traumatic, can wear them down in many little and big ways, their capacity for problem-solving diminished. Where there is illness or addiction, there is gross level detachment too. Their whole situation, a social condition, literally prevents healthy connections with healthy others. Lastly, from that world of "others" comes stigma, often played out in what ethno-methodologist Harald Garfinkel calls "status degradation ceremonies." There is personal shame too, internalized stigma experienced as embarrassment. Taken to its extreme, when employers do not need him, think Elliot

Liebow, he will not be able to make the rent. This is not about his having competing priorities, it is about the snowball that landed him in the shelter or on the street. His mind, the last recourse to battling his demons, might even be failing him, now what? Gainful employment solves a few problems.

While Sigmund Freud was developing an understanding for the inner workings of psychiatrically disabled people, Alfred Adler was studying the psychological roots of society and to what degree a person's social participation impacts their mental health. He referred to the need for social functioning to be measured by a person's "social interest."

"The Networker Effect: Being a good networker pays off—but it requires skill as well as shamelessness. It's not just for the elites." Joseph Schumpeter, The Economist, January 2015.

The Joseph Rowntree Foundation, a British-based independent social change organization, studied worklessness, a relatively new term that covers economic inactivity, not just unemployment. Simply put, what they found: Tackling worklessness and low pay reduces poverty and decreases public expenditure on welfare spending and tax credits, with indirect savings in other public service areas, including healthcare, crime, and social services. Say it again.

Half of all private non-profit or public service jobs that address homelessness, already paid for by government, could be turned over to the people they are serving, the homeless themselves. That would cover about 50,000 jobs in New York State alone, about half of which are in New York City. So, since we recommend that half of all jobs serving the homeless should go to the homeless, that takes care of jobs for about 12,000 sheltered New Yorkers. And that is only in the non-profit sector. This covers more than half of the able-bodied people living in our shelters. This would energize just about everybody else. There'd be ancillary support programs, preparatory programs, training programs, educational efforts, all for a purpose. This could be accomplished in just a few years through attrition alone. Think Eugene Lang.

In this era of Facebook, Twitter, Instagram, Snapchat, LinkedIn, and Pinterest, what with all the emailing and texting, our cellphones within reach always, our every device speaking to each other, we are just oozing with our need to stay connected. To be less socially networked, less in touch with those we love, whether sitting in our living rooms next to them or not, is to lead ourselves towards the very sort of social disconnection we seem to fear, a long and bumpy road, one that leads all the way to being alone on a street corner or in a shelter bed. It is an economic condition, always, but there is a psychological ledge that long term unemployment can push a person over.

If we look at life as a series of connections, interrelated thanks to our personal protean dynamic, a social machinery whose moving parts are greased by interactions large and small, then we begin to see what a rescue from a shelter bed would look like. No housing – what then? It's going to have to be just as relevant, the way that a variety of exercises can work the core. Face it. If nothing else, let's be Monday morning quarterbacks. A job is easier to create than an apartment. In many cases it is already there, unused. And a job makes housing more affordable. Did we say that already? What about the fact that it is the social machinery of connectedness? Are we repeating ourselves? A home will absolutely make things better, but employment takes care of everything, homelessness too. That's it. Maybe the term for the people who, were they not unemployed, would likely not be homeless, is "homelessly unemployed."

Thirty-five

Grand Central Terminal. Beneath its 130-foot-tall domed ceilings, in and around its 60 shops and 35 places to eat, there's a lot of what could be called "social" work going on or so any ethnomethodologist would say, for example, Harold Garfinkle. Micro-sociology. What else? It is jam-filled with on-the-spot apologies, a redundant aftermath of people smacking into each other, grunting in their self-centered efforts to "do it all" in an optimistic, can-do, New York minute. Some are working cell phones, others just the room, the happy ones singing to themselves that maybe today will be the day. So then, everybody is handcuffed to a dance of status calibrations, inside a jail of sound laid out on one big indoor sidewalk as out sized and massive as not wide enough.

~ ~ ~

Re-established for most out-of-towners and many New Yorkers alike as a premier place to window-shop or people-watch, in the 90's, Grand Central Terminal transcended its once relegated status as a mere thoroughfare, now a destination-point as well. The midtown rush, born of necessity, was not without charm. Through it all, through the expanse of a dozen gilded doors out onto Lexington Avenue, a long-established scene, newspaper hawkers sitting side-by-side next to black and white stacks of what New York cynics would call "tomorrow's fish wrap." Noticeably, with a casual-Fridays look, Goodwill-clothed perhaps, a self-styled businessman was just ten feet away, selling New York's newest street paper, BIGnews. You'd never know it, but that guy used to be homeless. Not now.

~ ~ ~

In different cities, all over the world, there were at the time about 75 street newspapers, all of them designed to be sold by homeless people. Plus, there were about 40 in the USA, same thing, most every paper polemic in nature, rallying against the rut that people without money are forced into, no input, no respect, offering the perspective of people otherwise ignored. With free batches given out to those who attend an orientation meeting and sign a code of conduct, they get to keep whatever money they make in sales. After he sells the newspapers, we give him, money in hand, additional copies can be purchased at a fraction of the cover price for resale. Work when you want to, when your schedule permits, when you're able to, don't work if you don't want to that day, or the next. But the next? Fine. That's the formula, approved by the International Network Street Papers association, as well as our own National Association for Street Newspapers Association. Street Papers offer a radical escape route? Radical? It's about employment. Imagine that. That's radical. But it is also for the literary writer or investigative reporter or person with something to say, or whomever wants to sell a service in the classified listings, but most likely of course to establish or to supplement his income.

I had been approached by John Bird, now Lord Bird of The British House of the Lords, then just a guy who started off his own such publication for the poor, Big Issue, still today one of the few street papers worldwide not so much polemic as entertaining. It grew very big. His founding purpose was to create a sales moment to be sure, but he insisted it was not about preaching to the converted so much as being a truly transactional experience. Previously unaware of each other, both the seller and the buyer benefitted. Perfect. "Nobody's perfect," sings Chrissie Hynde "not even the perfect stranger." Well, these two were as close to being perfect strangers, one of them, an unknown, not hiding so much as hidden, the other, out and about, with dollars to spare, which made the whole transaction perfectly strange and strangely perfect. Now at the point-of-sale, they're talking. By the time John and I met, the Big Issue had spread to four or five other countries as well. He had "discovered" me, he said, in his search for someone who was like-minded, that is, employment oriented, entrepreneurial by nature, involved with homeless people directly, all hands-on deck. Big Issue USA? He asked me, did I want to join forces with him in a publishing venture? "I love the Big Issue and the idea of street papers. Yes." Okay, first things first, in New York, not wanting to encroach on the city's street paper already there, one of those polemic scribes, Street News, the first street paper anywhere, we approached them. Did they want to partner, work with us, or at least have an insert? No, no, and no. The paper's publisher, Indio, wanted no part of working as he put it, with "the corporate Big Issue." And, it was true, Big Issue had corporate underwriters and quite a bit of advertising support. And so, we went on to visit several different cities in search of the best place to launch. Met some fascinating people. Bird was mercurial as in "it'd be wrong to take him at face value," but he was intellectually adventurous, and quite serious about his take on homelessness. Once a "rough-sleeper" himself, both charming and rough then, he was open enough to be "changeable," forever young? We returned to New York, then he back to London. We had a few conversations, and he flew me out to his offices where I met with his Chief of Operations. We agreed on how we'd work together in the states. First New York, where we'd try again to work with Indio, but either way we'd start up our paper, then we'd take it to those states in which there were yet to be any paper. I returned to New York. Further conversations were planned. Six months went by – no contact. I couldn't reach him. Then I reached his operations chief who told me John had traveled to California a half-year earlier and met a young woman with whom out there he settled down. Next thing, he "switched ideas," from one plan, his and mine, to another, his and hers. Alas, their relationship cooled and so too did he on the USA, deciding that maybe it was not the best place to launch a Big Issue after all. He returned to Europe and launched it in a dozen other countries besides maintaining his extraordinary success with it in the UK. It never happened as we planned it, but he did propel me into the street paper business. I was able to start something for us in New York. We decided on a different format, more about the arts, writing, photography, and outsider art, all of it with a focus on poverty. First, we'd start something in-house, we said, and we did. *Upward* was written by and for homeless men and women, with tips and thoughts on survival, short stories, and poetry, written exclusively by the homeless themselves and distributed for free in shelters. If it went well, we'd try to establish our own street paper, which we did. *BIGnews* was to be a magazine/street paper, an income producer, sold by the homeless for their profit.

After a lunch-meeting orientation session and a meet-and-greet with current vendors, the wannabe salespeople sign a code of conduct agreement, receive a vendor clip-on badge for when selling, then receive 10 copies of the latest issue of our BIGnews to be sold at one dollar apiece to the public, free as a start-up gift for them. They could keep what they took in sales, but if they wanted to continue selling, they'd have to buy future copies at $.25 apiece. They'd go on to make their profit, and we'd get back the cost to print. Spend $2.50 to make $10, 7.50 in profit. Sell one hundred each week, a common amount, and the take would be $300 monthly. Some people housed themselves by selling 3 or 4 times that many. Soon, we had more than a hundred vendors, many of whom would start each morning, after a cup of coffee at our offices, by purchasing as many as 25, or 50, or 100 copies for their day's work. Again, and again.

From a BIGnews article, *Can-Picking in Bedford Stuyvesant*:

> The street, when it is gotten close to, has the feel
> of the neighborhood in an intimate way, as if you
> are entering a bunch of houses and being

anthropological; and the trash cans and debris found on them tell stories of consumerism that I wished to ignore. The intricate patterns of the frost, and the dirt, and the stray pieces of paper, held secrets that I would rather not hear and cannot explain.

We launched. BIGnews was an outsider art, photography, and writing newspaper, which was more of a magazine. Both. It was a monthly. It was beautiful. And it grew. We had several advertisers and sponsors. At its peak over its seven-year life we were giving away or selling close to 20,000 copies a month to our homeless and formerly homeless vendors and they, of course, in turn, sold it to the public. There were about 120 people selling it around the city, several of them surviving on that income alone, others using it to supplement whatever else they had coming in. By then our writing groups grew large and were widely popular at the Center. We belonged to a national and international street paper network. The NYC Commissioner for Homeless Services herself had a column in the paper; writers like Robert Sheckley, Ben Cheever, Jim Knipfel, Lee Stringer, Kofi Annan, illustrators such as Nick Bertozzi, Dean Haspiel, and our group of regulars we'd come to rely on for high quality published material. They were artists James Jajac, Brad Frederick, Fernanda Cohen, and writers J.L. Navarro, John Ray, Jr., Michael Hunter, and Misha Firer. Excellence. BigNews was a legitimate part of New York's outsider art scene. Drawing various awards from within our industry, truly excited, we drew in a multitude of new volunteers, and garnered some great interest from several "underground" newspapers around the country as well as some in what we now call "the mainstream media." From Sylvester's *I Walk the Streets*:

> Most of the stores I knew back when were gone. Gone too were most of the people I knew or had known. But I wasn't looking for a place or a person in particular, I just was pressing forward,

not knowing when I'd tire and stop. You see, they call me Sly, and I walk the streets.

Homeless Soccer. In 2002, our participation in the street newspaper scene led us to our participation in the formation of a worldwide homeless soccer program. We were attending a newspaper conference in Capetown, South Africa. One evening, in a pub close to the hotel, editors from a number of street newspapers gathered together for a night out, from Scotland, Austria, England, Germany, and of course, the USA. Here was a bunch of soccer crazy countries, and then there was us. A friendly argument emerged – "I bet you that our vendors could beat your vendors in a soccer game. Oh yeah? Yeah." Two years later, it happened. What? Homeless soccer, that's what.

Four on four, a goalie plus three on each team on a field about the size of a tennis court, in 14-minute games. Once the game started, there was no break until the 7-minute mark. Not even stopping to insert or pull a player, "running" substitutions were required, with only a one-minute break at the 7- minute mark. Exciting, you could pass the ball to yourself, just bang it off a nearby wall at just the correct angle and then meet up with the ball again on the ricochet. Happened all the time and then, bang! Goal! Wow. It was an explosive fourteen minutes to be sure, so exciting.

Not in a soccer crazy country, how would we do it? How would we locate players? We decided that besides making general announcements, to find enough players what we'd do is approach a feeding line, let's say on 28th street, early morning, and wave to a group of people. When we got their attention, we'd roll a soccer ball in their direction. Always, someone would run off the line out to "greet" the ball, dribble it between their feet for a few steps and then, boom, kick it back to us. That was our soccer player! First, we'd introduce him to our street paper program. If they became a vendor, we'd invite them to soccer practice and from these few, we'd assemble our team. In determining who amongst all our players would be one of the eight we'd take with us on our trip to the tournament, often this meant we had to prioritize whichever players could obtain travel documents. Sometimes, it would prove impossible to take our best players, for perhaps they might not be able to obtain a birth certificate, for example, which they'd need to obtain their passport. Oh well, they may not make the final cut, but at least then, a process was underway to obtain their much-needed documents even if not in time for the big trip. Also, they still were gaining so much from the practices themselves, exercise, camaraderie, a break from their troubles.

Our street paper vendors would play against vendors from around the world in homeless soccer tournaments held each year in a different country. The Homeless World Cup. In our first competition, 2003, we took a team to Austria. Eighteen countries did the same. The players, most of whom had never even left New York City, let alone been on an airplane before, were excited beyond their wildest dreams to participate. It truly was amazing to see them discover new places, meeting and interacting with people from all over the world, the adulations of the roaring crowds in center-city Graz, Austria, upwards of 1000 attendees per game, proving we weren't alone in our fascination with this whole soccer program concept. What it did was draw people to the problem of homelessness, people who may never have otherwise paid attention, and then, that quickly, close, and upfront, they learned - Wow, these are real people, maybe the stereotypes don't tell the whole story. Mary Carillo, former tennis star and reporter for HBO's show, "Real Sports," followed us out there with a crew, and upon our return, did a segment about it all on the show, then followed up a year later with a replay complete with updates as to how the players were doing. To the cameras, we explained the benefits of participating in such an activity, for the homeless person, getting in shape, meeting deadlines, others reliance on them to "show up" at practice, the pre-game pressures too, and a number of other positives, the team building, even the preening about among their peers in new uniforms, being that they were now "part" of something. For the attending crowds came a chance for a double take on their view of "homeless" people, a chance to watch them as something other than people "on the skids." Taken together, given those many status-degradation ceremonies previously discussed, all in all, it proved to be a highly humanizing experience.

With us for about six months was another film crew who also traveled with us to Austria for our first overseas trip as a team, this one led by the Oscar-winning director James Marsh, pre-Oscar. He made a BBC2 funded fly-on-the-wall documentary, edited just a certain way, raw humanity, eye opening, a movie he called *The Team*.

The following year, we took a team to Sweden, then came Scotland the following year, and then in the year after that, after my departure from Grand Central, as I continued running the project myself, we traveled to South Africa. Before that trip, something different. We moved to expand the project around the country. This time, to see which team would represent the USA, we held an elimination tournament of 7 teams sent from 7 different states. Our team, The New Yorkers, came in first, meaning they would represent the USA. Amazing. We traveled overseas.

Nelson Mandala spoke at the opening ceremonies. The tournament, which had grown by that time to about 46 teams from as many countries, had become a worldwide media event, with tv or film crews from nearly every participating country.

The following year, we "turned" the project over to an aggressive pair of volunteers, good guys, two soccer-loving brothers who we had brought into the project in early 2004, after our trips to Austria and Sweden. Having visited us the previous year in NYC, to get our set-up help and advice, they then began running their own soccer program in North Carolina. About two years later, late 2005, we couldn't take our NY team to the World Cup because of what was culminating during these, our scandal years. Remembering them for their love of the game, we asked if they could take their team to Scotland for that year's tournament. An all-expense-paid trip, hard to turn down – and they didn't disappoint. Afterwards, the Scots asked that we try to keep involving the Carolina brothers. The younger brother, straight up, was easy to work with, the "innocent one," but the older one, less so. Think Eddie Haskell, on the old television show *Leave It to Beaver*. But still, their upbeat, can-do spirit was enjoyable to be around. We worked with them to run the USA elimination tournament in their hometown of Charlotte, which our NY team won, so off to Africa it was. For that trip, we took them along too. As it turned out, the older brother had been busily working behind the scenes to get control of the program. Wow. He knew that we were planning that the United States part of the tournament, the National Cup program, be moved around - next stop Washington DC, the idea being that all the participants should get a turn to host. However, he wanted it in his hometown again. Some mild behind-my-back "collusion" with a couple of homeless service providers was his modus-operandi, and that was all it took.

We were pushovers. Perhaps under the sway of post-trauma theatrics, the impact of ten years of scandal strife, we were dumbstruck by the sheer mischievousness of his behavior, so unexpected. It was unnecessary too, because by then, given their enthusiasm for soccer, and their strong desire to continue with the project, we would have, indeed, we did let it go without even an argument. Drawn from a combination of personal ambition and raw talent no doubt, purposefully then, and by way of orchestrated omissions, for example there is no mention of us in either of their professional biographies, the story of their involvement has been told as if they were the imprimaturs of the whole she-bang. Weird. Not on The Board, but Board-like behavior, no? Okay, so they are pretending that they started it all up, still, even if that could be another story to tell, indicative perhaps of the less than pure motives of some people in the non-profit world, oh well, all told, it is secondary to the more important story here, mainly, that the soccer program is still ongoing. Thank-you to BIGnews and the good Lord John Bird of England.

Jolting across the street, having just burst out of Grand Central Terminal, looking around, nobody appeared to be homeless. Could this really be midtown Manhattan? All through the years, the numbers of street people seemed to be steady, spiking now and then, always dozens and dozens, at rush hour, more like hundreds. Where were they now? I turned in to the alleyway, like I did every day since we were relocated from the former St. Agnes High School for Boys to this large basement room around the corner, walked the necessary twenty-five or so feet down its length, turned left at its end and into the center and through the metal detector I went.

Inside, through a descending basement hallway, past the kitchen to my left, and into a great windowless room, a 2500 square foot vestibule with 30-foot ceilings and hanging chandeliers circa 1999. Wonderful, right? But what about when two hundred people, right off the street, still clinging to their belongings, must fit in? Think "jig-saw puzzle." This crunching of so many people into such a small space occurred when the church, having sold the 30,000-square foot school building that was right around the block, that we had been in from the start, jammed us in their basement; only way to close their deal was to deliver the schoolhouse empty. Problem was, we were in it, and they wanted the 26 million dollars that they were going to get from the sale. So, they wanted us out. However, they did not want the negative publicity that would come from throwing us out. How could they "do that" to the homeless? How could they "do that" to midtown? Our humble program was in the middle of the Church's real estate dreams. We had no place to go. Would they dare to make the homeless homeless? No...in the very last hour, to facilitate the sale of the high school and of the air rights above it, they moved us into their recently renovated 2500 square foot basement.

Monthly, about 1500 people were coming off the streets for services ranging from meals to assessment to social work to job training. At opposite far ends of the great room was St. Vincent's Hospital's medical center, where they'd test our program attendees for among other things, exposure to tuberculosis, and Gouveneurs Hospital's mental health program. While the administration of our program was always caught up in the tug-of-war between public and private interests, perhaps where it should be, our own social services department was more focused on the problem at hand. As I walked in, they were now assembling for a staff meeting meant to develop plans for yet another one of our monthly Network Fairs to be held a few blocks away on Thursday next.

Crisscrossing through the room, I took a seat in the meeting just in time to hear a statistical summary of recent outreach events. The day before, a day like most others, eight new homeless clients walked in on their own for help, three more were brought in by the agency's street outreach program, and five more were brought to us by the New York Police Department Outreach Program. Sixteen new people. And there we were, working in direct contrast to the idea that we wanted people out of our neighborhood. I was in fact sitting with my team, figuring out how to bring in even more people, river to river, midtown.

Thirty-six

Sociologist Peter Rossi said in our interview with him in *Beyond Homelessness*, chronic unemployment itself is a disability... however, we add here, not incurable.

~ ~ ~

Driving the point home. Home. At least half of everybody's current staff positions, throughout the service delivery system, through attrition and expansion, need to go to the homelessly unemployed, and the underemployed, to anyone earning less than a full-time living wage. Because we would expect an effort be made to hire every homeless person one way or another, current social service efforts would need to be transformed as well. Led by their specialists, the most highly trained among them, they'd become supportive employment services. With all paths leading to employment, specialized programs would be formally linked together as well as with more generalized ones to create all sorts of credible pathways to employment, perhaps moving some people up an experiential staircase, one-by-one, skipping steps where possible, volunteerism, stipend-paying internships, sheltered workshops, on-site employment, fee-for-service opportunities, day labor, temporary, part-time, and full-time work, again, all of it supportive. Powerful and important, professional social work would become the thing we do to help a person stay on the job. All activity is productive, purposeful, and socially connective. Regarding all of it, think status-management.

~ ~ ~

An example, a non-profit program that serves homeless adults has a total budget that calls for the hiring of 20 staff among differing job titles, from cooks to case managers to administrators. They would be required then that 10 of those positions have to be filled by homeless adults drawn from the very population of people they are serving, not others like them, but them. For them, this is the best scenario. Best, because it's all happening in front of their peers, you see, they survived the vetting process. It speaks to the credibility of their public success, that they want everybody to know that their achievement was not luck but the result of a process. One feedback loop is replaced by another, the bounce-back effect reaching inside self-esteem like little else could. Leon Festinger - why should his work be ignored? Why keep it in the classroom? It needs to get out there.

Social Enterprise is the art in the heart of social service delivery. It provides work.

Trained social service providers are in the best position to offer supportive employment. Who better? If we can succeed at this, very soon after they will be able to pay their way into their own unaffordable housing. Like the rest of us. 172 work hours in a month at $15-$17 per hour equals $2400-$2900. The national average for an apartment is $993 so that'll do it. Not ideal, but a start, 40% or so of income towards rent. It should be 30%, but...

The whole of every homeless program's service *must* be delivered through the prism of employment. New rules: *Must*. Regardless of program type, whether treatment, rehabilitation, educational, hands-on instruction, special needs, or the norm, this prism is all.

Prevention? Social services programs are part of a growth industry. In February 2017, it added close to 100,000 jobs, now close to 13 million nationwide in healthcare alone. This does not include the ones considered "homeless related," such as client-care workers, case aides, and shift supervisors in shelters, even outreach workers on the streets. There are also many drop-in-centers nation-wide whose staff are not counted here. That's millions of jobs throughout the country, half of which would under this plan go to the most at-risk people being served. As for homeless people, given the numbers at any given time, if this were to happen in the programs and shelters that serve them, that might mean about one-quarter of a million jobs, more than enough. Income getting injected directly into their pockets, indirectly into their family's pockets, and into their social circles. Money spent, injected into the economy by way of a hard day's work. This should satisfy the left and the right. Thousands of people taken off the dole, getting living wage jobs making the most of their strengths, their firsthand knowledge, their "stake" in the process. They would help all of us help them. Our formerly homeless co-workers and colleagues would be doing what in pandemic modernity is called "essential work" too. Going straight to the heart of Elliot Liebow's refrain, right alongside their peers, here, for sure they will feel needed. That is a way to reduce homelessness – employ them. Snap.

People who cannot afford a place to live want to work just as much as people who can. Yet, when treated as not "ready," primarily because they are not "stable enough," they are steered away from this ideal against their will. Away they go, from something as essential to them as work, to something else. Instead, they're steered into long-term shelter stays en masse, a minority making it to supportive housing, all of it, restrictive in nature. Think *The Truman Show* meets *The Survivor.* What if instead of all that, this adult was given a fulltime $17 per hour job along with a support system that included the employer. Snap.

Viewing people through the prism of homelessness sets everyone back. If we structure our interactions with them through the prism of their housing needs, given that nothing in the real estate market is accessible or affordable, then what? Nothing is affordable. Nothing. So, they must just sit in their brick and mortar "refugee" camp shelter beds and wait. Just another case of no choice but dependency. Dependent on whom? We the people. Yet, rare is the adult who wants to have to be dependent on others to fix this or that about their lives. Sometimes we don't want the fix as much as we do want it. We may thank someone who helps us, from our hearts, while at the same time tying them to our predicaments in some blameworthy way, in part simply because they are seeing us at our worst, or for the embarrassment we feel in the exchange, their gift, our gratitude, their bounty, our need. Perhaps we condemn our benefactor along with the society that would have us suffer so - see George Orwell's *Down and Out in Paris and London* for a better explanation. Helping maintain a semblance of sanity, beggars have at least two faces. It's complicated.

For the unemployed person, full-time living wage work can mean so much, and for everyone else, there'd be financial benefits as well. Emergency welfare, unnecessary. Need for a shelter bed, gone. Ongoing Public Assistance benefits, gone. Healthcare, still needed, but not through Medicaid, as half would be getting it through their employer. Food stamps, no. Rental Assistance, no. Social Security Disability, reduced.

Side note: Diminishing typecasting from both sides of the equation, the way that good jobs tend to do, would be good for everybody. We worry that the best scenario would be that they'd need a lot of "hands-on" if not "eyes-on" supervision. Well okay. Let's give it to them. Can't we do that? We have hundreds of thousands of support staff working now. We can retrain and redeploy them. Employers could provide some of that oversight themselves too. The refrain shouldn't go that homeless people "aren't ready" but that "the rest of us aren't." Hey, it wouldn't be that bad. The social services industry can pull this off. Get ready. Get set. Go.

Thirty-seven

The onus is on us, the labelers, not them, the wrongfully labeled. Just from reading Howard S. Becker's *The Other Side,* we see that. Instead, bring them inside the mainstream. Outsiders no more, buoyed by a larger and deeper sense of belonging, their own strengths will emerge. They will pay into a home of their own and become more of a driver of their destiny than otherwise possible, but first, jobs, our great investment. If C. Wright Mills meets Carl Jung, our collective sociological imaginations can point the way.

~ ~ ~

If a service provision industry is to grow around a social problem, shouldn't the jobs go to the people it is growing around?

~ ~ ~

Most people who have serious problems in need of treatment are not homeless. How do they manage that? In large part, motivated by their desire to hold onto their jobs, use of an Employee Assistance Program, or health insurance that'll buy something equivalent, is how it's done. People in all walks of life, in the mainstream and well above, get to "treat" their problems this way, in privacy, sometimes at the behest of their employer, sometimes their family. It's how they hold onto their position and their place. Status management.

~ ~ ~

Who is in the best position to be the benevolent employer of record? A social services provider.

What about jobs from outside the social services system? The Comprehensive Employment Training Act in the 1970's reimbursed employers up to half of a person's salary for the first four or five months of employment. CETA was an example of government working with the private sector to employ those whose resume may not be all that attractive. Shifts in thinking and approach.

Suppose the employer puts up one-third of a living wage salary, about $5 per hour, and the government puts up the rest. A 66/33 split. Equivalent to the cost of unemployment insurance payouts, the public cost would be about $20,000 annually, less than the current $40k or $50k it costs to take care of a person who becomes homeless. Collaborative investment.

That's the start, better than a shelter bed, a drop-in-center chair, or a street corner. Less expensive too. Here, we don't need to find new land, fight to get it properly zoned, or wait for the politics to sway to our favor over the planned use of this or that building. No waiting on the staccato progress of construction, and no time lost waiting on bent knees for the subsequent lottery-drawing – which homeless person is going to win this time? Lotto is not a retirement plan.

Could homeless shelters become employment hubs? Could there be a national public-private work program, guaranteed employment for the able-bodied who live in our homeless shelters now. Let's rename them too. "Employment Hostels." The person is given a job to begin immediately and pays into a room and board situation by way of salary deductions and an employer contribution matching savings plan too. The way out. Hired upon entry at a living wage, a reasonable job description having been hashed out, they've become someone the housing market will make room for. Working, and ready to join the ranks of the housed, even if among those who are living in unaffordable housing, they have their best chance at stability.

Affordable housing? That's another fight, one better fought by the housed. As taxpayers and voters, they seem to have more clout than homeless people and their advocates do, an outrage, but true, as whatever affordable housing does get developed, they are the ones getting most of it.

What about: From the sweat on their palms to a city rebuilt? Yes, but it will not be a cakewalk. They will be somewhat "troubled" by their success. They will be on their own, some for the first time. They will no longer qualify for income-based government benefits, nor live with a social worker within hand's reach. With the necessary supports in place, it'll likely be transformative, and affordable. This sounds prohibitively expensive. Could it ever pay for itself? Well, as we said, HUD reports that it costs society in direct and indirect expenses about $40,000, for some $50K, per year, per homeless person. For that money, they are kept "in-wait." Applied to 25000 able-bodied adults in the NYC shelter system alone, that's 1 billion dollars annually. A living wage for all these same adults is only 60-70% of that, about $700 million. A public/private sharing of that wage could reduce the overall cost further, perhaps eventually half of that, or $350 million annually. Not to forget, at the beginning of this journey, while they are in the Employment Hostel and receiving pay for work done, 30% of their salaries, or about $200 million, would come back to the city from rental payments. $350 million minus $200 million equals $150 million. People would not need food stamps, part of what happens when a person earns a "living-wage," a savings of about $20 million annually. People would not need rental assistance, another savings, of about $40 million annually. There's more – and we're already down to an annual expense of about $90 million, less than one tenth of the current cost to warehouse. Look, it's a start. More to come.

Prevention? We can go with the flow. For example, in between the numbers of those who experience homelessness each year and those homeless at any given moment lies the turnover, usually about a 3:1 or 4:1 ratio. One reason that happens is that the shelter resident acquires just a little bit of income. Take notice. For just a little while, they are not homeless. Instead, they're saved by their sudden ability to pay somebody, anybody, who for a price lets them live at their place, doubled-up, couch-surfing, on their floor? Okay, it does happen, and since it does maybe we should be seizing on it. What can we do for them there, right then, before they have to take a step backwards, towards the streets, back to the shelter? Maybe, we can help them stay where they are, in place, at their friend's place, that one step away? Maybe we can help the person who is helping them? Peter Rossi said it this way: "Aid to families with dependent adults." No problem, these makeshift bed-and-breakfast landlords, the couch-surfing industry, offer no competition whatsoever to the hotel industry. None. I think that can be easily demonstrated. Can't we then incentivize naturally occurring social processes such as these? Yes, we can. Let's call it "on the spot prevention intervention."

What else? Adults everywhere want to feel connected. Instead, already socially adrift, detaching in real time, once they are homeless, they are sheltered, kept apart, often going missing from friends and family, and by way of obstruction, to top it all off, wrongfully labeled too. Understand that, then this: Employment is the most powerful and accessible social engine of connectivity. How about transforming shelters into effectively run employment hostels? Point already made twenty times.

The Big Remake, the start of the revolution that needs to come to those most sheltered and disconnected, can only come by way of a vast and thorough systemic overhaul, that would offer everybody either a job or a credible pathway to one. Every current staff person would have their job descriptions recalibrated to where they'd credibly make up the "support" part of "supported employment." While any place along the continuum could be someone's starting point, some people would need to run the whole gamut. They'll do that, no problem, if there are going to be jobs "waiting" for them, jobs for which they'd qualify, and for which they could apply. But why wait? A sheltered workshop, a stipend for a task while in transition off government benefits, funding to offset expenses perhaps, call it "supported volunteering" where transportation and meal costs are covered, even an unpaid internship as an on-the-job try-out, in-house employment, piecework, temporary employment, part- or full-time work, onsite or off.

As the system itself transitions to full supportive employment for everybody, a person could go from being in supported pathway-to-employment training, to a full-time job whose costs are shared program with an employer, to a job that was fully employer-funded.

When a person comes into to the shelter, nay, the "employment hostel," they could be treated as if showing up for work. Immediately upon entry, an application, the required I-9 form, and a W2 form would be completed, and an account opened. Boom. The person is hired. About one-third, or 30% of income, would go to the employment hostel towards room and board, laundry, and storage services offered, as well as use of an employment self-help center. In New York, where the living wage might be closer to $17 per hour, after taxes that's about $750 back to the hostel for monthly rent. The rest, about $1500, pays off debt, or child support, or gets things out of "hock" or into paid storage, or just to place into a savings account towards the move-out, all of it adding up as the person works towards self-sufficiency.

The job? The person is assigned work either on-site for the agency itself, or off-site, in a position to be developed by the city, now blessed with thousands of new employees. Come on, there's a lot of work to be done. The existing social service departments of agencies everywhere would be re-worked as "employee assistance programs" working to help people keep their new jobs. The emergence of a personal problem? Let's call it a "personnel" problem. The person can take a leave of absence to enter treatment, their positions to be held for their return.

~ ~ ~

So then, as we've said, first off, every single agency that receives government funding would have to hire from within, from among the people they serve, to the point where, at minimum, they comprise half of the staff. In New York alone, that would mean thousands of jobs for shelter residents; nationwide that would add up to a very large number. The city could pay all their unemployed, able-bodied, full-time residents a living wage, $15-20 per hour, depending on size of family or cost of living index in whichever locale, 8 hours per day, five days per week, for every week that they are there, or about $2400-$3000 per month. This makes them live-in employees. For those residents already working for wages below the living wage outside of the shelter, the city would arrange with the employer to make up the difference, to get them to that living wage. There'd be excellent meal services, bagged lunches to take to the job, an excellent laundry service, and sufficient storage space at the employment hostel itself, as well as access to daily showers. In family hostels, day care centers could be established and run in-turn by the adult residents themselves.

Area employers could recruit some people to work for them at huge "below minimum wage" savings, paying the city, let's say, a portion of total pay per hour, around 1/3, for whomever they took in as an employee, or intern.

There could be massive national infrastructure improvement program by way of this new "labor" force.

The city could also provide excellent supplemental educational support inside these newly formed employment hostels. English as a second language courses, Spanish speaking courses, writing and basic math refresher courses, computer-based courses that enhance skills. Residents could prepare for GEDs, as about half do not have high school diplomas, and they could acquire other skills through participation in on and offsite training programs. Through linkages with state university programs, life credits could be awarded towards college degrees.

Sounds crazy? In New York City alone, how crazy is 30 years of warehousing 25,000 able-bodied grown adults who want to work, and 40,000 others, many of whom might be in need as well of medical support, but who also would work at the snap of the finger, all of them with little hope?

That's right. Hire everybody. "Bad hires?" Not to worry. Give everybody a job, and then use existing social service departments to help them become more "ready." As an additional member of the city's workforce, they can be asked to do whatever the city needs done but hasn't done. If it's been because they've been understaffed, they are understaffed no more. If it's been because they haven't had the funding necessary, they are underfunded no more. With all these new staff, there can be more cooking, repairing, assisting, escorting, securing, cleaning, and maintaining.

Uh oh. Big problem. Truly empowered, what with their new-found financial self-sufficiency and resulting ebullience, the formerly homeless person's healthier self-esteem might make it quite difficult for those more accustomed to their acquiescence, who expect it. A side-effect, or an intended consequence?

Again. Think of Fountain House. Operationally, we'd be alongside them rather than on top, our relationship with an air of collegiality. It'd make for great differences in process, all of it real, no longer the righteous pride and the frustrated sighs of our housing-firsters, but the swelling egos of achievement and accomplishment in people who before were downtrodden, underachieving, and unfulfilled. Positive asymmetry.

Worried about all the people that would be knocking at the door of the newly created Employment Hostel and its pathway to employment system? The underemployed, or the unemployed, who are not homeless? Everyone who is working or not, who does not earn a living wage, you say, would be clamoring at the front door? Well, from them may come the next generation's homeless, right? Here, we can prevent some of that. With the current homeless shelter warehousing program swelling, and three times that many ready to take each person's place, what do we think we have now? It's been close to 40 years now this current way and it seems never-ending. One can speculate that this remake would not change that. Okay. But given that our current system would become less expensive, there'd be money for prevention. The dynamic energy of the many transitions toward success would ricochet throughout the city. As disconnections melted away, that would be a good thing.

Positive Cathexis meets the Reality Principle. Striving for Superiority meets the Creative Self. Thank you, Sigmund. Thank you, Alfred.

Uh-oh. The final push for my undoing as the last surviving founder of the business district's initiative had arrived, and boy oh boy, did I have it coming. You could say that The Board had upped the ante for my head. The Intern called me downtown to his office, the headquarters of the Department of Homeless Services. Glistening with the sweat of a manic episode, or so it seemed, he told me that he had determined that we were distracted because of our five-year old street paper, BIGnews. "Close it down! It's too distracting." But it provides an income to 100 plus vendors every month. The Commissioner has written for it. She said that our community has the lowest number of people living on the streets of any other drop-in-center, even though our drop-in center is by far the largest. We are not distracted. We are making more housing and employment placements each year. But...but... But nothing. The Intern was emphatic. What passion. "End BIGnews and all related activities, including your writing-groups, and fire the paper's editor immediately. He's your brother for God's sake! How do you think that looks?" \But we hired him four years ago – and you approved it. "Do it." What? "That's what." Huh? "And quit playing soccer. Try getting them housed instead. Did you hear me? Look at me. No more soccer!" Thanks, I said, but no thanks. Goodbye.

Back to the scandal years. Those three or four hundred people each day, those one or two thousand different people each month, the six thousand different people in just the first five years, all of them who came into the Center...could they have been all wrong? No. Our Center was all about walk-ins, word of mouth, the efforts of outreach, the largest such center in the country, popular on the streets for so many reasons, not the least of which was that always more than half of its staff were formerly homeless, off the streets themselves. We gave out memberships and they wanted to be members. Didn't that mean anything? Yes, it did. Suddenly, though I was no Fred Astaire, I sang "No, no, they can't take that away from me." Oh yes, they can.

Okay then, okay, go ahead, chop us down. No more street newspaper, it's messy, they said. You see, newspapers infer, we don't want that. We don't want homeless people on the street selling anything. We don't want them on the street. No more soccer program either, don't you see, you're encouraging fun, when they should be working with their case managers. Also, no more homeless people doing outreach, people on the street are too vulnerable. You must use professionals. Oh, and no more having people who are homeless cooking meals in your food services training program, they're not really learning anything. No more self-help center, they don't know what they're doing, so they can't self-help. How can you not see that? And no more hiring formerly homeless people, it's not the "real world," and no more micro-loans. If you're going to give someone something, give it to them. It's not fair to ask them to give back. No more of those Network Fairs, it crosses too many important barriers. Oh, and end those five-course meals of yours, they said, it's overkill. The homeless are tired. We want them to have a quiet place to rest while they wait for housing. Let the professionals lead the way. Cut the word multi- off your name "multi-services center," it's too confusing.

Now, you're not unique anymore. Now, you're like the others. See, you are not really doing more or better than any of them. We told you so. Now just do what you are being funded to do – get them housing, housing, housing.

As one man living in a large homeless shelter put it, "Advancement is a setback for some people."

The Intern threatened our social services program with its very existence. First my brother, then me, and he put the brakes on our more prolific programming too. Our seventeen-year effort that brought in thousands, that found housing and jobs for hundreds and hundreds of people, that made mid-town's revival possible, now never existed. Its website was wiped clean, all mention of those years and of me and mine, gone. The spoken history too. We were not just absent, we were invisible. And all the while, the chairperson of the drop-in-center's board was secretly drawing a paycheck from the city for some side work as a geographer, secret because of course, it was corrupt. On The Board herself, she was clear as to her loyalties: No problem, Mr. Intern, she'd say, oh yes, that Grunberg guy is the problem here. There are so many irregularities. For example, I asked him to sign my name on all kinds of checks when I just did not want to trek into the city, and he always complied. Maybe I shouldn't have asked him to do that but, even if he always requested my approval for each of these checks first, the fact is, he did it, and that was wrong. You don't sign someone else's name to a check. Who does that? Also, once I asked him to put a few of our work phones on his personal account because our account was maxed out. He did it. That showed poor judgement. He shouldn't have done it as it could appear that he was asking us to pay his bills. Appearances matter. And don't forget, he ran that pathway to employment program that lost in court. And don't forget the goon squad charges. Never should have happened and it happened under his watch...so, okay, I've got enough on him to turn the screws. He must go. What has he ever really done for us anyway? Thusly, she made all the changes requested by The Intern, and then some, she said. And then some.

~　　~　　~

And so, it came to pass. Look across New York's midtown now, look river to river. Look north to Boston, back down south to coal-torn country in the Appalachia. Look westward to southern Texas, and then, look up north in Minnesota. Don't stop there. Look across the west coast to Los Angeles and up to Seattle. Zig zags zoom. Pretty sad. Homeless people are everywhere. With few exceptions, they have no chance. Look.

CPSIA information can be obtained
at www.ICGtesting.com
Printed in the USA
BVHW030013130122
625993BV00009B/1241